1990

Nineteenth-century
French poetry

Nineteenth-century French poetry

Introductions to close reading

Edited by
CHRISTOPHER
PRENDERGAST

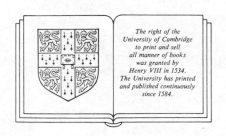

The right of the
University of Cambridge
to print and sell
all manner of books
was granted by
Henry VIII in 1534.
The University has printed
and published continuously
since 1584.

CAMBRIDGE UNIVERSITY PRESS

Cambridge

New York   Port Chester

Melbourne   Sydney

Published by the Press Syndicate of the University of Cambridge
The Pitt Building, Trumpington Street, Cambridge CB2 1RP
40 West 20th Street, New York NY 10011, USA
10 Stamford Road, Oakleigh, Melbourne 3166, Australia

First published 1990

Printed in Great Britain at
the University Press, Cambridge

British Library cataloguing in publication data

Nineteenth-century French poetry:
introductions to close reading
1. Poetry in French, 1848–1900
– Critical studies
I. Prendergast, Christopher
841′.8 09

Library of Congress cataloguing in publication data

Nineteenth-century French poetry: Introductions to close reading /
(edited by) Christopher Prendergast.
p.   cm.
Bibliography.
ISBN 0-521-34541-3. – ISBN 0-521-34774-2(pbk.)
1. French poetry – 19th century – History and criticism.
I. Prendergast, Christopher.   II. Title: 19th-century French poetry.
PQ432.N5   1989
841′.7′09—dc20   89-31434   CIP

ISBN 0 521 34541 3 hard covers
ISBN 0 521 34774 2 paperback

CE

CONTENTS

v

CONTENTS

PREFACE

I should like to express my gratitude to all the contributors to this volume, notably for their patience and good humour in the face of some – albeit necessary – editorial harassment. I am particularly grateful to Clive Scott, who, in addition to contributing his essay on Vigny, kindly agreed to write the discursive glossary on French versification. I also wish to express my thanks to Terry Moore and Kate Brett for their support as editors at Cambridge University Press.

I

INTRODUCTION

Christopher Prendergast

I

'I am inclined to think', wrote I. A. Richards in one of the great pioneering works on the study of poetry (*Practical Criticism*), 'that four poems are too many for a week's reading – absurd though this suggestion will seem to those godlike lords of the syllabus-world, who think that the whole of English literature can be perused with profit in about a year!'[1] He was speaking of the problems in the study of English poetry faced by native speakers. These problems are necessarily exacerbated when the poetry in question is not that of the mother tongue. If, as Richards also says in defence of his tonically restrictive view of the syllabus, '"making up our minds about a poem" is the most delicate of all possible undertakings', then this is *a fortiori* true when it comes to reading and studying poetry in a foreign language. The latter is arguably amongst the most testing of our literary experiences, and in many ways the most vulnerable to neglect, even in the specialist departments of that highly specialized world, the university. The present volume has been compiled with these problems in mind, and as such has a distinct pedagogic aim. It is addressed primarily to students, on the (perhaps overly pessimistic) assumption that, for a whole variety of reasons, the study of French poetry is rapidly becoming something of a poor relation in the family of the subject as a whole.

If this is generally the case (with of course many honourable exceptions), the contributors to this volume would like their essays – whatever theoretical and critical differences separate them – to be

I

seen collectively as an attempt to correct this unhappy situation, as a gesture towards both arresting the decline in interest and updating the subject in the light of developments in current critical preoccupations. The primary objective has been to do so in terms that for the 'average' student reader (whatever that individual may conceivably look like) are at once accessible and challenging. Getting the balance right between these two requirements, however, is not easy, and there may be moments when our envisaged (or imaginary) readers will feel that their resources have been excessively stretched; or, to put the point in less charitable fashion, that some of the contributors have been speaking more to each other than to them. That is one of the regrettable, but perhaps inevitable, consequences of the increasingly sophisticated professionalization of literary studies, arising in large measure from the impact of modern 'theory' (some of whose implications for the study of poetry are central to this project in ways I shall try to explain shortly). But, beyond these very real difficulties of level and address, there is a common belief of a quite straightforward sort underlying and organizing the volume as a whole. Although Richards's view as to the ideal curriculum would not necessarily be endorsed by all the contributors, the shared commitment of the undertaking is to sponsoring the virtues of what is called 'close reading', in the belief that, whatever we might mean, in the context of formal study, by 'understanding' poetry, its analytical pre-condition is close-up focus on the detailed verbal dynamics of theme, structure, texture and rhythm peculiar to poetic statement.

Accordingly, the present volume consists of a series of essays, each devoted to the analysis of a single poem by a major nineteenth-century French poet, in a chronological sequence from the early 'romantic' Lamartine through to the 'symbolist' Laforgue and Mallarmé. The reasons for focussing on the nineteenth century range from the purely practical to the strictly intellectual. In practical terms, restricting the scope of inquiry to the poetry of one historical period has helped to give a greater degree of coherence to what is by its nature a highly diversified enterprise. Furthermore, since it is normally with the nineteenth century that most students start with French poetry, a certain familiarity with the relevant corpus has been assumed as a context for the various analyses developed in the essays. This also explains in part the choice of 'canonical' poets and texts, although this should not be taken to imply some notion of a fixed and stable canon. A canon is always historically produced in function of specific interests and decisions (it was not that long ago, for example, that Nerval, the 'mad' poet, was held at the uneasy margin of the canonical map, or indeed taken off the map altogether).

The strictly intellectual reasons for restricting the volume to the nineteenth century I shall return to in more detail later, but broadly they have to do with questions of historical perspective. Some of these questions are of a very general character, theoretical as well as historical. They touch on the problematic relations between, on the one hand, nineteenth-century conceptions of lyric poetry (which continue to shape many of our own unexamined yet pervasive conceptions), and, on the other hand, the category of 'history' itself. One major problem here concerns the denial of, or blindness to, the historical determinations of poetry arising from an allegedly 'romantic' notion of lyric as unmediated private utterance (more of this later). In addition, and at a lower level of abstraction, the historical perspectives afforded by the study of nineteenth-century poetry are important by virtue of the strategic place of the latter in the general history of lyric poetry in France. With the benefit of hindsight we can now approach the nineteenth century as a place from which we can look at once backwards and forwards: backwards in that, at least in its initial phases (roughly what we call the 'romantic'), the nineteenth century is the moment of the confident, even assertive recovery of the lyric voice after its relative eclipse in the eighteenth century (this is part of Eric Gans's argument about the inaugural significance of Lamartine's 'Le Lac', as a poem that, through its obsession with 'origins', seeks to establish itself as a new, originating event on the historical stage of poetry); forwards in that, in the later stages of its own internal history (for the 'nineteenth century', is not of course some single homogeneous thing), it can also be read as an anticipation of the more uncertain, self-questioning poetic voice of modernity (Baudelaire, as Jonathan Culler argues, is here the pivotal figure). The nineteenth century can thus be posed historically in terms of principles of both discontinuity and continuity, as a time of break with a cultural past, and as advance notice of the insistently self-conscious voice of much twentieth-century poetry. It is thus one of the hopes of the present contributors that what is learnt here may prove to some extent portable knowledge, which can be taken into other areas of students' explorations of French poetry, notably that of the twentieth century.

But if the volume as a whole throws up, in a variety of guises, these larger issues, its methodological *parti pris* remains entirely committed to the strategy of close reading. These are not necessarily in conflict with each other; on the contrary, it would be one of our claims that each mutually demands the other: the larger issues cannot be adequately apprehended without passing through the filter of close textual analysis, just as the latter will not make much sense unless linked to wider cultural questions (including what it means to 'read' poetry and what the conditions of 'reading' are). For the practice of close reading itself is of course neither a-historical nor theoretically 'innocent' (although in some of its institutionally routinized incarnations it has tried to pass itself off as being both).[2] On the other hand, in the matter of poetry and the forms in which it is interpreted, general claims in the domain of theoretical reflection and historical explanation are worth little if they are not tried and tested in detailed analysis of specific texts. The following essays are offered as an invitation to make those connections. But we have also tried to take into account the difficulties of accepting the invitation. There are many reasons why this might be so in current circumstances. Apart from the normal interferences of everyday life (including supremely the invasion of that 'exacting silence' which Walter Benjamin saw as the condition of reading by the information-spewing technologies of the mass media), there are many other, more specific disincentives to the pursuit of disciplined and productive attention to the intricacies of verse in other tongues. Here I shall address just three areas which might be cause for potential discouragement: the question of linguistic competence; the 'technical' nature of the analysis of poetry; and the impact on literary studies of contemporary 'theory'.

II

The most obvious problem confronting the English-speaking reader of French verse concerns limitations of linguistic competence. This is not just a matter of charting the complexities of poetic syntax or the obscurer zones of poetic vocabulary (for example, our despair at finding no entry in a French dictionary for Mallarmé's famous 'ptyx'). More importantly, it is also the difficulty of catching the vast range of connotation and allusion imprinted by a culture in its language (or the other way round). Access to the connotative and allusive resources of poetry in the relevant language may well presuppose not only a native speaker, but also a formidable knowledge of the poetry's surrounding linguistic habitat. A case in point might be Michael Riffaterre's account of poetic discourse as the transformation of what, in *The Semiotics of Poetry*, he has called a 'hypogram'. Hypogram is technical shorthand for a repertoire of terms ('a pre-existent word group') governing 'normal' ways of describing a topic or a theme at a given historical moment. These terms and the statements they generate usually have the status of clichés, and it is the function of poetry to undo, transform and re-route the language of received ideas towards another, more novel mode of perceiving and representing the world. But the difficulty of Riffaterre's model for the student of French poetry who is neither native speaker nor erudite historical lexicographer will be at once obvious and forbidding: he or she might be forgiven for thinking that, in its emphasis on the importance of mastering the detailed linguistic environment of a given poem, Riffaterre's account will inevitably exclude the non-initiate from the club of competent readers of French verse. But this would be an unnecessarily pessimistic inference. In a sense, Riffaterre's language-orientated account is but another version of the idea of poetry as the site of a permanent dialogue between tradition and innovation, or of the idea of poetry's function as geared to strategies of 'de-familiarization' – making it new by making it strange. In these terms, however limited the student's historical knowledge of the language, Riffaterre's approach supplies a way of thinking about how one might start to track analytically the internal history of nineteenth-century poetry at the level of both its basic presuppositions and its operative vocabularies.

INTRODUCTION

But even on a more relaxed and flexible view of the pre-conditions of understanding French poetry, there are other considerations of a more technical sort that might deter the prospective student. If the language of poetry transforms a more general linguistic landscape, it does so in special ways. Exactly how special, and in particular what distinguishes poetry from prose, is a question that has greatly exercised the critical imagination, but without securing intellectually very satisfactory answers. Paul Valéry defined poetic discourse as 'une sorte d'extension et d'application de certaines propriétés du Langage'.[3] By 'propriétés', he meant largely the physical or material properties of words and their combinations ('le son, le rhythme, les rapprochements physiques des mots'[4]). These are the 'basics', the building-blocks of poetry. They are, however, not necessarily absent from prose (part of the lesson of Rimbaud's way with the prose poem or Laforgue's experiments with *vers libre* is the blurring of the poetic/prosaic distinction, and their example will be widely emulated in many areas of twentieth-century poetry). Perhaps the most we can say is that in what we recognize as 'poetry' the exploitation of the physical (and syntactic) properties of language is especially dense and systematic, and, as such, is the main source of its particularly charged semantic energies. Roman Jakobson (whose argument is briefly summarized in Ross Chambers's essay) saw these kinds of systematic regularity and repetition as the basis of what he called the 'poetic function' of language, which he sought to formalize as 'the projection of the principle of resemblance from the axis of selection to the axis of combination'.[5] What this means is that, in the formation of any linguistic act, we select from stocks or pools ('paradigms') of linguistic items which belong together in a given paradigm by virtue of their resemblances to each other (not only phonic but also lexical, grammatical, etc.); we then combine the selected items to form a chain or sequence (a 'syntagm'), as a phrase, a clause or a sentence. Under this description of how language works, the 'poetic function' stands out from the other, more pragmatic functions of language by its retrieval at the level of the syntagm (combination of elements) of the principle of similarity governing the paradigms. This produces concentrated patterns of resemblance and identity between the words of the poetic text, and is thus one

6

of the ways in which the language of poetry marks itself for identification as 'poetic'.

But if this is the most we can say, it is also much; for if this is what defines poetry as a distinctive mode of utterance, it may also be what makes us feel unable or unwilling to attempt to gain analytical purchase on it. Representing in analytical terms what is articulated in poetic terms (where 'articulate' should be understood as both expression and embodiment[6]), and in particular grasping how the material 'body' of poetry functions as a carrier or, better, a generator of meaning, is a critical art still in its infancy, despite the development of exceptionally sophisticated descriptive vocabularies. Nevertheless, one of the purposes of adopting the method of close reading has been to suggest to the reader ways in which the study of 'basics' might be usefully undertaken. In particular, the following general areas are variously addressed in the specific context of individual poems: sound pattern, metre and syntax. These suggestions naturally vary according to the focus of particular contributions, and range from passing observations made in the pursuit of some other interest to more sustained exposition (as in Clive Scott's reflections on prosody in his essay on Vigny's 'La Mort du Loup'). But collectively they may be taken as pointers towards further analysis, and above all as an invitation to leave behind the loosely impressionistic habits of talk acquired from an older belle-lettristic tradition (what presumably Richards in part had in mind when he spoke contemptuously of the 'critical chit-chat' and 'the stocks of imitation currency' we all too readily produce as a substitute for analysis[7]).

Sound

Nowhere perhaps are these habits more active than in our ways of talking about sound pattern in poetry, in particular the unreflecting extension into the complicated relation between sound and meaning of the model of onomatopoeia (the 'mimetic' fallacy). The *dream* that the sounds of words might imitate their sense has had a long philosophical and literary life, reaching back to Plato's *Cratylus*.[8] But, as Mallarmé pointed out (ruefully, since he himself was much tempted by the dream), if the Cratylist argument were correct, then 'jour' and 'nuit' ought to signify their opposites (though the claim that the 'ou' and 'ui' vowel sounds are respectively 'sombre' and 'clair' itself begs questions). In reality, the phenomenon of onomatopoeia in language is relatively rare. For example, Rae Beth Gordon shows how Nerval's 'El Desdichado' works systematically from a principle of echoing sounds, producing a kind of incantatory effect that doubles the theme of Orphic song to which the poem alludes in its closing stanza. The repetition of sound – the literal act of incorporating certain elements of some words into others (crucially the key word *étoile*) – parallels, or even 'performs', the poem's effort to overcome division and fragmentation; it is a way of 'tying subject to object' in the very body of language. But this is not at all the same as saying that the relevant sounds 'imitate' the meanings in question. Consider, for example, the sound-values of Baudelaire's 'Correspondances', a poem which explicitly explores the idea of the 'poetic' unity of being, where matter 'speaks' and the language of poetry is its translation ('La Nature est un temple où de vivants piliers/ Laissent parfois sortir de confuses paroles'). Matter, in this doctrine, includes the materiality of the poetic word itself; the phonic echoes of the poem should mirror the 'echoes' which are the poem's subject. But, as Culler shows in the context of a more general sceptical account of Baudelaire's relation to the doctrine of 'correspondances', if the echoing of the phonemes 'f' and 'r' in 'parfums frais' and 'chairs d'enfants' helps to link otherwise discrete ideas, the sounds themselves clearly have no *mimetic* relation to what the words designate; the 'echoes' in question are purely verbal and rhetorical – they form a phonetic *figure*, not a natural association.

The virtue of Jakobson's more formalist approach has been to remind us that sound and meaning are separate systems, whose interlacing is not natural but formal; phonic recurrence is a kind of knitting or coupling process that brings words together on the basis of sound similarity prior to or independently of any relation of semantic overlap between the words, but which, on that basis, invites the reader to consider possible relations of meaning between them. The most obvious case of this is homonomy – two words which sound the same (homophony) or are written the same (homography), but which have entirely different meanings: Gautier, for instance, rhymes 'nue' (as noun meaning 'cloud') with 'nue' (as adjective meaning 'naked'), and the identity of sound here draws us into a poetic world in which sound equivalences are related, though deceptively, to the poem's effort to assimilate the phenomenon of clouds to the forms of naked women. In other words, what is relevant here is not a notion of the 'natural' expressive values of sound, but rather a formal strategy of positioning and repetition. Thus, as Mary Ann Caws shows in connection with Leconte de Lisle's 'Midi', the sound cluster 'di' in 'midi' of the first line is recalled at the end in the word 'di/vin', suggesting by way of position (opening and closure) a set of thematic associations between the motifs of midday, heat, and a metaphysical experience of dissolution into the 'néant'. Similarly, the echoing of the sound of the verb-form 'est' in the sequence 'étés/épandu/tait/étendue/est immense/et les/et la/blés/s'éveille' reinforces, not mimetically but simply in the formal fact of repetition itself, the poem's insistent concern with placing itself under the sign of Being. Indeed, as some of the other contributions (notably the essays on Mallarmé, Verlaine and Laforgue) suggest, sound patterning can become a virtually autonomous, self-generating system which, so to speak, trails sense along the path of purely phonic associations, or – to put the point more positively – which acts to *produce* meaning in novel and unexpected semantic combinations. Riffaterre, in his account of sound pattern in Rimbaud's 'Mémoire', relates this process to an organized yet dislocating form of punning (the sort known by the rhetorical figure of 'syllepsis').

Metre

If sound pattern is one fundamental level of the reality of poetic language, metrical structure is another. Poems are not just sequences of phonically related items. They are also sequences organized in terms of rhythmic structures, as a distribution of stresses and pauses across the line of verse. Prosody, as the analysis of poetic metre, may often strike us as a return to the pedagogic dark ages, a lethal combination of the arcane and the tedious, a mere exercise in the inert quantitative listing of measures and accentuations. But, as Clive Scott here demonstrates in both his reading of Vigny's 'La Mort du Loup' and the discursive glossary at the end of the volume, prosody can go under very different descriptions, and connect intimately and powerfully with the very life of the poetic line. While it is concerned with rule-governed elements of versification, prosody is not, or should not be seen as, a system of fixed 'rules' prescriptively legislating more or less automatic, predictable readings of a poem's rhythms. 'The notion that verses must conform to metrical patterns', says I. A. Richards, '[is] the most damaging enemy to good reading ... it cannot be too much insisted that there is no obligation upon verses to conform to any standard'.[9]

Prosody nevertheless provides some of the means for making sense of the (often subliminal) role played by rhythm in our own activities of sense-making when we read a poem (what Scott has in mind when he says in the essay on Vigny that his purpose is 'to show how prosody projects, even creates thematic texture'). On this view, prosody is an attempt to clarify the principles, at once constraining and permitting, that govern an otherwise immensely variable spacing of stresses and pauses in the actual reading, oral or mental, of a poem. Thus, as Scott points out in the glossary, in the case of French regular verse, the two major prosodic constants are the principle of syllabicity and the principle of oxytonic stress: the foundation-stone of the integrity of the regular French line is the rule that it have a fixed number of syllables in it; and whatever words receive stress, it is always on the last syllable of the relevant words that the accent will actually fall. But the principles of syllabic regularity and oxytonic stress still leave partly open to individual interpretative choice the question as to *which* words in the line will count as the relevant ones for the purpose of stress. For example, in the case of the regular Alexandrine – the dominant form of the body of verse examined in this volume – there is, by prosodic rule, always an accent on the last accentuable syllable of the word at the end of each of the two hemistiches. But there is no rule, as distinct from conventions and preferences, for the determination of any of the other accents necessary to the constitution of the line's rhythm (although in a large number of 'normal' cases the syntactic structure of the line, its division into groups of grammatically related terms, will affect the decisions we make).

The consequence of this relative scansional liberty is to open up a wide range of rhythmic variation, according to shifting priorities of mood and meaning. Scott shows us that in 'La Mort du Loup' the different rhythmic configurations of Vigny's hemistiches correspond to different existential points of view in the unfolding of the poem's moral and affective drama (for instance, the equilibrium of the 3 + 3 configuration actualizes the theme of resolution, the overcoming of conflict and dissonance in the achievement of spiritual equipoise). For further, though less developed, accounts of the semantic riches disclosed by metrical analysis the reader should also consider certain moments in some of the other essays: for example, Eric Gans's observation that metrical variations in 'Le Lac' are directly related to the two distinct modes of discourse and the corresponding symbolic positions given to the woman and the poet respectively in the poem (the woman's 'weaker', less sustained and hence more vulnerable to extinction); Rae Beth Gordon's claim that rhythmic variation in Nerval's 'El Desdichado' (between the 'flowing' and the 'broken') is directly related to the poem's oscillation between a fear of fragmentation and a striving for unification; Victor Brombert's remarks on the mobility of the Alexandrine (in particular the transition from the *tétramètre* to the *trimètre* form) in Hugo's 'La Pente de la rêverie', as at once a mirroring and a desired mastering of the chaotic flux of Nature; Ross Chambers's description of stress, pause and run-over ('enjambement') in the closing stanza of Verlaine's poem as dramatizing the potential 'disordering' pressure of a certain experience of 'modernity' (represented in the speed and noise of the railway train) on the integrity of the poetic line itself.

Two general points flow from these various observations and examples.[10] First, metrical analysis is not simply description, it is also, and irreducibly, interpretation; scansion is always an account of how a rhythm is produced in the service of the production of meaning. Secondly, scansion reminds us of the relation between reading and time. As a written text, the poem permits a multiple and mobile scanning of its internal relations; it allows us to treat the text as a kind of 'spatial' entity within which one can travel back and forth. The idea of poetry as speech or oral performance focusses on the temporal plane of reading (especially reading for the first time), the negotiation of the poem line by line, where the realization of a rhythm involves a continuous adjustment of attention and expectation on the part of the reader. This is of course particularly marked in the case of the rhythmic indeterminacies of *vers libre*. For, while it is in the nature of regular French verse that the rhythm of one line cannot be fully predicted from that of the previous line, a measure of predictability is nevertheless assured by the standard requirement of syllabic parity and terminal rhyme. Late nineteenth-century experiments in free verse abandon that requirement, thus opening poetic rhythm to what, in the Appendix, Scott describes as the 'changing movements of the mind' in a manner cognate with the emerging techniques of stream of consciousness in contemporary fiction. Peter Collier analyses Laforgue's use of free verse in 'L'Hiver qui vient' as an attempt to capture the fluctuating rhythms of consciousness. But he also argues that free verse should be seen as more than just a mimesis of psychological reality; if *vers libre* dramatizes consciousness, it does so as a deliberate 'staging' of the life of the mind, as a *mise en scène* itself governed by convention and artifice, a kind of prosodic rhetoric challenging the literary authority of the institution of regular verse. In other words, the pertinent relation of free verse is as much with the literary as the psychological, or – to anticipate a later topic for discussion – engages a form of the 'intertextual' relation.

Syntax

The grammatical and syntactic properties of poetic language often go unremarked, perhaps for the paradoxical reason that they are so basic to linguistic intelligibility that we tend to take their functions for granted. One of the aims of the present volume is to retrieve some of these functions from that taken-for-grantedness. Two examples will briefly illustrate the kind of analytical attention to the text which this level of approach requires: verb tense and punctuation. As Scott points out in connection with 'La Mort du Loup', variations in verb tense (and mood) register not only shifts of narrative perspective, but also shifts of existential perspective; or, to put the point in slightly more technical terms, they articulate not just relations of temporality (the relation of action to time) but also relations of modality (the relation of subject to action). An example might be the past historic 'Je vis' in Hugo's 'La Pente de la rêverie', where, as Brombert suggests, the narrative tense at once denotes a past action and connotes an existential point of view (broadly, as the verbal sign of the poem's assumed visionary power and authority). Similarly, punctuation (which we might have thought to be quite unworthy of serious consideration) can also be shown to yield a wide variety of important effects. Caws maps these possibilities in some detail in connection with Leconte de Lisle (and others): the separating function of the comma can heighten other kinds of setting apart and aloneness; the suspensive syntax marked by the use of a semi-colon accentuates pause and uncertainty; while the mid-line full stop becomes the moment of a 'mid-line crisis', intimately connected with the poem's involvement with the themes of arrest, finality and death. Punctuation can also be of significance by virtue of its absence at line-ending (what is normally referred to as enjambement). Properly speaking, enjambement belongs to prosody, but, by its very nature, it also involves considerations of poetic syntax. As several of the contributors demonstrate, enjambement can perform a variety of functions, whether of a binding sort (as in the Nerval sonnet) or of a destabilizing sort (as in the Verlaine sonnet). But perhaps its most interesting feature is its capacity to generate moments of hesitation in the reading mind. Enjambement is a point of potential tension between metre and syntax; metrically, line-ending requires a pause, but syntactically enjambement requires run-over (*rejet*) into the next line for the completion of sense. The combination of pause and run-over makes for moments of uncertain anticipation whereby expectations can be either confirmed or displaced. The use of ambiguous syntax to equivocate expectations and introduce uncertainty into the reader's mind is crucial to the art of Mallarmé; as Malcolm Bowie shows in analysis of the sonnet 'Quand l'ombre mnaça...', metre and syntax describe a complex phrasal dance, a play of appositions, enjambements, analeptic and proleptic clauses, which decisively route any attempt by the reader to reduce the poem to a unified and stable 'propositional' sense.

III

A third major source of possible inhibition when approaching the analysis of poetry derives from the more general changes in literary criticism wrought by the so-called 'theory-revolution', or what

Roland Barthes, in notorious dispute with one of the self-appointed guardians of traditional literary study, called 'la crise du Commentaire'.[11] Indeed, as Caws here reminds us (herself citing Barthes's example), 'criticism' and 'crisis' are etymologically related. On the other hand, the forms which this notion of a putting into crisis has taken in the twenty-odd years since Barthes's intervention pose as many problems as they produce possibilities, especially for the would-be student of poetry. Apart from the intrinsically taxing intellectual demands of modern theory, there are at least two reasons why this might be so. First, in contrast to the immense prestige of narrative (producing that curious specialization within an already excessively specialized system of the academic division of labour, 'narratology'), the study of poetry has been far less an object of the new theoretical interest.[12] The second difficulty stems from what have rapidly become the dominant institutional and pedagogic forms in which students are now typically introduced to the whole culture of modern theoretical discourse; as the notion of 'crisis' has paradoxically settled into routinized rhetorical gesture, theory has become just another 'subject', often separated off, effectively ghettoized. We have many courses 'on' theory, doubtless well-packaged and instructive, but all too frequently leaving the student with very little idea as to how to unwrap the packages and carry over their contents into whatever concrete problems of literary interpretation and analysis he or she is confronted with. This is particularly marked in the case of poetry, where travelling across the gap separating the encounter with abstract theory and the demands of practical analysis must seem acutely strenuous.

Many of the issues in contemporary theory are present, tacitly or explicitly, in this collection of essays. Although some of the essays begin by sketching out the lineaments of a theoretical approach, we have on the whole eschewed extensive formal exposition of theoretical positions and debate, preferring instead to avail ourselves of the tactic of close reading in order to bring theory out of the ghetto; the emphasis here is resolutely on theory-in-practice. This has a double advantage: first, it enables a certain testing of theoretical positions in the detailed terms of practical criticism; secondly, and conversely, it also encourages bringing into theoretical reflection the assumptions that often lie unexamined in traditional forms of practical criticism (notably of course the assumption that practical criticism as such is a theory-free exercise). The various theoretical issues raised throughout the essays include: authorial 'intention'; the distinction between poetic language and ordinary language; the question of figurative meaning and the problem of metaphor; the nature of 'subjectivity' in lyric poetry; the status of allusions to and quotations from other poems; devices of *mise en abyme*; relations between poetry, society and history. These are of course very complex and wide-ranging issues. We have not tried to provide a 'primer' for them (there are already more than enough of these in existence), nor has any of the contributors been given a specific theoretical brief (in terms of either issue or treatment of it). Nevertheless, the diverse theoretical concerns of the volume as a whole have tended – more by coincidence than design – to fall into one or more of the following, and to a large extent interlocking, main categories: poetic 'voice'; self-reference; intertextuality; poetry and history. The following remarks are intended simply as a series of guidelines to what is more amply discussed and explored in the essays themselves.

Voice

The dominant mode of poetry in the nineteenth century is what we usually refer to generically as the 'lyric' (even the narrative mode favoured by Vigny is, as Scott shows in connection with 'La Mort du Loup', a clothing for what are essentially lyric interests). The lyric, as its putative origins in song suggest, assumes both a personal 'voice' and an intimate situation of address, often to a beloved (for example, the woman in Lamartine's 'Le Lac'), but which can also take the form of apostrophe to more general notions and entities such as nature, man, death, the muse, the reader and so on: Nerval's persona addresses a 'toi' identified with a lost love; Vigny's wolf addresses 'man', or rather that privileged minority held to be peculiarly receptive to the poem's message; Leconte de Lisle's poem apostrophizes 'Homme' *tout court*; Hugo's poem begins by addressing 'Amis'; Rimbaud's poem addresses a spouse ('O l'Epouse'); Verlaine's poem operates an implicit apostrophe (Chambers calls it 'pseudo-apostrophe') to an indeterminate 'Nom' which can be taken as referring to both a feminine beloved and the muse; Mallarmé's

sonnet apostrophizes the firmament ('Luxe, ô salle d'ébène...');
Laforgue's narrator addresses himself, or rather the 'tone' ('ton
ton') of his attempted self-representation in poetry. Accordingly,
we tend to think of lyric poetry on the model of private utterance,
as the 'expression' of a singular subject's inward life of thought and
emotion, moreover often identifying the lyric subject with the
biographical subject (the poet himself); and from there it is but a
step to construing the range of possible meanings articulated by the
poem as controlled by an authorial 'intention' (Caws talks briefly
about problems of intention in her account of Leconte de Lisle).

To think of lyric in this way, as the actualization or imitation of a
particular speaking voice, is certainly what the convention of lyric,
especially in the nineteenth century, invites us to do; and that
invitation is accepted, at least in part, by two of the contributors
(Gans and Gordon). Gans, for example, argues in connection with
Lamartine that the convention can be a source of considerable
poetic force, making possible the emergence of a new and 'strong'
individualized poetic register from the dying forms of neo-classical
literary culture. But many of the essays (including both Gordon's
and Gans's) are anxious to develop the view that this is primarily a
matter of *convention*: in the case of Lamartine, it helps us distinguish a 'romantic' – as against a purely Lamartinian – voice from
the inertly neo-classical; while, in the case of Nerval, Gordon suggests terms in which lyric voice can be understood as a device for
dramatizing not just the interiority of the poet but the more general
and impersonal processes of the Unconscious. Similarly, Bowie
shows how in Mallarmé's poem the very category of 'individuality'
itself is dissolved into the phenomenon of a generalized and intransitive Desire, anonymously circulating in the cosmos; while Collier
argues that in Laforgue's text the rhetoric of self-address works ironically to expose as an empty fiction the idea of a unique and coherent 'self' speaking in and through the text. Riffaterre shows how the
convention of apostrophe is ironized in Rimbaud's 'Mémoire' by
the insertion of the colloquial definite article in 'O l'Epouse', and,
more generally, frames his account of the complex linguistic and
rhetorical operations of the poem with the strong claim of its
absolute irreducibility to biographical interpretation.

In brief, many of the essays are committed to questioning the traditional assumption of lyric poetry as the natural home of private speech. In this regard, Chambers's essay takes us back to basics, inviting us to consider the absurdity of construing Shakespeare's 'Shall I compare thee to a summer's day' on the model of a literal speech-act by a speaker to a listener. Chambers argues that we should suspend or bracket, as a pure fiction, the idea of the poem as a record or miming of an actual address by someone to someone or something else, and instead take the I/You relation of the speech-situation in poetry as itself the object of interpretation. This is another way of making the claim entered by Caws in respect of Leconte de Lisle that a poem 'means' more than it (literally) 'says' and that this surplus of meaning becomes available only when we abandon empirical assumptions about speakers and listeners. Both the speaker and the apostrophe are thus better thought of as fictions serving the construction of a *figure*; they are metaphors, figures of speech. Thus, to take just one example, consider the address to the 'Amis' in 'La Pente de la rêverie': the speech-situation is not to be taken literally; it is less an instance of Victor Hugo sending messages to his friends than a figure serving the poem's thematic and ideological interests. More precisely, it is, as Brombert says, a 'rhetorical figure of authority', deceptively evoking a shared universe of understanding only to throw into sharper relief its real affirmation – the special cognitive and philosophical powers of the unique and solitary visionary artist.

Self-reference

The argument that 'voice' in lyric poetry is less the staging of a speech-act than the construction of a figure demanding its own interpretation is perhaps a difficult idea to grasp. But one other way of trying to get a grip on it is in terms of a preoccupation shared in one form or another by every contributor – the idea that poetry (and certainly the poetry of the nineteenth century) is in some important sense as much about itself as about speakers and interlocutors; that, as both Chambers and Culler put it, the poem contains its own *art poétique*, or, as it is more commonly put in contemporary theory, deploys a strategy of *mise en abyme*. In Verlaine's poem, according to Chambers, the implied apostrophe seems turned as much towards the muse as towards an absent beloved, and thus acts as one of the figures through which the poem 'theorizes itself', draws attention to 'its own situation as poetic discourse'. In the body of poetry examined here, the idea of the poem as containing and enacting its own *art poétique* can be seen as working in two quite different registers, which correspond more or less to two phases in the evolution of the self-consciousness of nineteenth-century French poetry. Although we will not find a cleanly linear historical development (indeed the two registers can be seen co-existing within a single poem), we can distinguish broadly between, on the one hand, a form of reflexivity that belongs largely to an earlier and highly self-confident phase, and, on the other hand, a reflexive mode that belongs to a later, more anxiously and sceptically self-aware questioning of the ambitions invested in the project of poetry.

These two different manifestations of *mise en abyme* can be illustrated by juxtaposing two material objects which, in their respective poetic settings, also serve as allegorical objects referring to the poems in which they appear: the lute in Nerval's 'El Desdichado', along with its transformation into Orpheus's lyre; the telegraph wires in Verlaine's 'Le Paysage dans le cadre des portières', explicitly compared in the poem to a form of writing, the *paraphe* (a scarcely legible scribble, usually of the initials of a proper name). Rae Beth Gordon points out that the seven double-strings of the lute mirror the fourteen-line structure of the sonnet, and that material echo reinforces the strong identification implied in the poem between poetry and song around the figure of Orpheus: at the moment of his victorious exit from the underworld in the last tercet, the lyric 'persona' of 'El Desdichado' becomes, not just thematically but in the very rhythm and texture of utterance, a reincarnation of Orpheus, who is himself often posed in the nineteenth century as a figure for the origins of human culture. The poem is thus 'about' itself in the sense that, via the references to Orpheus, music and song, it at once affirms and enacts a belief in the power of poetry to confer meaning and pattern on darkness and disorder.

This belief typifies the outlook of the romantic generation as a whole, and we will find similar dramatizations *en abyme* of that belief in the poems by Lamartine, Vigny and Hugo: 'Le Lac', according to Gans, celebrates its own capacity to conquer loss and mortality; its invocation of nature is a figure for its own imagined re-enactment of man's accession to language and meaning. Part of Scott's argument about 'La Mort du Loup' is that it contains a text within the text; it unfolds not just as narrative of hunter and hunted, but also as confident initiation of narrator and reader into hidden script, into its own secret and privileged space of revelation (the space of 'silence' in which the Vignyan 'Idea' is made manifest). Finally Brombert's account of 'La Pente de la rêverie' shows how Hugolian poetic rêverie is proposed by the poem as nothing less than a key to the mysteries of the cosmos; its metaphors (notably the metaphor of 'les yeux de ma pensée') do not merely serve a way of seeing – they make a statement about their own visionary status, their ability to bring light into darkness, to master a world (indeed *the* world).

Yet, if Hugo's poem is a self-affirming commentary on its own assumed power, it is also hedged about by uncertainty; it describes a journey of discovery, but comes up against a limit: the limit beyond which lies what Brombert calls the unsayable and the unrepresentable. Similar anxieties are to be found in Nerval; if *mise en abyme* in 'El Desdichado' is articulated as a victory over death through the euphoric identification with Orpheus, we should not forget that the Nervalian *abîme* is also a dangerous, life-threatening and ultimately unfathomable place. The abyss is that which is without ground (like the 'sans fond' of the poem 'Le Christ aux oliviers'), and, from that connotation, we might wish to return in a very different register to the reflexive meaning of the allusion to Orpheus: if poetry, through its ancient association with song ('chant'), creates the state of en-chant-ment, it is but a step to activating the negative senses of the title of Nerval's collection of sonnets ('Les Chimères') – the idea of poetry as chimerical construct, pure fable of the imagination, magical enchantment ungrounded in the realities of experience in a modern world that the great social thinker, Max Weber, was to describe, precisely, as a 'disenchanted world'.[13]

Baudelaire, in an essay on Gautier, described poetry as being akin to magic ('une sorcellerie évocatoire'). He meant it as a compliment to both poetry and Gautier, and, in a more general cultural context, as an assertion of the value of poetry in a secular, rationalized, commercial society, where the 'disenchanted' attitude was cognate with the growing dominance of an instrumentally utilitarian ideology. Yet the negative sense of magic as empty 'illusion', and even 'hallucination', is also relevant to the forms of poetry's self-understanding in the nineteenth century; for example, Rimbaud's criticism and renunciation of the poetic project in *Une Saison en enfer* rest on its negative identification with alchemy, magic and hallucination ('Puis j'expliquai mes sophismes magiques avec l'hallucination des mots!'). This in turn gives the terms of a very different kind of *mise en abyme* that will come more into the foreground in the poetry of the second half of the nineteenth century. In connection with this more sceptical mode, a key topic in the present volume is the question of metaphor, notably in the essays on Baudelaire and Gautier. Where Hugo (before encountering the limit at which his poetic construction disarticulates into an elemental 'cri') accords almost limitless power to his own metaphors, Baudelaire and Gautier, while also strongly wedded to a belief in the special aesthetic and cognitive value of metaphor, nevertheless enter certain doubts as to its 'grounded' nature. Jonathan Culler (working from the ideas of Paul de Man concerning the lack of 'ground' beneath metaphorical discourse) argues that – contrary to received opinion – Baudelaire's 'Correspondances' does not so much repeat as query the romantic notion of poetry as 'translation' of the metaphoric unity of being; that in the poem the fragile philosophical claims of metaphor are undone from within, by the self-deconstructing operations of the poem's tropes and figures (crucially, the undoing of the comparative status of the word 'comme' in the last tercet).

Similarly, Gautier's late poem, 'La Nue', is analysed by Christopher Prendergast as an inquiry, at once didactic and embodied, into its own metaphorical productions, where a major (though provisional) place is given to rational criticism and censure of the legitimacy of metaphorical imaginings. He also suggests that the poem emphasizes the ethical as well as philosophical problem of metaphor – the danger of metaphor as the site where imagination blurs the distinction between self and other, appropriates otherness to its own needs and desires; more specifically, Gautier's poem is seen as both reproducing and ironizing the appropriation of the otherness of woman by a fantasizing male imagination (the terms of the representation, or indeed suppression, of 'woman' are also an issue in the essays by Caws and Gans). Bowie too raises sceptical questions regarding metaphor in connection with Mallarmé's sonnet: he points out that in the phrase 'Luxe, ô salle d'ébène' it is impossible to decide which is 'figure' and which is 'ground', and further relates that particular uncertainty to the more general experience of systematic doubt informing Mallarmé's attitude to all the products of poetic invention. Similarly, Riffaterre shows that many of the interpretive difficulties in reading Rimbaud's poem turn on a principle of circularity whereby the distinction between compared and comparing terms, literal and figurative meanings, gets blurred.

All of which brings us back to Verlaine's analogy between the telegraph wires and the *paraphe*. Telegraph wires, like railway trains, are elements of the 'disenchanted world' in its guise as modern industrial society, in turn defined as the mortal enemy of the poetic imagination. Chambers describes the *art poétique* enacted by Verlaine's poem in terms of the attempt by the poem to negotiate a conflict between poetry and modernity, between a traditional conception of poetry as sonorous 'harmony' and the clashing dissonances of the industrial world. The *paraphe* (as rapid, incomplete, semi-legible scrawl) not only rhymes with *télégraphe*; the wires of the latter are seen as resembling it in the speeded-up, blurred perceptions from the moving train. For Chambers this analogy becomes the emblematic figure of the poem as a whole: the superimposition, from the point of view of both the perceiving subject and the writing subject, of train, telegraph and scribbled text gives a complex figure for the fate of poetry in the modern age – as writing invaded by 'vertigo' and menaced by 'blur', threatened with the loss of a stable perspective of meaning, fractured and fluid to the point of edging towards the indecipherable.

Intertextuality

But, if self-reference in nineteenth-century poetry can send us spinning vertiginously towards the 'abyss', this is not the only trajectory along which poetry takes its readers. Poems do not talk only about themselves, but also about, and to, other poems (although talking about other poems can be one of the ways a poem talks about itself, for example, in defining itself in relation to a 'tradition', either as belonging to it or coming to it in belated and therefore problematical ways). Thus we move from self-reference to other-reference, or from the intratextual (the poem exploring and commenting on itself) to the intertextual. Intertextuality is one of the major theoretical concepts elaborated in recent years for the discussion of poetry. Instead of the fiction of the singular, unified speaking 'voice' which dominates our habitual conception of lyric poetry, intertextual reading approaches the poem as a space of many voices, as a complex network of literary (though not only literary) seepages, interferences, convergences and collisions. As several of the essays (notably those by Collier, Culler and Riffaterre) demonstrate, the mechanisms, forms and functions of the intertextual relation can vary considerably. It is important to stress the variety, if only to distinguish the relative richness of the concept of intertextuality from the far thinner, traditional concept of 'influence' or 'source'. The latter suffers from being a somewhat mechanical notion; it implies a purely one-way, direct transaction between a poem and a literary past, whereby the former simply inherits and repeats, in a more or less passive manner, what is given to it by that past. Rigorously applied, the logic of such a view would result in obscuring, even obliterating, what is crucial to any historical understanding of literature, namely the principle of *change*. For, if continuity of form and theme is part of the relevant history of a given body of poetry, that history is not of course properly grasped as simply the endless repetition of the same.

Intertextuality, while incorporating the notion of influence, also supplies analytical means for considering other kinds of relation. The relation can be oblique and tacit rather than in the form of explicit echo or direct quotation (we 'hear' Lamartine and Hugo in Baudelaire's 'Correspondances' only distantly, allusively). It can also be indirect and generalized; it does not follow from scholarship's laborious listing of all the possible 'sources' for the theme of 'correspondances' in Baudelaire's sonnet that Baudelaire actually read them all; many of them may well have come to Baudelaire in indirect form, mediated by other texts. Culler in fact questions whether the apparent 'echoes' of these alleged sources in Baudelaire's poem are echoes at all, and thus poses the intertextual relationship as never a mere given but always a matter of 'interpretation'. Similarly, the fact that Lamartine's 'Le Lac' dramatizes, through the voice of Elvire, the genre of neo-classical elegy does not necessarily mean that Lamartine had personally read all the later eighteenth-century instances of the genre, which one could then theoretically list as potential source material for this aspect of 'Le Lac'. The intertextual relation here is, precisely, with the genre in general, the terms of its historical and cultural constitution, or, even more generally, with the establishment of a universe of the poetically 'sayable', a universe in part constituted by texts that the given individual poet may have never read, but which still press a horizon of possibility and constraint on the world of his own writing. Indeed, the temporal frame of intertextual reading can implicate the future as well as the past, texts which come after as well as before the poem under consideration. This is the intertextual perspective not of the author of the poem (who by definition cannot have such a perspective), but of the later reader, who may well bring her knowledge of subsequent texts into the field of interpretation; this, for example, is what Caws proposes, reading aspects of Leconte de Lisle's 'Midi' in the light of the midday theme in Nietzsche's *Also sprach Zarathustra* and Rimbaud's 'Aube'.

But perhaps the most interesting and important aspect of the concept of intertextuality is that it helps to describe a more restless, combative and dynamic role for a poem in its transactions with its predecessors (and contemporaries). Harold Bloom's theory of the 'anxiety of influence'[14] has been an important reference in this description: in Bloom's view, poems stand in anxious relation to their poetic forbears, at once subject to and yet trying to escape and undermine the latter's 'authority' in the effort to carve out an independent terrain of their own. This model works particularly well in accounts of romantic poetry (Bloom's favoured examples are the English romantics), where notions of 'uniqueness' and 'originality' become virtual obsessions. On the other hand, the model arguably suffers from an excessive emphasis on poetic dialogue and exchange as an arena of tense and tortured agonistic conflict (it is not, for example, very well equipped to deal with the kind of relaxed and playful poetic wit that characterizes, say, Gautier's engagement with the inherited poetic stereotypes of the 'éternel féminin' in 'La Nue'). The model has also been seen as excessively psychological in orientation, extending to the textures of poems a vocabulary of conflict, neurosis and repression that belongs more properly to the description of poets than to that of poems. If 'repression' is a relevant concept in the theory of intertextuality, it is better thought of less in terms of the psychic dramas of individual subjects than on the model of what Riffaterre here calls an 'unconscious of language', where certain meanings get repressed by virtue of incompatible semantic claims on words, and yet continue to lead a displaced, underground life elsewhere in the text (this is one of the main functions of syllepsis, as illustrated in the Rimbaud poem, for example, by the different semantic and syntactic paths travelled by the word 'souci'). Nevertheless, the idea of intertextuality as involving resistance to 'influence', or, more actively, transformation of prior literary discourse that has hardened into cliché and stereotype, remains an important one. Riffaterre shows how much of Rimbaud's poem is to be understood as oblique ironic reference to, for instance, a standardized language of water imagery, or to the hugely oversubscribed theme of 'sunset' in nineteenth-century elegiac writing. At the most general level, this form of the intertextual relation becomes an ironic questioning of the 'literariness' of poetry as such, and is thus a point at which intertextuality helps perform the function of 'self-reference'. Collier also proposes a similar value for the intertextual relation in Laforgue's poem, where, around the conventional poetic topos of the landscape of 'winter', different references and vocabularies, voices and styles, both co-exist and clash in a way that knowingly puts pressure on the whole tradition of lyric utterance.

History

The final theoretical issue I wish to raise here is one that this collection of essays does not address in any sustainedly direct way (and which indeed some of the contributors might wish to deny is an issue at all). If the essays are much concerned with both the intratextual and intertextual dimensions of poetry, they have less to say about the movement from the latter to the extratextual (what in certain theoretical circles is called the *hors-texte*), and in particular that order of the *hors-texte* we commonly refer to as 'history'. Some versions of contemporary theoretical work would argue that the question, posed thus, is mal-posed; that there is no 'outside' to which the language of poetry, or indeed, in the more radical claim of this body of work, language as such, directly leads us. In respect of poetry, this is, for example, the view of Riffaterre: poetry articulates 'reality' only by way of its re-working of prior literary and linguistic forms; the relation of poetry to world is always and irreducibly intertextual (thus, Rimbaud's city poems, for example, do not describe a historical Paris, but rather re-describe or transform previous descriptions of it).

These are deeply controversial and necessarily open-ended matters. Nevertheless, the question of history, of the place of poetry in history, still remains vexingly on the agenda of discussion. Or to put the point in a slightly more complex way, there is still much work to be done on how we might grasp both the history *of* poetry and history *in* poetry, the inter-relations of those two prepositions pointing towards the idea of a history of poetic forms caught up in, inflected by and in turn (though perhaps only modestly) inflecting a wider cultural and social history. In connection with the first (the history of poetry), intertextual analysis has a lot to teach us. It takes us away from unreflecting recourse to the fictions of pure 'originality' towards a conception of poetry as a dialogue or conflict of texts through time. Culler's account of the transitional significance of Baudelaire is a case in point ('The romantic line runs into this poem; the modernist line runs out of it'), while Riffaterre's reading of Rimbaud's 'Mémoire' considers its transformative energies against the wider historical background of forms of everyday linguistic usage.

On the other hand, it can be objected that the kind of history which intertextual analysis gives us is either too narrow or too generalized. In its former guise, it tends to see the history of poetry entirely as a matter of 'high' culture, as a dialogue of canonical proper names (the 'great poets'), with a corresponding neglect of other kinds of historical connection and context.[15] In its latter guise, it tends to evacuate from its field of vision the specifics of history in the name of something called Language, 'patterns' of language

135,308

25

tracing themselves out in what often appears to be relative independence from other kinds of historical determination. At least three of the essays in this collection go some way towards linking intertextual considerations with a richer and more precisely focussed sense of history. Gans's essay on Lamartine, Chambers's essay on Verlaine and Bowie's essay on Mallarmé give us some terms for grasping the vicissitudes of poetic 'voice' in the nineteenth century in relation to the emergence of a market society and its development into an industrial and consumer society. Lamartine's striving for a strong 'individual' voice against the dead forms of neo-classical literary culture (whose death is embodied in the death of Elvire) is seen by Gans as connected to the loss – and nostalgic idealization – of pre-Revolutionary communal forms of life and the elaboration of a corresponding strategy of survival in the impersonal modern world of the 'bourgeois marketplace', where the category of 'individual' has assumed greater centrality. Chambers notes the intertextual echo in Verlaine's poem of Dante's inferno, but makes sense of that echo by reading it in terms of the pressure on the late nineteenth-century poetic imagination of the sounds and sights of the new industrial society; the two-term relation (Dante/Verlaine) is interpreted in function of a third term, the 'outside' of a new economic and social formation (though this word 'outside' – which Chambers himself does not use – must still remain problematic in such an argument). Bowie draws attention to the lexical echoes in 'Quand l'ombre menaça ...' of some of the terms in Mallarmé's journalistic reports on the World Exhibitions of 1871 and 1872 in London. From this intertextual fact, Bowie – against the grain of the received view of Mallarmé as serenely indifferent to material reality – proposes a reading of the sonnet that takes us via the opening pages of Marx's *Das Kapital* towards a reflection on Mallarmé's art as caught in complex and ambivalent relation to the values of the contemporary commodity culture.

Finally, both the essays by Gans and Chambers not only give an account of how poems may be said to 'register' the imprint on sensibility of a specific history; they also give rise to speculations concerning the historical nature of lyric poetry as such, or, more accurately, of conceptions of lyric poetry. If they tell us about

26

history in poetry, they also tell us about the history of poetry, or rather the historicity of poetry, in the important sense of directing attention towards the fact that the notion of lyric as the expression of a private 'subjectivity' is essentially an invention of the nineteenth century itself. The personal voice and the atomic, solitary subject which we ourselves often take for granted as constituting a trans-historical essence of lyric are better understood as local constructions developed in response to a particular historical experience encouraging the divorce of the categories of 'public' and 'private'. To convert the emphasis on the private into a universal mode of lyric expression is to forget that history, and to overlook the fact that in other periods poetic 'voice' was understood as expressing concerns of a more public sort (something of the survival of those older public forms can be seen in Vigny, whose 'La Mort du Loup' Scott describes as combining exhortatory fable in the grand oratorical style and the more intimate mode of address we associate with the 'romantic' idea of lyric). If, in early nineteenth-century France, Lamartine decisively alters the conception of lyric by radically 'privatizing' it, this is both in response to historical developments and itself a historical development. Its logical terminus in the later nineteenth century might then be seen as Verlaine's reduction of experience to 'blur', a domain of inwardness so private, fugitive and fragmented that it threatens to exceed the capacity of language to name and represent it. The partial eclipse of a secure public framework for poetic expression is one of the most important of nineteenth-century themes, and it is of course still with us in the twentieth century. This is another reason for returning, with the help of these essays, to the nineteenth-century poets, if only to remind ourselves not just of a relation of continuity between then and now, but also of the reality of both then and now as historically produced.

NOTES

1 I. A. Richards, *Practical Criticism* (London 1929), p. 317.
2 For a trenchant critique of the tradition of 'practical criticism' from this point of view, *cf.* John Barrell, *Poetry, Language and Politics* (Manchester, 1988).
3 P. Valéry, *Œuvres* (Paris, 1957), Vol. 1, p. 1440.
4 *Ibid.*, p. 1510.

5 R. Jakobson, 'Linguistics and Poetics', in *Style in Language*, ed. T. A. Sebeok (Cambridge, MA, 1960), p. 358.

6 I am indebted for this point to Martin Swales, *German Poetry: An Anthology from Klopstock to Enzensberger* (Cambridge, 1987), p. 5.

7 Richards, *Practical Criticism*, p. 318.

8 *Cf*, G. Genette, *Mimologiques: voyages en Cratylie* (Paris, 1976).

9 Richards, *Practical Criticism*, pp. 230–1.

10 Both these points are cogently made by C. Scott, *A Question of Syllables* (Cambridge, 1986), pp. x–xi.

11 R. Barthes, *Critique et vérité* (Paris, 1966), p. 46.

12 An important exception is the collection of essays, *Lyric Poetry: Beyond New Criticism*, ed. C. Hošek and P. Parker (Ithaca, NY, 1985).

13 This opposition between 'enchantment' and 'disenchantment' (in the Weberian sense) has been described in connection with the theory of lyric by Jonathan Arac, 'Afterword: Lyric Poetry and the Bounds of New Criticism', in Hošek and Parker, *Lyric Poetry*, p. 347.

14 H. Bloom, *The Anxiety of Influence: A Theory of Poetry* (New York, 1973).

15 *Cf*. Arac, 'Afterword', p. 349.

2

THE POEM AS HYPOTHESIS OF ORIGIN: LAMARTINE'S 'LE LAC'

Eric Gans

Ainsi, toujours poussés vers de nouveaux rivages,
Dans la nuit éternelle emportés sans retour,
Ne pourrons-nous jamais sur l'océan des âges
    Jeter l'ancre un seul jour?

5   O lac! l'année à peine a fini sa carrière,
Et près des flots chéris qu'elle devait revoir,
Regarde! je viens seul m'asseoir sur cette pierre
    Où tu la vis s'asseoir!

Tu mugissais ainsi sous ces roches profondes,
10   Ainsi tu te brisais sur leurs flancs déchirés,
Ainsi le vent jetait l'écume de tes ondes
    Sur ses pieds adorés.

Un soir, t'en souvient-il? nous voguions en silence;
On n'entendait au loin, sur l'onde et sous les cieux,
15   Que le bruit des rameurs qui frappaient en cadence
    Tes flots harmonieux.

Tout à coup des accents inconnus à la terre
Du rivage charmé frappèrent les échos:
Le flot fut attentif, et la voix qui m'est chère
20   Laissa tomber ces mots:

«Ô temps! suspends ton vol, et vous, heures propices!
    Suspendez votre cours:
Laissez-nous savourer les rapides délices
    Des plus beaux de nos jours!

25 «Assez de malheureux ici-bas vous implorent,
     Coulez, coulez pour eux;
Prenez avec leurs jours les soins qui les dévorent,
     Oubliez les heureux.

«Mais je demande en vain quelques moments encore,
30   Le temps m'échappe et fuit;
Je dis à cette nuit: Sois plus lente; et l'aurore
     Va dissiper la nuit.

«Aimons donc, aimons donc! de l'heure fugitive,
     Hâtons-nous, jouissons!
35 L'homme n'a point de port, le temps n'a point de rive;
     Il coule, et nous passons!»

Temps jaloux, se peut-il que ces moments d'ivresse,
Où l'amour à longs flots nous verse le bonheur,
S'envolent loin de nous de la même vitesse
40   Que les jours de malheur?

Eh quoi! n'en pourrons-nous fixer au moins la trace?
Quoi! passés pour jamais! quoi! tout entiers perdus!
Ce temps qui les donna, ce temps qui les efface,
     Ne nous les rendra plus!

45 Eternité, néant, passé, sombres abîmes,
Que faites-vous des jours que vous engloutissez?
Parlez: nous rendrez-vous ces extases sublimes
     . Que vous nous ravissez?

Ô lac! rochers muets! grottes! forêt obscure!
50 Vous, que le temps épargne ou qu'il peut rajeunir,
Gardez de cette nuit, gardez, belle nature,
     Au moins le souvenir!

Qu'il soit dans ton repos, qu'il soit dans tes orages,
Beau lac, et dans l'aspect de tes riants coteaux,
55 Et dans ces noirs sapins, et dans ces rocs sauvages
     Qui pendent sur tes eaux.

Qu'il soit dans le zéphyr qui frémit et qui passe,
Dans les bruits de tes bords par tes bords répétés,
Dans l'astre au front d'argent qui blanchit ta surface

60   De ses molles clartés.

Que le vent qui gémit, le roseau qui soupire,
Que les parfums légers de ton air embaumé,
Que tout ce qu'on entend, l'on voit ou l'on respire,
Tout dise: Ils ont aimé!

✳✳✳

Few literary destinies are more touching than that of Lamartine. The author of one of history's few poetic best-sellers in 1820, a national political leader in 1848, he spent his last two decades in severe financial difficulties, composing vast, hastily written series of historical volumes in a futile effort to pay off the debts accumulated in his earlier years. In a photograph made in 1867 the elegant young aristocrat had to all appearances been transformed into an aged peasant.

Although at the end of his life Lamartine's poetry and novels in verse and prose were still widely read, the waning of the romantic era deprived his work of much of its popular appeal. Today he is remembered chiefly for a few poems from the 1820 *Méditations* and for one or two others, notably his mature masterpiece 'La Vigne et la maison'. But from the first, one poem has stood out from the rest: Lamartine is above all the poet of 'Le Lac'.

Other poems of the *Méditations* give the poetic pseudonym 'Elvire' to the woman who plays in them the same role as Beatrice in *La Vita Nuova* or Laura in Petrarch's *Canzoniere*. In real life, she was Julie Charles, the consumptive wife of a distinguished academician whom Lamartine had met during her visit to a sanatorium in October 1816 at Lake Bourget in the French Alps. The following summer, Lamartine returned to the lake, but Julie had become too ill to leave Paris, and died in December 1817. It is this absence that is commemorated in 'Le Lac'.

A poem or any literary work expresses a vision of man, an *anthropology*. Its significance is not reducible to the personal or even to the historical. We would not read 'Le Lac' if it were merely the commemoration of a particular adulterous love-affair. We read it as a model for human life in general, including our own.

'Le Lac' tells a story of love and death. But the most fundamental anthropological category, the one that distinguishes us from our animal brethren, is not love or death, but *signification*. What is significant to man is what signifies, because the signs of human language, as opposed to animal sign-systems, not only refer to other things but can themselves become objects of thought.

The ambition of any literary work is to provide an autonomous, self-contained model of the significant. Every poem is a microcosm, but this fact can only be put to productive use once we have understood something about the 'cosmos' to which its structure is analogous. The human cosmos is a world of meanings centred on a scene that is the origin of meaning. 'Le Lac' gives us an insight into the structure of this scene. Its claim is that the commemoration of the love consecrated by the beloved's death is the only task worthy of the human system of signification, that the scene on the lake is a privileged model, a hypothesis, of the origin of language.

How can language describe its own origin? The most common contemporary answers to this question are either that no meaningful model of this origin is constructible, or else that the task is trivial, since higher animals already possess forms of communication that differ only by degree from our own. Lamartine's poem offers the possibility of a third, more meaningful answer. The art-work does not formulate a theory in conceptual terms, but presents to the reader's imagination a structured model of the originary scene.

The sign is created from the locus of an absence. The fear of death is the beginning of linguistic communication. Because man is the only species that poses more of a threat to its own survival than the external agencies of nature, his first use of language is to control the violence of intraspecific aggression. Man alone envisions his own death because man has put death at the origin of his culture. It follows from this that even 'natural' death must be given cultural significance. Death is the privileged point of contact between the personal and the universally significant. The Greek word for 'sign', 'sema', is also the word for 'tomb'. In 'Le Lac', the stone on which the poet has returned to sit alone hints at this theme. The whole of the lake is a metaphorical tomb/sign for the victim whose martyrdom it witnessed. Elvire was here, she is no more; in this place she and the poet became aware of their mortality. The locus marked by the sign is the place where the human voice acquired both the need and the power to produce language.

Even in its richest vein, that of Victor Hugo, French romantic poetry never attains the depth of metaphor of the great English and German poets. France has no Wordsworths or Hölderlins. What it does have, in its best moments, is *structure*. Writing in what was still very much the idiom of late eighteenth-century elegy, Lamartine transforms the lake and its surroundings into the locus of a dialectical opposition between neo-classical and romantic hypotheses of origin, as revealed in differing conceptions of time, poetry and language.[1] The secret of 'Le Lac' is its dramatization of this opposition in the contrast between the pathetic voice of the dying Elvire and the strong new voice of the romantic poet.

The contrast in voice is emphasized by a difference in versification. Of the sixteen four-verse strophes of 'Le Lac', the first five and last seven consist of three alexandrines followed by a six-syllable hemistich. In the middle group of four, the verses spoken by Elvire, the second alexandrine too is cut in half, producing a rhythm noticeably hastier and less sustained than in the rest of the poem. Not merely the speakers and the verses, but the occasions for these two modes of discourse are different. The classical writer, like Elvire, celebrates the present, not the past. Classical works locate human truth in a present enactment. The ambivalent advantage of cultural lateness allows the romantic to develop a more complete anthropological model than his predecessor. The presence of classical literature retains in secularized form the urgency of ritual; the retrospective romantic vision is a step closer to the objective stance of the scientist.

Only memory can preserve the past against loss, and cultural memory, including the memory from which language is constructed, requires a content of natural experience. Language must be independent of any specific scene; otherwise it would not serve us as a means of communication. But the first shared signification can only be the memory of a shared experience. The origin of signification, the origin of language, must take place in a specific place at a specific moment. The poet's unique personal revelation becomes a model for the production of public meaning. The discovery procedure is individual, but what is discovered is not only of general significance but the model of a collective event. The first person singular is absent from the last third of 'Le Lac', after having figured prominently in the other two parts. The natural phenomena that surround the lake-as-centre play a role analogous to that which a human collectivity would have played in a sacrificial ritual. The human witnesses are gone, but because the locus remains, the trees and the rocks can offer adequate testimony to the sacral moment.

The love that Lamartine wants us to remember is an adulterous affair parasitic on the social order. From its beginnings in the High Middle Ages, the literature of romantic love founded its hypothesis of origin on a scene of sexual desire detached from its reproductive goal. Love's spiritual, as opposed to its biological, function can be liberated from the concrete order of things within which the latter remains fixed. The lover stands at the periphery of a circle whose centre is the inaccessible female figure. The resulting deification of the beloved creates a personal model of religious revelation in which the woman's death is assimilated to a process of sacred transfiguration. The paradigmatic example of this is Beatrice's role in the *Divine Comedy*.

The power of this hypothesis depends less on the absence of physical possession than on the inviolability of the scene of desire on the periphery of which the lover remains. Desire gives significance to lived experience by providing a centre around which this experience may be organized. The deferral of sexual satisfaction is the prerequisite for the metonymic attribution of significance to the objects which seem to promise or refuse this satisfaction. In the Renaissance this system came to be articulated in elaborate codes of poetic language.

In its original form, romantic love was the basis of the neoclassical aesthetic that made possible the transition from the classical culture of antiquity to the modern romantic culture of which 'Le Lac' is an important early expression. The term 'romantic' by which this kind of love is designated emphasizes its connection with romanticism, but unfortunately implies that the literature it inspired was fully emancipated from the system of classical aesthetics. Yet however personalized the scene of desire, romantic love never sees this scene as a whole, only the woman at the centre of it. The revelatory event of love is the encounter between the peripheral lover and the central beloved that constitutes the scene. This aesthetic system is mimetic in the classical sense; the work remains the enactment or making-present of the significant event. The disappearance of the scenic centre through the woman's death occurs outside the work's commemoratory structure; as in Petrarch's *Canzoniere*, it divides the poems into two groups, *ante mortem* and *post mortem*.

By the time of the late neo-classical elegy exemplified by Elvire's complaint, the mortality of the central figure was no longer the occasion for an apotheosis; it had become a morbid obsession. The male self's vulnerability to desire that had been emphasized in all the old poetry from Dante through Maurice Scève and Ronsard was forgotten in face of the pathetic fragility of the central female Other. The poet's elegy expressed a detached pity rather than the anguish of loss. The scene of desire was no longer experienced as a conversion to a new system of meanings but as a consciousness of mortality that emptied out all preceding systems of meanings. Death no longer seemed assimilable by a traditional culture that had lost faith in its own immortality.

But this emptying-out of the old aesthetic was at the same time a preparation for the new. As Elvire's words show, the classical 'event' of love has become no more than a revelation of mortality. The present is wholly absorbed by its future decay, to the point where the neo-classical literary voice abandons the very attempt to make present through mimesis that had until then been the hallmark of all secular art. The stage has been set for the romantic artist who will transcend the passivity of present experience by constructing a hypothesis of origin that no longer requires the originary event to generate its own representation.

The French Revolution destroyed the social order that had sheltered the old aesthetic. By the time the Restoration had brought a temporary end to the political upheavals the Revolution had occasioned, Western man had acquired an experience of historical evolution that definitively cut him off from his traditional past. A society was being created in which significance was based not on tradition but on exchange. But the mediate values of the new era, like the exchange-values of goods, had to be traced back to 'use-values' in a world anterior to the market-place. The romantic art-work puts into circulation the artist's originally incommunicable intuition of primal experience. The intimate scene becomes the retrospective referent of the language of the public scene. The classical model of cultural communication as shared presence survives only as it does in 'Le Lac', as a transcended form within the new.

The link between Elvire and the old regime is the demise of both. Late classical culture's obsession with time reflects its vulnerability to history. Time refused to suspend its flight not only for the individual members of old-regime society, but for the society itself. But the failure of late traditional culture suggests a lesson to later generations; in the face of the impermanence of human institutions, the permanence of the material world makes it a guarantee of the enduring significance of originary human experience. Elvire's despairing words assimilate this intimate experience to the forms of a dying culture; the poet affirms the invulnerability of intimacy to the revolutions of history. Like the natural surroundings of Lake Bourget, the scene of origin is prehistorical. Historical change has taught the romantic poet that the origin of meaning must be situated anterior to human time.

The tripartite structure of 'Le Lac' corresponds to a temporal dialectic of thesis, antithesis and synthesis:

1 After lamenting the oceanic flux of time ('Ainsi, toujours poussés vers de nouveaux rivages...'), the poet addresses the lake as the locus of a cyclical temporality ('l'année') that has been broken by his beloved's absence, and evokes a shared memory ('t'en souvient-il?') of her presence.
2 In the remembered scene of the preceding year, the woman laments the irreversibility of time viewed as a linear ('Coulez', 'Le temps m'échappe et fuit') rather than a cyclical process, a river more than an ocean, and surely not a lake.
3 The poet at first despairs of this irreversibility ('ce temps qui les efface, / Ne nous les rendra plus!'), then appeals to the presence, both cyclical and timeless, of the natural phenomena surrounding the lake ('Vous, que le temps épargne ou qu'il peut rajeunir') to preserve the memory of their love.

The first strophe presents the image of the ocean endlessly driven toward new shores as an allegory of man's passage through time. There is no vantage point on the shore from which one may observe this flux; like Pascalian man, the poet is 'embarqué'. At this stage in the poem, no specific time or place has been given significance;

man's voyage on the sea is as inescapable and unstructured as the movement of life toward death. The figure of time as 'l'océan des âges' is midway between the linear and the cyclic. In the dialectic of the poem it corresponds to an original chaos, an unordered movement that permits us to conceive a human order only as an opposing motionlessness ('jeter l'ancre'). In contrast, the waters of the lake share the periodic movement of the poetic 'versus', returning always to the same place.[2] Here the poet is not borne by the waves; like Rousseau contemplating Lake Bienne at the end of the Fifth Promenade of the *Rêveries*, he sits on the shore.

In the second and third strophes, the poet evokes Elvire's absence in pathetic contrast to the movements of the lake which are identical ('ainsi') to those of the previous year ('Regarde! je viens seul . . . / Où tu la vis s'asseoir!'). This prompts him to make the lake his accomplice in recalling his beloved's former presence. But all that is recalled of this presence is her voice, which expresses not the plenitude of the moment of happiness but its fragile vulnerability to the very process of time referred to in the first strophe ('L'homme n'a point de port', 'Il coule, et nous passons'). Elvire's four strophes express a despair at the swiftness of time typical of late neo-classical elegy. Her first hemistich, 'O temps! suspends ton vol,' is in fact a quotation from 'Ode sur le temps' by Thomas, a minor eighteenth-century poet; one wonders if Lamartine expected his readers to recognize this.

It is of interest that Lamartine eliminated from his manuscript two strophes immediately following Elvire's lament that had attempted to evoke the timeless 'moment d'ivresse' between the two lovers:

> '. . .
>   Il coule, et nous passons!»
>
> Elle se tut: nos cœurs, nos yeux se rencontrèrent;
> Des mots entrecoupés se perdaient dans les airs;
> Et dans un long transport nos âmes s'envolèrent
>   Dans un autre univers.
>
> Nous ne pûmes parler: nos âmes affaiblies
> Succombaient sous le poids de leur félicité;
> Nos cœurs battaient ensemble, et nos bouches unies
>   Disaient: Eternité.

This blissful moment is described as that of the dissolution and cessation of language ('mots entrecoupés', 'Nous ne pûmes parler'), in contrast with the despairing voice that had preceded. The plenitude of the act of love puts an end to a speech which conveyed only absence. Yet the apparent timelessness of the lovers' happiness can itself only be given meaning through its assimilation to an act of speech ('Disaient: Eternité).

Two mouths united in a kiss would hardly be able to speak. Like the 'Tout dise: Ils ont aimé!' at the end of the poem, 'disaient' is both straightforward and metaphoric; in Richards's terms, it is vehicle and tenor at once. The mouths 'say' Eternity by their kiss more than by mouthing the words. This is not an unsubtle finesse, but it is unsatisfactory, not because of the intrinsic absurdity of the figure, but because 'saying' eternity is but another way of revealing that one is not eternal.

With the elimination of these two strophes, the 'moment d'ivresse' disappears from the poem itself. The poet's language will claim no superiority over Elvire's in its ability to recreate such moments; its advantage lies in its retrospective capacity to view the lake as the locus of a *scene*, defined as a circle composed of a periphery and a centre. This superiority of the lake-as-scene as a model for the generation of meaning had not been accessible to Elvire, for whom time's linear flow has neither the ocean's chaotic ambiguity nor the lake's cyclic stability; her speech was made *on the water*, that is, within the flux of time. Modern man is swept down the river of time ('point de rive') that Heraclitus had observed from the bank. The lake is equivalent to a river when one finds oneself floating on it; thus the central figure of the original scene is not conscious of her centrality. Only in retrospect do the lake's borders lend human significance to the temporal process. The lake acts as a mirror retained by its frame, maintaining an eternal reflection of the events that took place upon its surface.

The poet's first reaction is to reproduce in universal terms the sentiments of his beloved. Where she had said, 'Le temps m'échappe et fuit', he exclaims, 'se peut-il que ces moments d'ivresse/... S'envolent loin de nous ...?' His apostrophe to 'Eternité, néant, passé, sombres abîmes' remains in the same mode of discourse. By addressing himself to abstractions he guarantees that there will be no reply. This silence creates a dramatic tension that finds its release in the climactic turning point between the twelfth and thirteenth strophes. The new series of apostrophes, 'O lac! rochers muets! grottes! forêt obscure!' parallels that of the previous strophe, but now all is changed. These are not abstractions, but material realities that can be imagined by the reader. Nor are they a mere series of unconnected natural objects; they are the constituents of a scene centred on the lake. That the human imagination has an inherent attachment to such scenes of origin is the great discovery of this poem, and of nineteenth-century poetry in general.

These natural phenomena are sources of metaphor rather than logical homologies. That there is no single romantic hypothesis of origin is clear from the familiar schoolbook contrast between 'Le Lac' and other romantic poems that use Nature imagery differently: Hugo's 'Tristesse d'Olympio' where the permanence of Nature is only 'lent' to the lovers, or Vigny's 'La Maison du berger' where it disdainfully opposes itself to them. In telling Nature to remember, or in reproaching it with its indifference, or in any other variation of this poet–Nature dialogue, the poet enjoys the freedom of a theorist constructing an independent hypothesis. What all these romantic interpretations of the relationship between man and Nature have in common is the poet's own innocence, his lack of any complicity with the mortal movement of time that separates the human past from the present and renders the locus more permanent than the event enacted on its stage.

The critical transition between the abstract figures of time and the natural objects that appear in the thirteenth strophe is in fact the passage from a classical to a romantic hypothesis of origin. 'Time', 'eternity' and the rest appear to us as imageless abstractions, as they indeed appeared to the readers of Lamartine's time. But as Elvire's apostrophes demonstrate, time is a vestigial but still bloodthirsty classical divinity. Such divinities incarnate a violence which is not really that of natural processes but that of the human community. Men justify their sacrifices by referring them to gods who incarnate their intraspecific aggressiveness. The great classical tragedies reveal the human origins of sacrificial violence. In contrast, the feeble neo-classical elegies of a traditional society that has lost faith in its values hide these origins by converting the gods into depersonalized abstractions.

The appeal to time is tantamount to an admission that the culture has lost control of the means for the creation of significance. Before the romantics, neo-classical poets locate their pathetic scenes of sacrifice in natural settings, but these settings illustrate rather the absence of human witnesses than the presence of natural ones. The passage from seventeenth-century tragedy to eighteenth-century elegy reflects the weakening of the traditional community, the emergence of a new intimacy that had not yet acquired the means of self-affirmation. Pre-romanticism contains all the thematic material of romanticism without its affirmative strength; its 'privacy' reveals only the deprivation of communal solidarity that is expressed by the word's etymology (French *privé*, 'deprived').

Elvire's lament exemplifies the weakness of late classical culture better than a real neo-classical poem could do, for we know as we hear it that the voice that pronounced it has been stilled. Hers is the cry of a victim appealing pathetically to a god who has been reduced to no more than a figure of speech. Her prayer concentrates on the central fact of death at the expense of its locus. Only someone unconscious of her location would feel herself more on a river than on a lake. We sympathize with Elvire's plight, but are given no imaginary means to resist it; she performs on a featureless stage.

The romantic poet discovered the cultural importance of the locus in which language is generated. In this place we too can stand, not merely witnessing the present but reliving the past, not only perceiving the abstract sign but imagining its absent material referent. In its celebrated nostalgia for Nature, romantic culture in fact pays homage to the stage-setting of human events. Thus the poet's counter-appeal to the trees and the rocks has a different focus from his beloved's lament. He requests not mercy but language. Although this language is dependent on the previous violence done to the woman, the objects he addresses are themselves non-violent and peripheral. Elvire demands the postponement of an inevitable event, whereas the poet solicits what culture is able to give, significant commemoration after the fact.

This difference between romantic and pre-romantic poetry is not a mere difference of degree. All literature expresses anthropological knowledge, but romanticism's concretely retrospective character permits a greater degree of assimilation of imaginary constructions to theoretical models than any previous literary mode. Petrarch's laments for Laura were not preceded by the 'moment d'ivresse' of possession. What he lost was the occasion for desire, not its fulfilment. Neo-classical desire is always ahead of itself, projected toward its 'sacred' object, even when this object is no more. Romantic desire uses the past as its edenic guarantee; this is what gives it its cognitive edge. To contemplate the empty locus of a lost ideal intimacy is to add an additional layer of structure to the anticipatory figures of the classical mode of desire.

The neo-classical lover plays a part in a scene that the romantic views as a whole. While the one stands at the periphery of the circle that contains the sacred figure of his mistress, the other stands outside the circle altogether. Observing the frame as well as the portrait it contains, the romantics comprehend its structural relationship to its central figure. Returning to the empty frame from which the picture has been removed, as in Baudelaire's 'Le Fantôme' ('Comme un beau cadre ajoute à la peinture . . .'), the poet recognizes it as a model *en creux* of his beloved's former presence. She is revealed to have been from the start more absent than present, more dead than alive, a figure of inaccessibility that exemplifies the interaction between the sacred ritual centre and its peripherally located worshippers.

The romantic hypothesis of origin does not simply contradict the classical; it includes it in its synthesis. In 'Le Lac', both voices agree on the primary importance of the originary event, the love-scene in the boat. But whereas Elvire attempts to live the scene as self-sufficient, as though it could generate out of itself the language that will preserve its significance, the poet makes language a compensatory response to a preceding violence. When Elvire speaks, all else is silent, as at the first instant of creation. Her hypothesis of origin is unreflective, wholly implicit in the fact of her speech; she uses language to prolong the present rather than to re-present it. Her final words addressed to her love ('Hâtons-nous, jouissons!') are an incitement to sensual activity as a Pascalian *divertissement* from the truth of inevitable death. Unlike Elvire's, the poet's language makes no claim of having been present at the origin. The poet's command to Nature to speak its remembrance of their love, first made in the imperative ('gardez, belle nature'), is given its definitive expression in the hypothetical mode of the subjunctive ('Que ... Tout dise'). Elvire wanted action, not words, whereas even when the poet addresses time, it is words he is after: 'Parlez: nous rendrez-vous ces extases sublimes ...'

In this apostrophe to time, the poet feigns a preliminary acceptance of his beloved's implicit 'theory'. To see whether time, that is, the human consciousness of time as mortality, is truly the origin of language, it is given its chance to speak. This request is not an imperative but a question: the beneficiary of the sacrifice, unlike mere spectators who can only remember, should be able to provide an understanding of what has occurred. If the classical hypothesis is true, then the scene of origin, conceived as an awakening to the necessity of death, must contain its own understanding. But merely to ask the question is to reveal the limitations of the old view. The classical hypothesis fails because non-human temporality cannot provide an answer to man's question; the romantic hypothesis generates its own. The poet need not be the original speaker in order to furnish the words for the originary speech. The origin takes place in two phases, event and sign, present and past, presence and re-presentation. The significance of the event, its very constitution as an event, is inseparable from our commemoration of it.

The poet's voice is opposed to the beloved's by his attribution to the lake of the ability not to 'suspend time' but to retain its objective reality through time. The years pass, but the lake remains as the locus of what has occured. The 'bruits de tes bords par tes bords répétés' offer a paradigm of poetic language, whose rhythms make time their servant rather than their master. The permanent-in-time surroundings of the lake can be asked to 'say', not 'Eternité' perhaps, but 'ils ont aimé': not 'they are eternally present' but, more modestly, 'it remains eternally true that they have been present'. The last three strophes, although divided by periods, really form one long sentence that emphasizes the productivity of the poet's new discovery. Once the lake has been recognized as a scenic centre, its shores provide an inexhaustible wealth of signifying material.

The poet's cry 'Que ... Tout dise "Ils ont aimé!"' is not a reflection of meanings he finds in Nature but an assignment of a human meaning to natural phenomena, a command that only men are equipped to carry out. The resolution of the poem's original figure of human life as a voyage on a boundless ocean is the confinement of its significance to the captured water of the lake. The lake, unlike oceans and rivers, is a bounded place to which one can return, to which one can 'cycle' back. In their association with this locus, trees and rocks and even the moon can be described as not merely in contiguity with it but *centred* on it: '... ces rocs sauvages/Qui pendent sur tes eaux', 'l'astre au front d'argent qui blanchit ta surface'. Finally, all sense data are pressed into the service of this new centrality: 'Que tout ce qu'on entend, l'on voit ou l'on respire ...' The creation of a centre reorganizes the entire natural universe around a unique human experience.

The poet speaks to Nature with a new voice, but his beloved has become a silenced victim of history. This relation of surviving male and mourned woman appears in a surprising number of romantic works. From Goethe's Werther on, suicidal males are not lacking in the romantic repertory (Senancour's Obermann, Musset's Rolla, the nameless hero of Flaubert's early work *Novembre*). But the martyred Self, both subject and object of language, is an ambiguous and never fully mature figure. It is rather the model of 'Le Lac', the distant archetypes of which are the late medieval love-epics of Dante and Beatrice, Petrarch and Laura, that dominates the romantic scene from its inception in Rousseau's *Nouvelle Héloïse*, through Chateaubriand's *Atala* and *René*, Constant's *Adolphe*, Vigny's 'La Maison du berger' (where the woman is only 'menacée'), Balzac's *Le Père Goriot* (where the woman's role is played by an old man), Hugo's *Contemplations* (where the woman is the poet's daughter), to its derisory end in Charles's posthumous cult of Emma in *Madame Bovary*.

All these works oppose two species of martyrdom: the 'classical' female variety whose victim actually dies, and a 'romantic' male variant whose victim continues to live in inconsolable mourning for his loss. (As Lamartine put it in a famous line from another poem of the *Méditations*, 'Un seul être vous manque et tout est dépeuplé.') Female martyrdom is associated with the traditional order that perished with the Revolution; the man lives on, as he must, within bourgeois society. The romantic's elegy for classical culture is the lament of the atomic individual for a network of interpersonal relationships. The historical nostalgia of romantic literature protests against the emerging market-society of the industrial era by idealizing the 'feudal' relations of the pre-revolutionary past. These relations are 'feminine' in that they are established directly between persons rather than through the intermediary of an exchange-system. They are the essentially familial relationships of traditional society (*Gemeinschaft*) as opposed to the impersonal ones of the modern world (*Gesellschaft*). But the romantic does not merely lament the passing of a bygone age; he assimilates these social forms to his individual experience of childhood intimacy which is in fact a by-product of the rise of the bourgeoisie. The woman's death is associated with the adolescent's forcible emergence into an impersonal world. Woman is part of romantic man's intimate prehistory; her death is a sacrifice that is prerequisite to the survival of the male self in the bourgeois market-place.

The death of the poet's beloved in 'Le Lac' was motivated by a real event. But we need not accuse Lamartine of having murdered Julie Charles to note that his poetic alter ego profits from Elvire's death. In the absence of any *ante mortem* poetry like that of Dante and Petrarch, this 'profit' constituted at the time of the *Méditations* Lamartine's entire poetic capital, to which the subsequent decades added unfortunately rather little.

In 'Le Lac', the man, the woman, and the natural environment play three different roles in the scene of which the lake is the stage. In this scene of metaphoric ritual, the woman is the central victim; the natural 'witnesses' called by the poet are passive peripheral observers who illustrate the romantic hypothesis that language does not originally emanate from the sacred centre, but from its human periphery. In religious terms, it may be God who teaches us to speak, but it is man who pronounces the words.

But the role of the poet himself, who was present beside his beloved at the original scene, is less clear. Although he proclaims his innocence, we are tempted to see him in the role of the executioner who penetrates to the centre of the circle in order to slay the ritual victim. His appeal to Nature to immortalize his love is destined to absolve him of blame in Elvire's death. The romantic hypothesis of origin, however great a theoretical advance it represents over the classical, remains in part a cultural alibi. Language is indeed generated on the periphery of the scene of origin, but the innocence of the peripheral 'observers' is suspect. The sinister aspect of the 'noirs sapins' and 'rocs sauvages' expresses a veiled allusion to this hidden guilt.

The universe of romanticism is close enough to the revolutionary era for history to take the blame for the death of the past. After the failed revolution of 1848, in which Lamartine himself played a noble but ineffective part, the artist will increasingly realize his own complicity in the sacrifice his poetry celebrates. As the post-romantic poetic Self becomes conscious of its dependence on the Other's expulsion for its very existence, the 'natural' romantic death-scene will become the explicit product of human violence. The Parnassians, without always understanding why, are obsessed by archaic spectacles of ritual cruelty. Baudelaire, the century's most lucid analyst of the 'Satanic' guilt of the poetic ego, openly plays the role of a sacrificer coveting the object of his desire as a potential victim. Finally, Mallarmé's *œuvre*, dominated by 'tombeaux' and tableaux of mysterious oceanic drownings, makes the reconstruction of the scene of the Other's death the sole constitutive experience of the Self. This lucid depersonalized art attains the limit of the romantic aesthetic that situated the scene of universal origin within the intimate experience of the differentiated individual. Henceforth the strong claim of originary significance that had made romantic art the heir to the classical 'pursuit of the absolute' would have to be renounced. In the modernist aesthetic that emerged in the early years of the twentieth century, Self and Other, survivor and victim, would no longer be meaningfully differentiated.

No reader of Lamartine's day made a thematic analogy between the scene of 'Le Lac' and the origin of signification. No one spoke of the poem as the expression of an anthropology. Yet the specific scene on the lake was felt as a model of a more general phenomenon. It was intuitively understood that the poet's exhortation to Nature to commemorate the lovers' meeting marked a new stage in culture's triumph over the irreversibility of time. The reader does not expect the wind and the reeds to 'say' 'Ils ont aimé!' but he has learned that he can say it for them, that the power of speech is the possibility of attributing meaning to the locus of an event. Lamartine's originality was to have discovered, or rather, rediscovered for modern man the meaningfulness of the circular scene of origin surrounding the central object of desire.

The systems of mass communication inherent in modern indus-trial civilization have weaned the contemporary reader from the romantics' faith in the personal. We can no longer accept their naive equation of the intimate with the significant; too much in our lives tells us the contrary. The 'unique' loses its lustre when it must be mediated through a publicity apparatus. Thus today's poetry no longer expects the reader to relive the origin of humanity in the poet's love affair. We have learned to seek this origin in apparently more fundamental, albeit less intuitively accessible, experiences, like Freudian 'primal scenes' or the child's apprenticeship of language. These scenes of origin avoid the ambiguity of adult or even ado-lescent experience; they antedate the child's exposure to, or at any rate his absorption of, models of social behaviour that borrow their values from outside the intimate sphere.

But whether or not our experience of modernity has dimmed our enthusiasm for Lamartine's masterpiece, we should recognize the seminal role of 'Le Lac' in nineteenth-century poetry's advancement of our anthropological understanding. Today's critics set Mallarmé far above Lamartine in their poetic pantheon. But the mirror of the 'Sonnet in "x"', framed by 'éternel oubli', in which the dead body of a collectively murdered 'nixe' is transformed into the constellation of the Great Bear ('des scintillations sitôt le septuor') that is the emblem of original human signification, borrows its most important structural elements from 'Le Lac'. In his description of the scene of significance emptied of its central object, Lamartine belongs to the modern age. 'Le Lac', the first great French romantic poem, already expresses the anthropological intuition that would provide the foundation for Symbolist poetry: that originary significance is constructed by the Self from the specular reflection of the Other's death.

NOTES

1 I use the term 'neo-classical' to refer to the aesthetic practised during the
   period that extends roughly from the Renaissance through the French
   Revolution. As the term suggests, the neo-classical aesthetic is an
   extension of the classical aesthetic which it attempted to revive. The
   'classical' side of the familiar opposition between the classical and the
   romantic is in fact neo-classical.
      I will also use the term 'pre-romantic' to refer to the late neo-classical
   culture exemplified by Elvire's lament. The 'weakness' of this culture
   may be said to anticipate the 'strong' solution that romanticism would
   bring in the wake of the Revolution.

2 The Latin word *versus* from which 'verse' is derived comes from the
   verb *vertere* meaning 'to turn'. The rhythm of poetry is produced by the
   periodic turning-back that begins each new line.

3

THE RHETORIC OF CONTEMPLATION: HUGO'S 'LA PENTE DE LA RÊVERIE'

Victor Brombert

Obscuritate rerum verba saepe obscurantur.

GERVASIUS TILBERIENSIS

Amis, ne creusez pas vos chères rêveries;
Ne fouillez pas le sol de vos plaines fleuries;
Et, quand s'offre à vos yeux un océan qui dort,
Nagez à la surface ou jouez sur le bord.
5   Car la pensée est sombre! Une pente insensible
Va du monde réel à la sphère invisible;
La spirale est profonde, et quand on y descend
Sans cesse se prolonge et va s'élargissant,
Et pour avoir touché quelque énigme fatale,
10   De ce voyage obscur souvent on revient pâle!

L'autre jour, il venait de pleuvoir, car l'été,
Cette année, est de bise et de pluie attristé,
Et le beau mois de mai dont le rayon nous leurre
Prend le masque d'avril qui sourit et qui pleure.
15   J'avais levé le store aux gothiques couleurs.
Je regardais au loin les arbres et les fleurs.
Le soleil se jouait sur la pelouse verte
Dans les gouttes de pluie, et ma fenêtre ouverte
Apportait du jardin à mon esprit heureux
20   Un bruit d'enfants joueurs et d'oiseaux amoureux.
Paris, les grands ormeaux, maison, dôme, chaumière,
Tout flottait à mes yeux dans la riche lumière
De cet astre de mai dont le rayon charmant
Au bout de tout brin d'herbe allume un diamant.

48

25 Je me laissais aller à ces trois harmonies,
    Printemps, matin, enfance, en ma retraite unies;
    La Seine, ainsi que moi, laissait son flot vermeil
    Suivre nonchalamment sa pente, et le soleil
    Faisait évaporer à la fois sur les grèves
30 L'eau du fleuve en brouillards et ma pensée en rêves.

    Alors, dans mon esprit, je vis autour de moi
    Mes amis, non confus, mais tels que je les vois
    Quand ils viennent le soir, troupe grave et fidèle,
    Vous avec vos pinceaux dont la pointe étincelle,
35 Vous, laissant échapper vos vers au vol ardent,
    Et nous tous écoutant en cercle, ou regardant.
    Ils étaient bien là tous, je voyais leurs visages,
    Tous, même les absents qui font de longs voyages.
    Puis tous ceux qui sont morts vinrent après ceux-ci,
40 Avec l'air qu'ils avaient quand ils vivaient aussi.
    Quand j'eus, quelques instants, des yeux de ma pensée,
    Contemplé leur famille à mon foyer pressée,
    Je vis trembler leurs traits confus, et par degrés
    Pâlir en s'effaçant leurs fronts décolorés,
45 Et tous, comme un ruisseau qui dans un lac s'écoule,
    Se perdre autour de moi dans une immense foule.

    Foule sans nom! chaos! des voix, des yeux, des pas.
    Ceux qu'on n'a jamais vus, ceux qu'on ne connaît pas.
    Tous les vivants! – cités bourdonnant aux oreilles
50 Plus qu'un bois d'Amérique ou des ruches d'abeilles,
    Caravanes campant sur le désert en feu,
    Matelots dispersés sur l'océan de Dieu,
    Et, comme un pont hardi sur l'onde qui chavire,
    Jetant d'un monde à l'autre un sillon de navire,
55 Ainsi que l'araignée entre deux chênes verts
    Jette un fil argenté qui flotte dans les airs.

    Les deux pôles! le monde entier! la mer, la terre,
    Alpes aux fronts de neige, Etnas au noir cratère,
    Tout à la fois, automne, été, printemps, hiver,
60 Les vallons descendant de la terre à la mer
    Et s'y changeant en golfe, et des mers aux campagnes
    Les caps épanouis en chaînes de montagnes,
    Et les grands continents, brumeux, verts ou dorés,
    Par les grands océans sans cesse dévorés,

49

65 Tout, comme un paysage en une chambre noire
Se réfléchit avec ses rivières de moire,
Ses passants, ses brouillards flottant comme un duvet,
Tout dans mon esprit sombre allait, marchait, vivait!
Alors en attachant, toujours plus attentives,
70 Ma pensée et ma vue aux mille perspectives
Que le souffle du vent ou le pas des saisons
M'ouvrait à tous moments dans tous les horizons,
Je vis soudain surgir, parfois du sein des ondes,
A côté des cités vivantes des deux mondes,
75 D'autres villes aux fronts étranges, inouïs,
Sépulcres ruinés des temps évanouis,
Pleines d'entassements, de tours, de pyramides,
Baignant leurs pieds aux mers, leur tête aux cieux humides.
Quelques-unes sortaient de dessous des cités
80 Où les vivants encor bruissent agités,
Et des siècles passés jusqu'à l'âge où nous sommes
Je pus compter ainsi trois étages de Romes
Et tandis qu'élevant leurs inquiètes voix,
Les cités des vivants résonnaient à la fois
85 Des murmures du peuple ou du pas des armées,
Ces villes du passé, muettes et fermées,
Sans fumée à leurs toits, sans rumeurs dans leurs seins,
Se taisaient, et semblaient des ruches sans essaims.
J'attendais. Un grand bruit se fit. Les races mortes
90 De ces villes en deuil vinrent ouvrir les portes,
Et je les vis marcher ainsi que les vivants,
Et jeter seulement plus de poussière aux vents.
Alors, tours, aqueducs, pyramides, colonnes,
Je vis l'intérieur des vieilles Babylones,
95 Les Carthages, les Tyrs, les Thèbes, les Sions,
D'où sans cesse sortaient des générations.

Ainsi j'embrassais tout, et la terre, et Cybèle;
La face antique auprès de la face nouvelle;
Le passé, le présent; les vivants et les morts;
100 Le genre humain complet comme au jour du remords.
Tout parlait à la fois, tout se faisait comprendre,
Le pélage d'Orphée et l'étrusque d'Évandre,
Les ruines d'Irmensul, le sphinx égyptien,
La voix du nouveau monde aussi vieux que l'ancien.

105 Or, ce que je voyais, je doute que je puisse
Vous le peindre. C'était comme un grand édifice
Formé d'entassements de siècles et de lieux;
On n'en pouvait trouver les bords ni les milieux;
A toutes les hauteurs, nations, peuples, races,
110 Mille ouvriers humains, laissant partout leurs traces,
Travaillaient nuit et jour, montant, croisant leurs pas,
Parlant chacun leur langue et ne s'entendant pas;
Et moi je parcourais, cherchant qui me réponde,
De degrés en degrés cette Babel du monde.

115 La nuit avec la foule, en ce rêve hideux,
Venait, s'épaississant ensemble toutes deux,
Et, dans ces régions que nul regard ne sonde,
Plus l'homme était nombreux, plus l'ombre était profonde.
Tout devenait douteux et vague; seulement
120 Un souffle qui passait de moment en moment,
Comme pour me montrer l'immense fourmilière,
Ouvrait dans l'ombre au loin des vallons de lumière,
Ainsi qu'un coup de vent fait sur les flots troublés
Blanchir l'écume, ou creuse une onde dans les blés.

125 Bientôt autour de moi les ténèbres s'accrurent,
L'horizon se perdit, les formes disparurent,
Et l'homme avec la chose et l'être avec l'esprit
Flottèrent à mon souffle, et le frisson me prit.
J'étais seul. Tout fuyait. L étendue était sombre.
130 Je voyais seulement au loin, à travers l'ombre,
Comme d'un océan les flots noirs et pressés,
Dans l'espace et le temps les nombres entassés.
Oh! cette double mer du temps et de l'espace
Où le navire humain toujours passe et repasse,
135 Je voulus la sonder, je voulus en toucher
Le sable, y regarder, y fouiller, y chercher,
Pour vous en rapporter quelque richesse étrange,
Et dire si son lit est de roche ou de fange.
Mon esprit plongea donc sous ce flot inconnu,
140 Au profond de l'abîme il nagea seul et nu,
Toujours de l'ineffable allant à l'invisible . . .
Soudain il s'en revint avec un cri terrible,
Ebloui, haletant, stupide, épouvanté,
Car il avait au fond trouvé l'éternité.

✳✳✳

Even the title of this densely metaphorical poem is a metaphor. But this metaphor is doubly deceptive. The word 'pente', meaning slope or incline, suggests an appealing surrender to one's natural inclination. This notion of ease and pleasure is soon echoed by the expression 'Je me laissais aller...', which evokes passive hedonism, and by the image of the river flowing in a 'nonchalant' manner toward the sea (ll. 25–8).[1] But the word 'pente' also connotes danger. The downward movement, though gradual and at first perhaps even imperceptible, does none the less imply a descent, an irresistible sliding downward, a fall.

The other substantive in the title is equally ambivalent. 'Rêverie' may well refer to pleasant daydreams, to carefree, playfully associative mental pictures such as we all indulge in. But the word also has an older meaning in French, namely that of an all-absorbing meditation or reflection. It can even suggest an addiction to the world of dreams which may turn out to be chimerical and self-destructive.

The double signal of pleasure and danger, precisely because the downward movement is not immediately obvious, is further stressed by the ominous Latin epigraph ('Obscuritate rerum verba saepe obscurantur') which twice in the same short sentence refers to darkness. This double darkness ('Obscuritate' and 'obscurantur') is specifically related to the poetic activity through association with the word 'verba' referring to language. What the epigram states is that the darkness of 'things' ('rerum') casts a pall on our words. Both reality and its verbal representation are thus linked to the pervasive presence of an enigma. The 'chambre noire' of the poet's mind (l. 65), and the occult visionary insight implied by the expression 'yeux de ma pensée' (l. 41), only confirm this motif of a truth hidden in darkness.

Beyond these early signals, some general features are noticeable even at a first glance. The poem progresses by accumulating heavy blocks that correspond to no fixed form. The forward movement seems to depend on the mobilization of large masses, bringing about a sense of crescendo and amplification. The occasional displacement or disappearance of the caesura contributes to this effect of enlargement. The strategically situated trimeter ('Les deux pôles!/le monde entier!/la mer, la terre ...', l. 57) confirms, in a pivotal position, the overwhelming impression of monumental mobility. Form, with Hugo, is most often in the service of movement. In 'La Pente de la rêverie', repeated changes of speed help convey the theme of nature's transformational dynamics, as valleys become gulfs and continents are devoured by oceans (ll. 60–4).

But the opening lines of the poem contain other determining signals. The first word ('Amis') is an apostrophe that imposes the poem's *voice*. The imperative structure of the first two lines ('ne creusez pas ... / Ne fouillez pas ...'), compounded with the insistent negative form, imposes a hortatory offer of advice and a warning that is essentially a rhetorical figure of authority. The figura of the poet here defines itself by addressing a plural in the name of friendship. Yet in spite of this act of communication and implicit communion, the distance established from the outset between the singular of the poet and the plural of the friends repeatedly indicates that the auctorial voice conceives of itself as *one* confronting *many*. The poem about reverie and solidarity is also a poem about solitude. At the end, the poet finds himself alone ('J'étais seul', l. 129); his mind is 'seul et nu' (l. 140). But even earlier, he searches in vain for an interlocutor as he proceeds on his quest through nightmarish Babelic structures.

Hugo demonstrates from the outset that he is a master rhetorician. His apostrophic exordium involves a subtle play of language that is intimately related to the didactic thrust of the poem. The ever so slight variance between the singular of the title ('rêverie') and the plural in the first line ('rêveries') has far-reaching implications. 'Rêverie', in the singular, points to an all-absorbing, all-encompassing mental activity. Its overwhelming nature is far removed indeed from the plural 'rêveries' which presumably occupy the friends in a carefree, fragmented, superficial manner. The banality of such indolent daydreaming is further suggested by the banality of the accompanying adjective: '*chères* rêveries'. That the plural in this context implies a sense of distance and dissociation is moreover indicated by the somewhat condescending possessive adjective preceding the banalized plural ('*vos* chères rêveries'). Despite, and to some extent because of, the hortatory solicitude of the beginning, the voice of the poet dissociates itself from the unsubstantial surface joys to which the patronizing advice would seem to confine the 'friends'.

What is indeed most significant about the entire first section is the contrasting imagery of surface and depth. All the metaphors of these first ten lines develop along the double axis of horizontality and verticality. The friends' reveries are to remain safely above ground, in the innocuous ambience of the 'plaines fleuries' (the banality of this image is also deliberate); they are to remain 'at the surface' of any body of water or play cautiously along the banks. Contrasted with this unexalted horizontality there are the key verbs *creuser* and *fouiller*, both of which are also metaphors of intellectual and spiritual effort aimed at uncovering a hidden truth. The adjective 'profonde' and the verb 'descend' further insist on this vertical thrust. As for the image of the ocean, it appropriately combines horizontality and verticality through the reference to an apparently placid surface ('océan qui dort'), and hints at the deceptive nature of this calm surface and at the dangers lurking beneath.

The key image of this first section is however that of the spiral. 'La spirale est profonde, et quand on y descend / Sans cesse se prolonge et va s'élargissant ...' The notion of a spiralling descent is particularly interesting because it combines, as it were, the two axes. (Could one not almost speak of a horizontal descent?) Moreover, the spiral leading to the nether regions unavoidably brings to mind Dante's *Inferno*, except that in Hugo's poem the spiral has a broadening effect ('va s'élargissant') and promises to lead to a vision of the invisible sphere, promises in fact to lead – though dangerously, like all epic voyages – to a confrontation with an enigma, and ultimately to a revelation coming from below.

The poem thus inscribes itself in a tradition rooted in antiquity; the hero's perilous quest leads him to the nether regions. The 'voyage obscur' of the section's last line introduces a whole series of travel images; the 'longs voyages' of the absent ones and of the dead (l. 38); the caravans, sailors, ships, and lines of communication established between one world and another (ll. 51–4); the double ocean of time and space (l. 133); the return of the awestruck explorer who reached the ineffable and the invisible, and glimpsed eternity. (ll. 141–4).

The difficult and fearful contact between the world of surface reality and the hidden 'sphère invisible' determines the progression and the grammar of the poem. Here too Hugo shows himself to be a master of language, as he provides a virtuoso performance with syntax, and most specifically a dazzling poetic control of verb tenses. The entire first section is in the present indicative ('la pensée est sombre'; 'la spirale est profonde', 'on revient pâle'), which clearly corresponds to a timeless general truth. The temporal scheme in the second section (ll. 11–30) switches from the present to the imperfect, and this is of course the appropriate tense for the impressionistic description of the cityscape and the springtime interplay of sun and rain. The imperfect is also the appropriate tense for evoking the state of mind as it allows itself to surrender to the sensations of the fleeting moment ('Je me laissais aller ...'). Above all, the insistent imperfect places the entire section under the sign of the glance ('je regardais ...') and of the alluring pleasure of the eye.

But everything suddenly changes when we reach line 31. The third section begins with a dramatic shift in tone and mood. In obvious contrast to the leisurely array of imperfects, the dramatic preterite preceded by the emphatic adverb *alors* ('Alors ... je vis') underscores the semantic gap that separates the verbs *regarder* and *voir*. If the previous section evokes the delights of 'looking at', we are now thrust into the experience of 'seeing'.

For the mind can begin to see only when the eyes no longer gaze at sensuous surfaces. *Voir*, as opposed to *regarder*, is indeed for Hugo the verb of vision ('Je vis' is repeated in line 43); and the 'passé simple' obviously marks the time of insight and revelation, suggesting not a latent state but a dramatic moment. But most telling perhaps, in the overall perspective of the poem, and in the larger perspective of Hugo's writings, is the fact that visionary activity and visionary grasp can occur only in darkness, when the visible world of surfaces and objects has vanished (as it begins to do in lines 29–30), and the physical eyes no longer see. The expression 'my mind's eye' ('yeux de ma pensée', l. 41) thus takes on its full meaning. The voyage in question is 'dark' precisely because Hugo's visionary poetry is always thematically linked to the notion of occultation, and to a broadening downward movement that reaches toward a spiritual totalization from below. This totalization is also suggested here by the progression of verb tenses. The trajectory of the poem leads from the present, to the imperfect, to

the preterite and finally to the summed-up experience in the pluperfect associated with the return: 'Car il *avait* au fond *trouvé* l'éternité.'

The banal neo-classical diction of the 'Parisian' scene (section 2) is
thus highly functional. The trite prettiness of the trees and the
flowers, the string of clichés involving the beautiful month of May,
the playing children, the amorous birds, stress the sense of a bland
spectacle and a passive spectator. This decorative theatricality is
further highlighted by the multicoloured blind which the poet raises
in order to enjoy the scene. The platitudes of the diction and the
images correspond thematically to what Jean Gaudon, in his discussion of the poem, calls the 'platitude' of the world of reality.[2] The
so-called real world is of course, in this context, the surface world of
appearances.

Until this point, the poem projects a confined perspective, strictly
speaking limited by the aperture of the window (a symbolic eye),
and the illusion-producing interplay of sun, rain and mist. But this
mist, which becomes a fog, also marks the threshold. The epigram-
matic concluding line of this section stands in sharp contrast to
'Alors ... je vis' that opens the following section. What has
happened between lines 30 and 31 is like a fade-out.

The descent into an illuminating darkness is immediately characterized by a new development in the use of the plural. The
broadening effect initiated by line 31 is largely dependent on the
enumeration of the 'friends' (the poets, the painters, the absent ones,
the dead – all part of the 'troupe grave') and is repeatedly under-
scored by the pronoun *tous*. This collectivizing and totalizing
pronoun occurs in fact five times in quick succession, leading to the
still broader, transcendental notion of a 'nameless crowd', reaching
out, by means of 'immense foule', to the very notion of immensity.

The 'foule sans nom' which serves as a transition between sections
3 and 4 also signals the grand opening on to the world of the
unknown, the world of chaos, the world of the unsayable. The
succession of verbless substantives ('Foule sans nom! chaos! des
voix, des yeux, des pas') and the total disappearance of the caesura
introduce us into a world that seems to be devoid of purpose, shape
and order. Yet in that awesome universe of confusion, the poet's
efforts provide a link, or better, a bridge from one world to another

– though it is a bridge as tenuous and fragile as the silvery spider thread floating in the air from one tree to another.

But it is the following section, (ll. 57–84), the longest one, that is truly the heart of the poem. Here totalization becomes the subject, as *tous* shifts to *tout* ('Tout à la fois'; 'Tout, comme un paysage'; 'Tout dans mon esprit'), preparing the 'Ainsi j'embrassais tout ...' of line 97. The accumulation of substantives corresponds to the survey of the total panorama: 'le monde entier'. This panorama, however, cannot be surveyed. It is not an inert topography that can be mapped out. New perspectives constantly open up on to unsuspected horizons. Massiveness does not exclude mobility. On the contrary: the larger the masses, and the more impressive the monumentalization, the more cataclysmic this universe appears. Cities come into view and go under, entire epochs emerge and vanish, geography itself as well as the seasons are in perpetual mutation. Nature is flux. To be more precise: in the terms of the poem – it is one of Hugo's permanent themes – decomposition and destruction are the very conditions of the creative and re-creative process. For all creation is violence. Hence the stress on volcanic energy, on the *devouring* activities of the oceans.

This dynamic and ferociously transformational world evoked in the poem is also torn by the winds. Yet these winds also make ever new perspectives possible. Hugo uses the word *souffle* ('souffle du vent', l. 71), a word with a complex resonance, denoting the breath of God as well as the creative energies of the poet. The word is repeated in line 120 ('Un souffle qui passait ...') and later associated with the verb *ouvrir*, associated, that is, with revelatory glimpses, and more specifically with apocalyptic vision. The darkness and the turmoil that allow for the 'opening up' to the mind's view of endless horizons ('mille perspectives' and 'tous les horizons', ll. 70, 72) are the precondition of visionary poetry. The key verb remains *voir*: 'Je vis soudain surgir' (l. 73); 'je les vis marcher' (l. 94); 'Or, ce que je voyais' (l. 105). And what is seen is not only all of history and prehistory, but the bottom of the abyss. It is a fearful descent, a descent ultimately into the deepest recesses of the self.

This interiorization of totality is made very clear by a line that immediately precedes the allusion to the revelatory agitation of the wind: 'Tout dans mon esprit sombre allait, marchait, vivait.' The darkness is thus located inside the poet's mind, as is the sense of totalization. Many years later, Hugo was to write that a poet is a world enclosed within a human being ('Le poète est un monde enfermé dans un homme'). Such a fascination with the inner abyss is intimately bound up with Hugo's motif of the skull-as-prison. It is a fascination that ultimately reflects the pride and anguish of poetic creation. The 'intérieur' of the Babylons of this world (l. 94) corresponds to this inner vision of frightening architectures, and in particular of the favoured image of an inverted Tower of Babel.

If all creation is process, and if that creative (and destructive) process is destined never to be completed, then the Tower of Babel is a most appropriate symbol. The image seems, moreover, specifically relevant to the pride and anguish of writing, for the biblical Tower is an image charged with negative as well as positive connotations. Reaching up to the sky, having language as its foundation, it is also threatened by language. The multilingual Tower ('Tout parlait à la fois'; 'Parlant chacun leur langue et ne s'entendant pas', ll. 101, 112) remains an enigmatic edifice — at the same time an emblem of constructive incompletion and confusion.

Attentive readers of the poem may be struck by an apparent contradiction in the sections dealing with the Tower of Babel. In line 112, Hugo evokes the thousand workers all speaking different languages and not understanding each other. The confusion of tongues is of course consonant with the Biblical account in Genesis. Yet only a few lines earlier, Hugo wrote that 'everything' was talking all at the same time, making itself understood ('Tout parlait à la fois, tout se faisait comprendre', l. 101) The contradiction is, however, resolved if we understand that these two different experiences bring out the uniqueness of the poet's figura. For unlike common mortals ('mille ouvriers humains') the vatic explorer is the privileged decipherer of any secret language, whether it be that of Orpheus or that of the Sphinx. Baudelaire, in his essay on Hugo, stated that the poet must be a 'déchiffreur'.[3] But it is clear from the beginning of the poem that such singularity is also a condemnation to solitude.

The structure of the poem confirms this essential vocation. After the section where decipherment is initiated (ll. 97–104), after the lines that project a Pascalian image of the infinitely large where there is no longer either circumference or centre (ll. 106–8), after the passage where darkness covers darkness and all shapes disappear, the poet's voice proclaims his utter aloneness. 'J'étais seul' (l. 129). But here the fade-out is altogether of a different nature from the one produced by the lowering of the curtain of fog on the early Parisian scene. At the end, darkness and solitude have a heroic quality. But this heroism, which depends on the visionary destiny, also condemns the hero victim to the impossibility of articulating his vision, of giving an account of the unsayable and the indescribable.

And this is the significance of the inarticulate *cri* with which the poet returns from his voyage to the end of the world. This cry denotes the impossibility of any logical or even comprehensible utterance. It suggests pain, alarm, distress and horror. But it also refers implicitly to one of the notions dearest to the Romantics: the dream of unmediated communication. Ironically, the cry also seems to imply that the entire poem – certainly not a laconic one – is a hopelessly inadequate verbal enterprise.

The 'cri terrible' is the result of a confrontation with ultimate reality, and with the effort to account for this confrontation. As such, much like the Tower of Babel, it is symbolically associated with the act of writing, and the competing demands of *mimesis* and *poesis*. Some years later, Baudelaire was to write in one of his prose poems, that the confrontation with Beauty is a duel 'où l'artiste crie de frayeur avant d'être vaincu' ('in which the artist cries out with terror before being vanquished').[4] Baudelaire, we know, had read 'La Pente de la rêverie' with great care and admiration. It is not at all certain, of course, that Hugo ever considered himself 'vanquished' – but the poem unquestionably stresses in a self-referential manner the pain of expression and the glorification of expression because it is a cry of pain.

The network of images in 'La Pente de la rêverie' depends throughout on a series of opposites that seem to negate each other: stasis and movement, passivity and activity, prudence and perilous quest, horizontal and vertical axes, liquid and solid elements, multiplicity and unity. But one must distinguish between subject, motif, theme and visionary mode. The subject of the poem seems to be the danger of indulging in reverie. At that level, the poem is a warning to others, but perhaps primarily to the self. The motif is the epic descent to the nether regions, and is inscribed in a tradition that harks back to antiquity, thus justifying the noble diction of the poem. As for the central theme, it is the grand vision of the *vates*, the blinding insight of the seer who requires darkness in order to see. In later texts dealing with the tragedy of history and revolution, Hugo refers to Moses's being dazzled by the face of God. The poet, in his role as visionary prophet, is equally dazzled by the face of the great Mystery. Indeed, the first adjective in a string of adjectives referring to the figura of the poet as he utters his terrible cry is *ébloui* (blinded, dazzled, l. 143).

In the end, the true subject of the poem is the poet himself, and his tragic vocation. The poetic experience is not merely the result of a surrender to dreams and nightmares; it is an act of will. 'Je voulus la sonder', Hugo writes about his desire to sound the double ocean of time and space (l. 135). The deliberate choice of the preterite, rather than the more common imperfect, stresses the volitional nature of the experience. The poet as hero – that is the message of the poem.

But poetry is more than the poem. Hugo never lost sight of this priority. And at the level of poetry, much like the world's creative processes which are never terminated, so too the poem is never an end in itself. It participates in a larger enterprise. In the cosmic description provided, all is movement. An analogue is established between cosmic and poetic creation, between the work of God the supreme *auctor*, and the *author* of the literary text. Such an analogue does not merely reveal a self-glorifying stance; it implies a philosophical outlook, a world view. For Hugo, all is flux, energy, dynamics. Literary order comes out of chaos, but must continue to thematize it. There are no barriers between the living and the dead, just as there are no lines of demarcation between Death and Life. The past and the future are alive in the present. All is moving forward, but also upward and downward. All is process, and also progress. All is alive, even the inanimate. And true poetry, even when it seems to be striving for form, never stops reaching beyond itself.

NOTES

1 'La Pente de la rêverie' is poem XXIX in the collection *Les Feuilles d'automne* (1831). The numbers in parentheses throughout the text refer to the lines of this poem.
2 Jean Gaudon, *Le Temps de la contemplation* (Paris, 1969), p. 48. Gaudon relates this aspect of the poem to the broader question of visionary occultation in Hugo's work.
3 Charles Baudelaire, *Œuvres complètes* (Paris, 1961), p. 705.
4 *Ibid.*, p. 232.

4

THE DESIGNS OF PROSODY: VIGNY'S 'LA MORT DU LOUP'

Clive Scott

I

	Les nuages couraient sur la lune enflammée	3+3+3+3
	Comme sur l'incendie on voit fuir la fumée,	(1+5)+3+3
	Et les bois étaient noirs jusques à l'horizon.	3+3+1+5
	– Nous marchions, sans parler, dans l'humide gazon,	3+3+3+3
5	Dans la bruyère épaisse et dans les hautes brandes,	4+2+4+2
	Lorsque, sous des sapins pareils à ceux des landes,	1+5+2+4
	Nous avons aperçu les grands ongles marqués	3+3+3+3
	Par les Loups voyageurs que nous avions traqués.	3+3+4+2
	Nous avons écouté, retenant notre haleine	3+3+3+3
10	Et le pas suspendu. – Ni le bois ni la plaine	3+3+3+3
	Ne poussaient un soupir dans les airs; seulement	3+3+3+3
	La girouette en deuil criait au firmament.	4+2+2+4
	Car le vent, élevé bien au-dessus des terres,	3+3+4+2
	N'effleurait de ses pieds que les tours solitaires,	3+3+3+3
15	Et les chênes d'en bas, contre les rocs penchés,	3+3+4+2
	Sur leurs coudes semblaient endormis et couchés.	3+3+3+3
	– Rien ne bruissait donc, lorsque, baissant la tête,	6+1+5/5+1+1+5
	Le plus vieux des chasseurs qui s'étaient mis en quête	3+3+4+2
	A regardé le sable, attendant, à genoux,	4+2+3+3
20	Qu'une étoile jetât quelque lueur sur nous;	3+3+4+2
	Puis, tout bas, a juré que ces marques récentes	3+3+3+3
	Annonçaient la démarche et les griffes puissantes	3+3+3+3
	De deux grands Loups-cerviers et de deux Louveteaux.	4+2+3+3
	– Nous avons tous alors préparé nos couteaux,	4+2+3+3
25	Et, cachant nos fusils et leurs lueurs trop blanches,	3+3+4+2
	Nous allions, pas à pas, en écartant les branches.	3+3+4+2
	Trois s'arrêtent, et moi, cherchant ce qu'ils voyaient,	3+3+2+4/4'+2+2+4
	J'aperçois tout à coup deux yeux qui flamboyaient,	3+3+2+4
	Et je vois au-delà quelques formes légères	3+3+3+3
30	Qui dansaient sous la lune au milieu des bruyères,	3+3+3+3

Comme font, chaque jour, à grand bruit, sous nos yeux,	3+3+3+3
Quand le maître revient, les lévriers joyeux.	3+3+4+2
L'allure était semblable et semblable la danse;	2+4+3+3
Mais les enfants du Loup se jouaient en silence,	4+2+3+3
35 Sachant bien qu'à deux pas, ne dormant qu'à demi,	3+3+3+3
Se couche dans ses murs l'homme, leur ennemi.	2+4+1+5
Le Père était debout, et plus loin, contre un arbre,	2+4+3+3
Sa Louve reposait comme celle de marbre	2+4+3+3
Qu'adoraient les Romains, et dont les flancs velus	3+3+4+2
40 Couvaient les Demi-Dieux Rémus et Romulus.	2+4+2+4
– Le Loup vient et s'assied, les deux jambes dressées	3+3+3+3
Par leurs ongles crochus dans le sable enfoncées.	3+3+3+3
Il s'est jugé perdu, puisqu'il était surpris,	4+2+4+2
Sa retraite coupée et tous ses chemins pris.	3+3+5+1
45 Alors il a saisi, dans sa gueule brûlante,	2+4+3+3
Du chien le plus hardi la gorge pantelante,	2+4+2+4
Et n'a pas desserré ses mâchoires de fer,	3+3+3+3
Malgré nos coups de feu qui traversaient sa chair	2+4+4+2
Et nos couteaux aigus qui, comme des tenailles,	4+2+1+5
50 Se croisaient en plongeant dans ses larges entrailles,	3+3+3+3
Jusqu'au dernier moment où le chien étranglé,	4+2+3+3
Mort longtemps avant lui, sous ses pieds a roulé.	1+5+3+3
Le Loup le quitte alors et puis il nous regarde.	2+4+2+4
Les couteaux lui restaient au flanc jusqu'à la garde,	3+3+2+4/3+3+5+4
55 Le clouaient au gazon tout baigné dans son sang;	3+3+3+3
Nos fusils l'entouraient en sinistre croissant.	3+3+3+3
– Il nous regarde encore, ensuite il se recouche,	4+2+2+4
Tout en léchant le sang répandu sur sa bouche,	4+2+3+3
Et, sans daigner savoir comment il a péri,	4+2+2+4
60 Refermant ses grands yeux, meurt, sans jeter un cri.	3+3+1+5

II

J'ai reposé mon front sur mon fusil sans poudre,	4+2+4+2
Me prenant à penser, et n'ai pu me résoudre	3+3+3+3
A poursuivre sa Louve et ses fils qui, tous trois,	3+3+3+3
Avaient voulu l'attendre, et, comme je le crois,	4+2+(1+5)
65 Sans ses deux Louveteaux la belle et sombre veuve	3+3+2+4/3+3+4+2
Ne l'eût pas laissé seul subir la grande épreuve,	3+3+2+4
Mais son devoir était de les sauver, afin	4+2+4+2/4+6+2
De pouvoir leur apprendre à bien souffrir la faim,	3+3+4+2
A ne jamais entrer dans le pacte des villes	4+2+3+3
70 Que l'homme a fait avec les animaux serviles	4+6+2
Qui chassent devant lui, pour avoir le coucher,	2+4+3+3
Les premiers possesseurs du bois et du rocher.	3+3+2+4

III

Hélas! ai-je pensé, malgré ce grand nom d'Hommes,   2+4+5+1
Que j'ai honte de nous, débiles que nous sommes!   3+3+2+4
75 Comment on doit quitter la vie et tous ses maux,   2+4+2+4
C'est vous qui le savez, sublimes animaux!   2+4+2+4
    A voir ce que l'on fut sur terre et ce qu'on laisse,   2+4+2+1
Seul le silence est grand; tout le reste est faiblesse.   4+2+3+3
– Ah! je t'ai bien compris, sauvage voyageur,   1+5+2+4
80 Et ton dernier regard m'est allé jusqu'au cœur!   4+2+3+3
Il disait: «Si tu peux, fais que ton âme arrive,   3+3+1+5/3+3+4+2
A force de rester studieuse et pensive,   2+4+3+3
Jusqu'à ce haut degré de Stoïque fierté   4+2+3+3
Où, naissant dans les bois, j'ai tout d'abord monté.   1+5+4+2
85   Gémir, pleurer, prier est également lâche.   2+2+2+5+1/2+4+5+1/4+2+5+1
– Fais énergiquement ta longue et lourde tâche   1+5+2+4/1+5+4+2
Dans la voie où le Sort a voulu t'appeler,   3+3+3+3
Puis après, comme moi, souffre et meurs sans parler.»   3+3+3+3/3+3+1+2+3

(Bracketed hemistichs indicate that the first accent in the hemistich is only slight)

✳✳✳

Vigny has yet to make his reputation as a poet. His verse has for a long time been respected more for its moral than for its poetic qualities – firmness, self-denial, straightforwardness. He strives to mount on 'leaden wings',[1] and this leadenness has several sources: Vigny's verse narratives often seem over-conscientious in their detail, not to say pedantic, and yet he is still unable to avoid glaring *invraisemblances*; Vigny's verse narratives call on metaphor and image to give them a wider resonance and moments of perceptual intensification, yet Vigny's metaphors are more important for their syntactic structures than for their intrinsic value as images,[2] and many are simply inappropriate or incoherent; Vigny's verse narratives are autodestructive in the sense that they are self-paraphrasing: the moral which emerges at the end supersedes and makes otiose the narrative which apparently brought it forth; Vigny's verse-art is dour and uninventive.[3] But the critical tide is turning. François Germain, who provides the most exhaustive list of *invraisemblances* in 'La Mort du Loup',[4] vindicates Vigny in these terms: 'De la part d'un homme qui connaissait l'art de chasser ... tant d'invraisemblances ne sauraient être fortuites, et si Vigny ne raconte pas une chasse, c'est qu'il pense à autre chose ... La vérité de la chasse ... est

... utilisée comme un langage qui traduit avec une force exception-
nelle la crainte de la mort' (pp. 67–8). The work of both Germain
and Jean-Pierre Richard,[5] among others, has helped to establish not
only the coherence but the motivatedness of Vigny's imagery; and
this concern with motivation – psychological, emotional, existential – has transferred Vignyan ideas from the realm of 'philosophy' to that of spiritual biography and confession, from the
didactic to the expressive. In his 1947 edition of *Les Destinées*,
V. L. Saulnier can still, in his introduction to 'La Mort du Loup'
and under the heading of 'Les Leçons', confidently enumerate a set
of moral precepts which merely take Vigny at his word –

Une leçon générale, donc: pour mener à bien la tâche d'homme il ne faut
pas mesurer sa peine: il faut, surtout, renoncer à gémir et à se plaindre ...
Au-dessous de cet enseignement général, plusieurs moralités particulières.
La première: l'admiration des animaux qui souffrent sans se plaindre.
D'autres concernent directement la conduite de l'homme et du poète:
valeur de la solitude pour l'édification et la culture de la personnalité;
nécessité de la Discrétion, contre l'impudicité de ceux qui s'avouent nus
(pp. 124–5).

André Fayolle (1959),[6] on the other hand, drawing on Vigny's
Journal d'un poète, argues for the poem's being an enactment of a
constellation of concerns and memories alive in the poet's mind at
the time of writing (30–31 October 1838): the death of his mother
(26 December 1837) reminds him of the death of his father, of his
father's physical and moral uprightness in death – 'L'horrible
douleur de l'agonie le redressa violemment; il mourut droit, sans se
plaindre, héroïquement'; and this leads on to an expression of pride
in his own literary work, work which has enabled him to support
his mother, work made necessary by the loss of the ancestral estates
during the Revolution; the following day (27 December 1837),
Vigny returns to memories of his father and to the tales of wolf-
hunting he told. However, the retrieval of Vigny's poetry as spiritual autobiography still leaves unanswered many of the traditional
objections to the specifically literary qualities of his verse. In my
own analysis, I want to address these issues, in particular by
pushing the argument for Vigny's coherence, for the irreducibility
of his poetic design, into the area of versification, and thereby to
demonstrate his prosodic resourcefulness. I shall preface my proso-

dic investigation with a more general thematic exploration of 'La Mort du Loup', not only to provide a structural and semantic context within which the prosody can exhibit its expressive efficiency, but also to show how prosody projects, even creates, the thematic texture.

It would be easy to equate the overall structure of 'La Mort du Loup' with that of the fable: a narrative about animals leads into a moral relevant to man. But it would be mistaken. For one thing the wolf's dying words are not a deduced lesson but an exhortation, an exhortation which the narrative does not of itself *necessitate*. For another, although the wolf's words are in a sense addressed to humanity at large – the wolf's conduct is, after all, exemplary – in another sense they are addressed privately to the intimate self of the poet and to a reader conceived of as a peculiarly *appropriate* listener. At the poem's close, the wolf looks into the poet's heart and his look speaks both to and through the poet; this ultimate convergence of poet with wolf has already been prefigured in several ways, in, for example, their both being an isolated, fourth member:

Trois s'arrêtent, et moi, cherchant ce qu'ils voyaient (l. 27)

... et n'ai pu me résoudre
A poursuivre sa Louve et ses fils qui, tous trois,
Avaient voulu l'attendre ... (ll. 62–4)

But just as the wolf *selects* the poet as his addressee, by an act of intimate recognition, of reciprocal identification, so the poet's (and poet's/wolf's) text selects the reader and equally implies a process of recognition. One of the ways by which this latter is engineered is the recurrent use of the perfect tense; for while the past historic is event-orientated and does not necessarily imply (implicate) a listener, the perfect tense is listener-orientated, the tense of direct address, and its present-tense element (the auxiliary) is not just the present of the continuing consequence of event, but is also the present of the moment of relation. In other words the poem, not through any explicit moral, but by almost masonic procedures, identifies the reader as appropriate, as able to understand, or converts the reader to the required appropriateness. Thus the reader, too, is the first-person protagonist of the poem, the hunter after signs, the one who is left behind by the rest of humanity (the hunters) to recognize, and be recognized by, the look/voice which is the sign made manifest, the Idea.

The poem, then, works not to transform narrative into moral, but to transform narrative into lyric, where by 'lyric' I mean not so much a different kind of discourse (emotionally charged, song-like, etc., although it is the wolf's swansong) as a different kind of receptivity to discourse. The function of the narrative is one not of demonstration,[7] but of spiritual preparation for, of initiation into, a proper state of receptivity; as Vigny puts it, albeit rather more negatively: 'Les poèmes comme je les ai faits ont un inconvénient, c'est que l'esprit n'est pas préparé à entrer en matière sur-le-champ. Dans *La Maison du Berger*, le récitatif préparera au chant' (*Journal*, 12 February 1841). In fact we might do well to adopt the terms Vigny applies to *La Maison du Berger*: the hunt and the wolf's death are the recitative, the wolf's words the aria.

It is for this reason that the poem's many *invraisemblances* are not intrusive. It is for this reason that the 'griffes puissantes' of the wolves have none of the aggressive or sadistic connotations attributed to them by Richard in his antithetical thematology of the 'front' and the 'pied': '"Les *pieds* lourds et puissants de chaque destinée", pèsent "sur *chaque tête* et sur toute action." Pied dont l'imposition se complique parfois d'incision ou de griffure, et qui devient alors cet organe d'une possessivité toute sadique: l'*ongle*.'[8] The wolves' 'ongles', or 'griffes', mark the sand with signs, are the styluses of a hieroglyph; what the hunters hunt is the wolf; what the poet hunts is the wolf's words, the text within the text – one is reminded of the fisherman in 'La Bouteille à la mer' who unconsciously fishes for the bottle with its 'inner' text:

> Un pêcheur accroupi sous des rochers arides
> Tire dans ses filets le flacon précieux.
> Il court, cherche un savant et lui montre sa prise;
> Et, sans l'oser ouvrir, demande qu'on lui dise
> Quel est cet élixir noir et mystérieux.

'La Mort du Loup' is about the excavation of a holy text, the idea, the diamond buried in the earth, the pearl hidden in the oyster.

But in the thematics of the poem, the 'griffes' have another equally positive significance. They are what sustain the wolf in its upright position (ll. 41–2). And the uprightness of the wolf corresponds to the 'tours solitaires' (ll. 13–14), the relics of a noble ancestry, isolated but resistant. Furthermore these descriptions, by their lexicon and underlying existential stance, bring to mind the opening lines of 'La Colère de Samson', which, as it were, transform the wolf's 'ongles crochus' into tent-pegs:

> Le désert est muet, la tente est solitaire.
> Quel pasteur courageux la dressa sur la terre
> Du sable et des lions? ...

This tent is a temporary mansion, a mansion of self, erected by the nomadic traveller out of his very privation.

If the upright wolf is the poet's real father both by biographical insinuation and by moral persuasion, then the leader of the hunters, 'le plus vieux des chasseurs' (l. 18), is his false, adoptive father, not only because his tracking skills are in the service of the wrong kind of objective, but because his posture is supine – the version of the poem which appeared in the *Revue des Deux-Mondes* has at lines 19–21:

> A regardé le sable en s'y couchant; bientôt,
> Lui que jamais ici l'on ne vit en défaut,
> A déclaré tout bas que ces marques récentes ...

These inept lines echo the description of the oaks at lines 15–16, and prefigure that of half-sleeping mankind at lines 35–6. Later the theme returns in the motive for the dogs' servility at lines 70–1. Of course the wolf himself is ultimately forced into this supine position, but it is only after having discharged himself of his look (l. 57), a look which is itself a repetition (l. 53), a look which is the search for the blood-brother, a look which is eloquent with the hidden text for those who know how to read it. And this text is a verticality restored, the reaffirmation of an upward-climbing principle of self-disciplined resignation:

> Jusqu'à ce haut degré de Stoïque fierté
> Où, naissant dans les bois, j'ai tout d'abord monté.

> (ll. 83–4)

Silence is, of course, the necessary condition of the emergence of speech, but the speech that emerges merely confirms that silence, explains its motives and contents, before being re-absorbed into it.[9]

The hunt of the poet turns out to be a hunt for silence; the hunt of the other hunters, is a hunt for a situation – the encirclement of the wolf – in which silence can finally be dispensed with. For the poet, silence becomes an ethos, the hidden teleology of the experience; for the other hunters, silence is the silence of stealth, treachery, a means. W. N. Ince finds the comparison between wolf-cubs and hounds at lines 29–36 justified by pathetic contrast alone, but otherwise 'clumsy and inappropriate, even incoherent'.[10] But the comparison serves at least two purposes: it implies an equation between noise and servility, or between noise (including complaint, lament, demagogy, false effusiveness) and mankind; it equally depicts a silence ostensibly motivated by a stealth, by a fear, but which is, in fact, if stealth at all, a stealth of a completely different order. This is a stealth compelled upon the wolf-cubs by a knowledge of their condition; it is not a stealth of deceit, a stealth by which certain acquisitive ends may be achieved; it is a stealth, or rather a silence, which is a guarantee, or safeguard, of a freedom, the freedom to dance. The silence of the wolf-cubs, therefore, is not only compared and contrasted with the noise of the dogs and what that implies about commerce with, and the commerce of, humanity; it is, by extension, compared with the silence of the hunters. One might then argue that the 'sans parler' of the poem's final line echoes the 'sans parler' of line 4 only the better to measure its distance from it, both spiritual and textual. But for the poet–narrator, this is a distance which is traversed, one silence transformed into another. And it should be said that even the silence which pervades the opening of the hunt is not exclusively composed of stealth; it is, too, a silence of attentiveness, of awe even, in anticipation of some imminent metaphysical encounter. Is this an exaggeration? Not really. The hunters walk in stealthy silence. But the discovery of the wolf's tracks produces, commands, a silence of a different intensity:

> Nous avons écouté, retenant notre haleine
> Et le pas suspendu ...   (ll. 9–10)

And it is as if this silence communicated itself immediately to the surrounding landscape, to be interrupted only by the weathercock:

> – Ni le bois ni la plaine
> Ne poussaient un soupir dans les airs; seulement
> La girouette en deuil criait au firmament   (ll. 10–12)

The signs of the wolf invest the natural theatre with a silence as imperious as it is redeeming.

This is the point at which we might begin to dip into the poem's prosody. It will not have escaped the reader's notice that lines 9–11, quoted above, consist exclusively of trisyllabic measures, a pattern broken in line 12 by the creaking weathercock; nor that the first line to mention silence, line 4 – 'Nous marchions, sans parler, dans l'humide gazon' – also has a 3+3+3+3 configuration; nor that the silence of the playing wolf-cubs summons a 3+3 hemistich:

> Mais les enfants du Loup se jouaient en silence   (l. 34)   4+2+3+3

And it is partly because of this conspicuous connection that the final line of the poem is more appropriately read as 3+3+3+3 rather than 3+3+1+2+3; not only, at this point in the poem, has suffering been passed beyond, not only is it as nothing in the perspective of 'Stoïque fierté', and of death itself, but the text is already imbued with the silence of which the words are only a reflection, and also with that post-verbal silence for which the poem has been a quest.

But while it would perhaps be unconvincing to suggest that all instances of the 3+3 hemistich are infiltrations of the text by silence, it is none the less true that the rhythmic equilibrium of this hemistich actualizes that deeper equanimity which is the source of Vignyan resolve. All sense of vicissitude, contained in hemistichs of unequal measures (2+4, 4+2, 5+1, etc.) has been erased, or ironed out; 3+3 is that levelling of consciousness which is a prerequisite of silent meditation and the emergence of the Idea. It might then seem odd that the 3+3 hemistich has a part to play at the very height of conflict (e.g. lines 44, 45, 47, 50, 51, 52, 55–6). But this final battle is presided over by the upright and unalarmed spirit that inhabits lines 41–2:

> Le Loup vient et s'assied, les deux jambes
>   dressées,   3+3+3+3
> Par leurs ongles crochus dans le sable enfoncées.   3+3+3+3

The inevitable outcome is already anticipated by the wolf, and although the action is violent, bloody, the wolf determines the tempo and sequence ('*Malgré* nos coups de feu...'), removes the vicissitudes of hope, despair, anger from it. He overcomes the destiny he undergoes; he ritualizes his own death. But the wolf's heroism is not merely in an attitude; it is in a struggle, too, and that struggle is not a struggle for survival, but a struggle to install the rite, to make visible the guiding principle. After all, the 3 + 3 hemistich is not a rhythmic constant in these lines, but something glimpsed or only intermittently achieved, until the climax, the couplet (ll. 55–6) prior to the narrative peroration (lines 57–60):

> Les couteaux lui restaient au flanc jusqu'à la
> garde,
> Le clouaient au gazon tout baigné dans son sang;   3+3+3+3
> Nos fusils l'entouraient en sinistre croissant.   3+3+3+3

The wolf compels the hunters into his own ceremony at the same time as he annihilates contingency, the chances and particularities of his own manner of dying; indeed he withdraws from event into his own spiritual space ('...sans daigner savoir comment il a péri'), leaving the hunters, apart from the poet, empty-handed. And the 3 + 3 hemistich is peculiarly this spiritual space, the space of steadied self-collection, of undemonstrative aloofness, occupied by a sense of one's own worth and the self-justifying nature of that worth. Finally, in this quiet apotheosis, the wolf accedes to complete possession of himself.

One of the basic oppositions of the poem is that between animals who have made a pact with man and those, like the wolves, who have remained obstinately independent, between the 'animaux serviles' (l. 70) and the 'sublimes animaux' (l. 76). This latter creates a 2+4 hemistich in which the expansion of the second measure is as if triggered by the *coupe enjambante* (see Appendix) which, by lengthening the accentuated vowel of 'sublimes', allows the poet's admiration and emotional involvement to be made manifest, as indeed does the pre-posing of the adjective. An identical set of rhythmic and grammatical features governs the hemistich 'sauvage voyageur' (l. 79). It would be structurally convenient if the 2+4 second hemistich turned out to be the consistent sign of the wolf, an enunciatory movement which although subject to the predominantly falling cadence of the second half of the line – supposing that the pitch-curve of the alexandrine most frequently creates an 'accent circonflexe', rising to a peak at the caesura, and then falling towards the line-ending, thus ╱ ‖ ╲ – enacts, even in its dying fall, a process of growth and protraction. And we might be encouraged to hold to this hypothesis in the light of some of the further evidence: the wolf-cubs are associated with 'Rémus et Romulus' (l. 40); the she-wolf is described as 'la belle et sombre veuve' (l. 65); the wolf is first perceived as 'deux yeux qui flamboyaient' (l. 28); and the look that those eyes first fix on the assailants is equally in a 2+4 second hemistich ('... et puis il nous regarde', l. 53), as is his final resignation ('... ensuite il se recouche', l. 57); finally, what life is for the wolf attracts a similar configuration, both in 'subir la grande épreuve' (l. 66) and its reformulation 'la vie et tous ses maux' (l. 75).

Again, I do not want to suggest that all other instances of the 2+4 second hemistich follow on consistently from these; this is a long poem, and besides, the poet does not enjoy sufficient freedom of choice, nor does language naturally comply with its own indications. But the coincidence occurs with frequency enough for us to propose the following. The poem dramatizes a search and a moment of recognition; the poet's two apostrophes (ll. 76, 79) are essential parts of the moment of recognition, of a naming, not of the wolf, but of the rhythmic configuration, in its most vivid and unequivocal embodiment, unequivocal, too, in the poet's own identification with it. In other words, this hemistich no longer merely acts as an accompaniment, a decorative leitmotif, for the wolves; it is the very existential shape of both wolf and poet, the shape that emerges from the quiet, even subliminal, evidence of its previous occurrences. Even though every single instance of the 2+4 hemistich does not apparently comply with the foregoing hypothesis – e.g. 'criait au firmament' (of weathercock, l. 12), 'cherchant ce qu'ils voyaient' (l. 27), 'la gorge pantelante' (of attacking dog, l. 46) – we should remember that rhythmic configuration is above all modality, or a certain affective or moral/ideological perspective. In other words, each rhythmically different hemistich is a different kind of impulse of enunciation, a different lens through which semantic contents are inspected, a different way in which syntax and lexicon are semanticized. Put in narrative terms, each rhythmically different hemistich provides a different focalization or indeed a different point of view. What I would like to suggest, therefore, is that when a 2+4 second hemistich occurs, it has a wolfish kind of tonality or perspective, even though its contents may not be explicitly wolf-related. In view of our thematic observations, it is not difficult to see the 'cries' of the weathercock as the revolt mastered and suppressed in the wolf's 'Stoïque fierté'. The 2+4 of line 27 is an anticipation of that of line 28 identifying the desire to see the wolf with being seen by it, with the desire to be seen by it. And the case of the attacking dog might be explained in two ways: first, the couplet 45–6 as a whole is governed by 2+4 initiated by the wolf's own action 'Alors il a saisi', and even though the second hemistichs of this couplet are not rhythmically identical, they share striking grammatical and acoustic similarities – each has a feminine noun in /g/ and hence a common /a/ of definite article and possessive, both nouns are accentuated syllables followed by an articulated e (*coupe enjambante*), both are qualified by present participial adjectives, and the hemistichs share a double /ã/ and a double /l/; the 2+4 of l. 46 therefore enacts the seizure of the doggish by the wolfish. But the second hemistichs of this couplet suggest something further, that this dog ('le plus hardi') of all dogs deserves to be the wolf's opponent. If the dogs have the task of cornering the wolf so that the hunters may dispose of him, then this dog has shown an independence of spirit, a lack of servility, which imitates the wolfish.

In order to demonstrate how a rhythmic configuration can, in narrative verse, indicate narratorial point of view, I would like briefly to consider a 2+4 second hemistich which at first sight seems resistant to the preceding analysis:

> Que j'ai honte de nous, débiles que nous sommes!(l. 74)   3+3+2+4

The passage in which this line occurs, just prior to the wolf's 'speech', is liberally strewn with 2+4 hemistichs, both first and second. This is the point at which the poem's real poem, indeed the poem's real poet, begins to emerge in the process already described whereby the narrative is transformed into the lyric. And this process is clearly delineated by Vigny, stage by stage, in the poem's third section. Lines 73–8 continue the meditative strain and dawning realizations of the second section – 'Me prenant a penser' (l. 62) leads into 'Hélas! ai-je pensé' (l. 73). These are lines of interior monologue. Lines 79–80 are the threshold of full revelation. The poet addresses the shade of the posthumous wolf, in words suspended between thought and speech. And in lines 81–8, the wolf expresses what the poet dimly perceived or had been led dimly to perceive by the wolf. The wolf addresses the poet in a speaking look. But this account may not be quite accurate, for while it is clear that the poet is the 'speaker' of lines 73–6, lines 77–8 spring from a more ill-defined and ambiguous source, may indeed be considered to be the words of a kind of ventriloquial wolf; these words have the same magisterial impersonality as line 85, and they are as if responded to by the poet, as if attributed to the wolf, in line 79:

> – Ah! je t'ai bien compris, sauvage voyageur

These observations suggest that the narrator is narrated by the wolf, that the wolf is the true narrator/poet. His rhythmic point of view is conspicuously present in lines 73–80 because the poet merely rehearses the wolf's judgements, is his mouthpiece or medium. The wolf's power to speak only emerges at the end, but his ability to speak has been implicit or tacit throughout the text, inhabiting the 2+4 rhythmic configuration. And it is hardly surprising that the act of utterance/narration originates in the act of bystanding and seeing, that the ability to speak is directly related to the ability to see and that the verb of penetrative sight, of significant seeing ('regarder') should belong exclusively to the wolf, whereas the poet is caught in the shallower perceptual mechanisms of 'apercevoir' (ll. 7, 28) and 'voir' (ll. 27, 29).

In considering lines 45–6 and 73–80, we have willy-nilly drawn into our discussion instances of first-hemistich 2+4. I do not now wish to embark on an exhaustive analysis of these, but merely to make a few remarks relevant to them. No 2+4 first hemistich occurs until line 33, that is, until the appearance of the wolves. Because it is part of the 'impulsive' syntax and rising pitch-curve of the first hemistich, what the 4 measure encodes is no longer the expansion of spiritual transcendence, or the attainment of the plateau of stoicism, but a taking possession, a confident decisiveness, even when the actions are not violent or dynamic:

Le Père était debout ...	(l. 37)
Sa Louve reposait ...	(l. 38)
Couvaient les Demi-Dieux ...	(l. 40)

It is only fitting that the security of man, physical rather than moral, however, should find ironic expression in the same rhythmic pattern:

Se couche dans ses murs l'homme, leur ennemi (l. 36) 2+4+1+5

It is equally fitting that the final section should be initiated by this hemistich:

Hélas! ai-je pensé ...   (l. 73)

Paradoxical though this opening cry of despair may seem, it is a cry not of surrender but of recognition, a recognition of failure which produces, by the stabilizing mechanism of thought, a corresponding determination. And the first-hemistich 2+4s which immediately follow are pervaded by the same inspiriting purposiveness:

Comment on doit quitter ...   (l. 75)

C'est vous qui le savez ...   (l. 76)

A voir ce que l'on fut ...   (l. 77)

If the second-hemistich 2+4 has more to do with the wolf's stoicism, the first-hemistich 2+4 has more to do with his 'fierté', with the drive and self-assurance that is inextricably linked with the impassive acceptance, the refusal to seek help or solace.

Before moving on to explore other rhythmic configurations, it would be appropriate here, having just singled out the verbal group 'apercevoir', 'voir' and 'regarder', to consider something of the prosody of verbs. It is common practice in verse analysis to examine tense from the point of view more of modality than of temporality. In the loose and constantly reinvented temporality of the poem, all time is *durée*, inner, experiential, qualitative, elastic; in verse, tense describes not the relation of action to time so much as the relation of the subject to action, in terms of psychological proximity to, or distance from, action, in terms of impulses, responses, associations. There is some tense-variation in 'La Mort du Loup', but the variations are organized in clearly delimited sections. The opening description (apart from the simile in line 2) is in the imperfect; the 'marchions' of line 4 describes the extended trek that precedes the action proper initiated by the perfect tense in line 7; background description continues in the imperfect. The 'allions' of line 26 closes

75

the sequence of perfect tenses, providing a bridge between them and the historic present which makes its appearance at line 27 and is accompanied by imperfects in subordinate clauses (with the intervention of the omnitemporal present in the simile at lines 31–6). The scene of the death (ll. 37–60) shifts between the imperfect, perfect and historic present, this last dominating the wolf's final moments (ll. 57–60). The second part of the poem (ll. 61–72), for all its finite verbs, is permeated by the play of infinitives, by possible or as yet unfulfilled action; this is only fitting since this section installs a lull prior to the final exhortation, and a change of key as *recueillement*, cogitative inwardness, become the new source of action. These infinitives undergo a transformation into the imperative in the closing 'speech', as we move from the infinitive string at line 85 to

Fais énergiquement ta longue et lourde tâche

and this speech has as its immediate context a passage (ll. 73–81) monopolized by the perfect and a present slung ambiguously between the punctual and the omnitemporal.

We have already had occasion to speak of the perfect tense as the tense of address, of dialogue, of bearing witness, of the event offered to the listener and shared with him. This presupposition of an auditor gives the tense something more than a narrative function: it does not simply tell the event, as the past historic does; it narrates with a kind of inbuilt justifying mechanism (the auxiliary), it is event with *apologia*, with an assumption of continuing responsibility for the event. The past historic, on the other hand, like the one in the opening line of 'La Flûte':

Un jour je vis s'asseoir au pied de ce grand arbre

locks the event away in the personal history of the first person and presents the event as an incontrovertible, definitive and irrevocable something. Rhythm has a complex and changing relationship with these modalities, sometimes reinforcing the ostensible modality, sometimes driving one tense in the direction of the modalities of other tenses.

Likelihoods of accentuation and thus of foregrounding are all a question of syllables. Because the first and second person plural forms of the present tense of the auxiliary 'avoir' have two syllables, it is likely that together with their pronouns ('nous', 'vous'), they will create a separate trisyllabic measure and thus receive an accent, as indeed they do at lines 7 and 9:

> Nous avons /aperçu//les grands ongles marqués
> Nous avons/écouté,//retenant notre haleine

The same effect is produced by the pluperfect form in line 8, with the addition of a relative pronoun:

> Par les Loups voyageurs//que nous avions/traqués

and again in l. 24, even though the pronominal 'tous' attracts the accent:

> Nous avons tous/alors//préparé nos couteaux

This distribution of the verb-form over two measures (two hemi-stichs in line 24), usually with an accentuation of each element (auxiliary and past participle), has the obvious effect of distancing the protagonists from the action, of imbuing action with a certain deliberateness, even labouredness. The action of the past participle is as if motivated by the auxiliary, but this motivation is the motivation not of desire or impulse, but of method and of the sheer need to recount. This squares well with the spirit of the hunt at this point: a quest whose motives are buried, invisible, perhaps non-existent, beneath uninspected procedures and grim determination. Only gradually will the purpose of this quest reveal itself, and then only to those able to read the signs, to see.

When the perfect tense engages the first and third persons singular, however, and syllabic quantity is reduced (monosyllabic pronoun at most + monosyllabic auxiliary), the rhythmic measure tends to reach directly through the auxiliary to an accentuation of the past participle, creating a more purposeful, single-minded and spontaneous contact between agent and action; no sooner has the auxiliary activated intention than the action is already completed in the past participle. It is again fitting that this pattern should first appear with the investigations of the 'plus vieux des chasseurs' at lines 17–23; as mentioned earlier, the 'vieux chasseur' is temporarily the poet's adoptive father; he it is who makes the first contact with the wolf, who introduces the notion of decipherment into the hunt and the valorized verb 'regarder'. This last, and the form of the perfect tense in which the auxiliary is unaccentuated, throwing the voice directly on to the achieved action of an accentuated past participle, are transferred to the poet's real father, the wolf:

Il s'est jugé perdu ...	4+2
Alors il a saisi ...	2+4
... comment il a péri	2+4

The only exception to this particular mechanism is at line 47, where the auxiliary is negativized:

Et n'a pas/desserré//ses mâchoires de fer	3+3+3+3

It is in the negativized auxiliary that one perhaps feels most strongly the colouring of justification and vindication; the verbality of the verb is in the gesture of refusal, for, after all, in negative forms of the perfect, the past participle is not an action – it is, if anything, an action cancelled by the auxiliary – but rather a piece of information. And ultimately this characteristic rhythmic shape of the third-person-singular perfect tense is shared with the first-person poet, most interestingly perhaps at line 73, the opening of the final movement:

Hélas! ai-je pensé ...	2+4

Here the process of thought itself has acquired, as it were, the same *a posteriori* force of revelation, the same affirmative actionality, the same instinctive speed, as the wolf's defence of himself. In comparison, the earlier phrase 'Me prenant à penser' (l. 62) is still operating in the mode of the initial first-person-plural perfects ('Nous avons écouté', etc.), in which action is approached tentatively, stealthily, from a distance. And I use 'stealthily' advisedly, for it seems to me that the verbal forms analysed above have a real enough connection with the modes of action discussed in our 'thematic' treatment of silence. When the auxiliary is accentuated, the agents stand off from the action, approach it with the kinds of circumspection which bespeak a faint-hearted conformation to agreed procedures.

We speak of the accent falling on the auxiliary in the first-person-plural form, and with justification, since the accentuation produces a segmentation which divorces auxiliary from past participle. But we might equally speak of the accent falling on a morpheme, on the *ending* of the first-person-plural of the present-tense ending of 'avoir'. The accentuation of the ending (*désinence*) is nowhere more apparent than in the forms of the imperfect:

> Les couteaux lui restaient au flanc jusqu'à la garde,
> Le clouaient au gazon tout baigné dans son sang;
> Nos fusils l'entouraient en sinistre croissant.   (ll. 54–6)

One argument for insisting on tense in verse as three-quarters modality is this rhythmic insistence on the ending. This is the point in the action at which, as we have already intimated, the hunters are left empty-handed, without bringing their activities to fruition. The wolf withdraws from them. The imperfective nature of the imperfect tense not only makes their assault on the wolf a backgrounded, almost decorative, setting for the wolf's death; it suspends the hunters in the amber of duration, in a past left hanging by the present of lines 57–60, in which the wolf performs his own death. As we have already noted, too, the imperfect tense appears frequently, perhaps characteristically in this poem, in subordinate clauses governed by present or perfect tense main clauses:

> Trois s'arrêtent, et moi, cherchant ce qu'ils voyaient,
> J'aperçois tout à coup deux yeux qui flamboyaient   (ll. 27–8)

> Et n'a pas desserré ses mâchoires de fer,
> Malgré nos coups de feu qui traversaient sa chair
> Et nos couteaux aigus qui, comme des tenailles,
> Se croisaient en plongeant dans ses larges entrailles   (ll. 47–50)

In the latter instance, the iterative imperfect is, thanks to its subordinatedness, given an almost spectral existence, reinforcing the 'Malgré'. It is as if the particular 'eventfulness' of the verbs 'traversaient' and 'se croisaient' is absorbed into the accentuated ending, dissipated in the general sense of persistence conveyed by the ending. Despite the brutality of these actions, emphasized by the simile ('commes des tenailles'), they are relegated to a role of accompaniment, their repeatedness expending itself in exasperation, in an inability to do any more than affirm that repeatedness. In lines 27–8, on the other hand, the imperfect provides a durative substratum to which the poet wishes to pierce through, the space occupied by the wolves, momentarily 'on the other side' and soon to be inhabited. This is a persistence of another kind, a vision to be acceded to; and as it is acceded to, so the historic present becomes more naturally the tense of real events, of the experience that matters.

It is, of course, in the present tense in particular that accentuation falls on the stem rather than the ending, that the rhythmic pulse coincides with specific action, with the semantic centre of the word, rather than with action's temporal or modal *inflection*. Which is not to say that the present tense has no modality, but merely to say that its modality is as it were fused with, and projected by, the accentuated stem. And not surprisingly perhaps, the modality of the present tense, in this poem at least, has much to do with imperativity, the imperative of impulse as much as the imperative of injunction. In the line:

> Et je vois au-delà quelques formes légères   (l. 29)   3+3+3+3

the poet both responds to a need to see and enjoins upon us the same need. Equally in the line

> Le Loup le quitte alors et puis il nous regarde   (l. 53)

– where I prefer a 4+2+2+4 reading rather than a 2+4+2+4 one, both because the two 'le's' create an acoustic continuity between noun and verb and because by isolating 'alors', as 'et puis' is isolated, one underlines the stage-by-stage, ritualized, controlled nature of the wolf's conduct – the wolf must morally quit the dog, just as he 'commands' us to quit it, to think no more of it, before turning to issue the challenge of the look. And this, too, he must do, not merely to affirm his 'Stoïque fierté', but also to seek out his blood-brother; the wolf must find his poet as the poet must find his wolf. And, of course, we must look at his look if we are ever to hear its message; his look asks us to look for its meaning. When, in the last lines of the poem, the look finally does speak, it does so not unnaturally in accentuated imperatives:

> Il disait: «Si tu peux, fais que ton âme arrive   (l. 81)
> – Fais énergiquement ta longue et lourde tâche   (l. 86)

(The former of these lines might be read $3+3+4+2$, but I prefer $3+3+1+5$, precisely to lift the 'fais' and thus set in unequivocal motion the sequence of imperatives.) And it is hardly surprising that an accentuated third-person-singular form of the present tense, adrift from its personal pronoun, sounds remarkably like an imperative:

> Refermant ses grands yeux, meurt, sans jeter un cri   (l. 60) $3+3+1+5$

This last quotation provides a starting point for the proposal that the $1+5$ hemistich is, in fact, the most imperative of rhythmic configurations. The abrupt, peremptory single-syllable opening is followed by definition, qualification, accomplishment, in a less urgent, but no less magisterial expansiveness. The first syllable of the $1+5$ hemistich is a moment of resolve or resolution, a triumphant moment, a moment of illumination, of destiny conquered, a moment entered into and enjoyed in the spaciousness of the following 5:

> ... où le chien étranglé,
> Mort longtemps avant lui, sous ses pieds a roulé (ll. 51–2) $1+5+3+3$

> – Ah! je t'ai bien compris, sauvage voyageur   (l. 79) $1+5+2+4$

And it might be argued that the reverse is true when the measures of this hemistich are reversed: $5+1$ provides a movement of sudden constriction, of expansiveness denied, freedom cut off, life denied:

> Il s'est jugé perdu, puisqu'il était surpris, $4+2+4+2$
> Sa retraite coupée et tous ses chemins pris   (ll. 43–4) $3+3+5+1$

> Gémir, pleurer, prier est également lâche   (l. 85) $...//5+1$

Perhaps the most striking lines in relation to this reversal of values are at 36:

> Se couche dans ses murs l'homme, leur ennemi $2+4+1+5$

and at 73:

> Hélas! ai-je pensé, malgré ce grand nom d'Hommes $2+4+5+1$

Prior to the encounter with the wolf, man might have grounds for believing in his superiority and dominion, in his powers of subjugation. But after the encounter, this anthropocentric confidence, this self-glorifying assertiveness, is undone, shown to be baseless and illusory. Line 73 is bitterly ironic, the capital letter serving only to underline an unfounded pretentiousness, the plural form dissolving the singleness of principle into the multiplicity of the acquisitive and cowardly mass. It would be easy to imagine that 'Hommes' is another instance of Vigny's awkward compromises with verse-demands, that the plural is enforced upon him by the plurality of the rhyme-partner 'sommes'. But this would be to depreciate the obvious and inevitable implication: man is profoundly exiled from the wolf's discovery of strength in unaided selfhood, in solitude and singleness; for man the strength which masks an inveterate moral cowardice is borrowed from his fellows (the hunting party), but since his fellows are likewise borrowers, this strength is a fabrication of the group, created by the group but not inhering in it. The poet, in the second section of the poem, is symbolically dissociated from the group by his lack of borrowed strength ('sur mon fusil sans poudre') and it is in the ensuing meditative solitude that he can at last spiritually dissociate himself from the group and attain to the self-knowledge and the self-sufficiency the wolf exhorts him to; ultimately it is not the 'nom d'Hommes' which is 'grand', but silence alone (l. 78).

As a coda to this analysis, we should remind ourselves that this poem is not just an unfolding of themes or a pursuit of argument through images, but a narrative whose drama is an intrinsic part of its persuasiveness. And we should remember that rhythm has a crucial function in narrative too, regulating its tempo and dramatizing the verse-texture. To examine fully the purely narrational operation of rhythm would require more space than we have at our disposal, but some sketchy indication of what is involved can briefly be given. Although, for example, we have concentrated on the expressive value of the $1+5$ hemistich, we might equally point out that Vigny sometimes uses the initial monosyllabic element to lift and suspend temporal conjunctions —

Lorsque, sous des sapins pareils à ceux des landes   (l. 6) $1+5+2+4$
Rien ne bruissait donc, lorsque, baissant la tête   (l. 17) $6+1+5/5+1+1+5$

— or relative pronouns —

Et nos couteaux aigus qui, comme des tenailles   (l. 49)   4+2+1+5
Où, naissant dans les bois, j'ai tout d'abord monté   (l. 84)   1+5+4+2

– so that the reader teeters on the brink of an imminent revelation, postponed and circumstantiated by an intervening parenthesis, a revelation which emerges only in a following line or hemistich. These monosyllabic measures create narrative thresholds which the reader must cross on his journey deeper into the text and into the text's meaning. On occasion, too, Vigny uses the 1 + 5 hemistich to intensify or superlativize a preposition:

Et les bois étaient noirs jusques à l'horizon   (l. 3)   3+3+1+5

This horizon belongs as much to the minds of the hunters as to the landscape. The hunters need the totality of this darkness to cover their stealth; but paradoxically they need the light (l. 20) to discover the wolf's tracks. But this is the darkness, too, of irrelevant purpose, of lost souls wandering the globe and expending their energies in unseeing pursuits. Only the poet throws off this blindness, achieves sight, thanks to the light shining from the wolf's eyes (l. 28).

The 4 + 2 hemistich also contributes to the drama of the narrative. This contracting hemistich, whose second measure halves its first, throws the reader abruptly on to the inescapable fact or the defining quality:

La girouette/en deuil//criait au firmament   (l. 12)
Il s'est jugé/perdu,//puisqu'il était surpris   (l. 43)
Et nos couteaux/aigus//qui, comme des tenailles   (l. 49)
Tout en léchant/le sang//répandu sur sa bouche   (l. 58)
Seul le silence/est grand;//tout le reste est faiblesse   (l. 78)

Some of these examples already have a certain tragic resonance: the dissyllabic measure acts like the passing of an irrevocable sentence (ll. 43, 58), a summary, dispassionate observation, heroically clear-sighted. There is more pathos when the dissyllabic measure expresses a certain resistance, a certain perseverance, in the face of imminent annihilation, a last defiant gesture:

Jusqu'au dernier/moment//où le chien étranglé   (l. 51)
Il nous regarde/encore,//ensuite il se recouche   (l. 57)
Et ton dernier/regard//m'est allé jusqu'au cœur!   (l. 80)

In the end, of course, it is impossible to make any clear distinction between the narrative and the expressive, between *énonciation* and *énoncé*, but we should bear in mind that prosody does not just make meanings, it also involves the reader in the making of meaning.

We assume that rhythm is a *sine qua non* of poetry and yet also assume that to make this observation is sufficient. To justify rhythm on the grounds of its suspected physiological source (the pulse of our very being) and its 'natural' agreeability to the ear (eurhythmy) is inadequate, and particularly so for French verse. French verse-rhythms are not a matter of 'footsteps hitting the pavement' (Lawrence), of beat, of regular recurrence; they are rather the mathematics of verbal disposition, the music of syntactic segmentation, of the relative spans of phrase, and of their combination. Rhythm is one of the languages of poetry, an inconspicuous, often subliminal rhetoric, which sensitizes and directs our responses to verbal configurations. The foregoing analysis has tried to indicate how prosody implements its designs and to demonstrate that when it comes to orchestrating these designs into a finely tuned and coherent whole, Vigny is no clumsy amateur.

NOTES

1 See Geoffrey Brereton, *An Introduction to the French Poets: Villon to the Present Day* (London, 1973), p. 119.
2 See, for example, Frank Paul Bowman, 'The Poetic Practices of Vigny's *Poèmes philosophiques*', *Modern Language Review*, 60 (1965), pp. 359–68, and Nicholas Osmond, 'Rhetoric and Self-Expression in Romantic Poetry', *French Literature and its Background*, Vol. 4: *The Early Nineteenth Century*, ed. John Cruickshank (London, 1969), pp. 26–30.
3 'La platitude glaciale refuse l'émotion. Le vers bien découpé, bien balancé et sans surprise, résonne sentencieusement aussi bien dans la description que dans la méditation' (Jacques Gaucheron, 'Vigny en poésie', *Europe*, 56, no. 589 (1978), p. 9.
4 The passage is too long to quote in its entirety, but an extract will give the flavour:
Les personnages de Vigny chassent 'à la rencontre', ce qui se conçoit pour le lièvre ou la perdrix, mais certainement pas pour le loup. De toute manière, cette chasse est impraticable de nuit; l'homme, en effet, voit très mal dans l'obscurité alors que les animaux, et notamment le loup, se

conduisent aussi sûrement qu'en plein jour ... Nous n'insisterons pas sur quelques invraisemblances manifestes: le chasseur qui, malgré son grand âge, relève des empreintes dans une forêt par une nuit noire, la louve, encore couchée quand les hommes sont assez près pour la distinguer dans l'ombre, le loup dont tous les chemins sont coupés alors que sa louve en trouve un pour s'enfuir, qui fait front assis sur son train de derrière et qui ne tente même pas de lutter ...

(*L'Imagination d'Alfred de Vigny* (Paris, 1961), pp. 66–7).

5 J.-P. Richard, 'Vigny', *Etudes sur le romantisme* (Paris, 1970), pp. 161–76.

6 André Fayolle, 'A propos de "La Mort du Loup"', *Revue d'Histoire Littéraire de la France*, 59 (1959), pp. 530–1.

7 An entry in *Le Journal d'un poète* (11 March 1860) would have us think otherwise. Describing his method of composition, Vigny speaks of discovering a fable 'qu'il faut inventer assez passionnée, assez émouvante pour servir de démonstration à l'*idée* et la *démonstration* incontestable s'il se peut'.

8 J.-P. Richard, 'Vigny', pp. 165–6.

9 'Eh quoi! ma pensée n'est-elle pas assez belle pour se passer du secours des mots et de l'harmonie des sons? Le silence est la Poésie même pour moi' (*Le Journal d'un poète*, 17 February 1832).

10 W. N. Ince, 'Some Simple Reflections on the Poetry of Alfred de Vigny', *Symposium*, 23 (1969), p. 281.

5

THE LYRIC PERSONA: NERVAL'S 'EL DESDICHADO'

Rae Beth Gordon

Je suis le ténébreux, – le veuf, – l'inconsolé,
Le prince d'Aquitaine à la tour abolie:
Ma seule *étoile* est morte, – et mon luth constellé
Porte le *Soleil noir* de la *Mélancolie*.

5 Dans la nuit du tombeau, toi qui m'as consolé,
Rends-moi le Pausilippe et la mer d'Italie,
La *fleur* qui plaisait tant à mon coeur désolé,
Et la treille où le pampre à la rose s'allie.

Suis-je Amour ou Phébus ? ... Lusignan ou Biron ?
10 Mon front est rouge encor du baiser de la reine;
J'ai rêvé dans la grotte où nage la syrène ...

Et j'ai deux fois vainqueur traversé l'Achéron:
Modulant tour à tour sur la lyre d'Orphée
Les soupirs de la sainte et les cris de la fée.

✴✴✴

The first impression this sonnet makes on the reader is one of inscrutability. Indeed, Nerval's commentary on the eight poems that comprise *Les Chimères* was that 'ils ne sont guère plus obscurs que la métaphysique d'Hegel ou les *Mémorables* de Swedenborg, et perdraient de leur charme à être expliqués, si la chose était possible'.[1] None the less, Nerval's personal belief was that everything signifies, and that the occurrences, places and names one encounters every day are signs of one's destiny, meant to be deciphered. In fact, in the sonnet, each name, place and event is a sign rife with meaning for the destiny of El Desdichado, the Disinherited One. Long before

86

the reader has unravelled the individual knots of meaning, that at least is evident. In romantic lyric poetry, the 'I' often represents the poet himself, whose personal values, emotions and strivings are cast in a fictional form that only partially veils the autobiographical 'I'. This is the case with 'El Desdichado' despite the persona's seemingly far-fetched claims that he is the Prince of Aquitaine or that he has twice crossed the river of Hades. Nevertheless, the question of the autobiographical self is itself immensely complicated in Nerval. His madness consisted in identifying with many legendary and mythic personages, and the strength of these identifications gives to these figures an extremely personal resonance once they are set down on the page. They are, simultaneously, symbols or moulds into which Nerval casts his identity, and beings from whom the poet believes himself to be descended.[2] In his own life, the experience of fragmentation and division was played out to extreme limits, since he saw himself in a multitude of personae. Yet, once these fragments of the self were activated within a given poetic text, one could see parallels and correspondences that formed a tremulous unity. In the end it all falls apart, but each text is an effort towards this creation of the self. Because the imperatives of poetic form – rhythm, syntax, rhyme and other sound-patterns – direct the narrative in which these figures are 'caught', these representatives of the 'I' are set into play through language, not through the poet's personal experiences. Rather than constructing a text out of the experiences of the self, Nerval constructs a personal identity through the interplay he sets in motion in the text. Therefore, rather than trying to 'get back' to the specific personal experiences that prompted each of these identifications, the reader will trace the trajectory of each figure as it moves towards the creation of the self. That is why the Nervalian text re-problematizes the earlier correspondence in lyric between the poet and the 'I' in the poem. Whereas the 'I' already sees these figures as parts of itself, the poet adopts the personae in this sonnet as a means of working out a coherent identity and poetic destiny.[3]

The primacy here of the personal quest is immediately clear from the repeated use of 'Je', 'mon/ma', and the question '(Qui) suis-je?' The personal quest presents itself as a quest for the person. The romantic experience of fragmentation of self and loss of a coherent identity, lived out by Nerval, is re-lived in this poem. Thus the text presents an initial paradox: it is so 'obscure' that it is probably impossible to 'explain', yet it calls out for decipherment (since we need to make sense of the signposts along the path travelled by the 'I' in order to comprehend his victory in the last verse). In addition, many of the nouns in the sonnet are metaphors or symbols (*'fleur'*, *'étoile'*, *'Soleil noir'*, etc.), and symbols exist, like metaphor, to suggest another level of meaning. Nerval went beyond any previous efforts on the part of romantic writers in elaborating a highly personal set of symbols. (A symbol as conventional as *'fleur'*, for example, acquires an unexpected meaning tied to the new contexts in which it is placed, yet its traditional meaning never completely disappears.) That is because he projected himself intensely into much of Western and Eastern mythology, making what were conventional symbols in poetry speak in the most dramatic way possible for his own personal quest. Is there a way both to respect the mystery of these *Chimeras* and to answer the questions they pose?

The first line of the sonnet illustrates this initial and essential problem.

> Je suis le ténébreux, – le veuf, – l'inconsolé,

The dashes are palpable representations not only of loss (of light, of spouse, of consolation), but also of the lacunae that are inevitable in the personal history of the subject, 'Je', and therefore in the comprehension of this *histoire* (history and story/narrative) by the reader.[4] We might therefore suppose that a simultaneous discovery of meaning will take place: on the part of Je – a piecing together of his identity; and on the part of the reader – a growing coherence of meaning emerging in the narration of El Desdichado's quest.

But does the reader uncover meaning at the same time as the Je recovers it? If not, what are the steps the reader takes to construct meaning?

> 1   Je suis le ténébreux, – le veuf, – l'inconsolé,
> 2   Le Prince d'Aquitaine à la tour abolie:
> 3   Ma seule *étoile* est morte, – et mon luth constellé
> 4   Porte le *Soleil noir* de la *Mélancolie*.

In the first quatrain, embedded within four appellations for *Je* and three attributes that further describe him, is a lone image of someone who is not the subject,[5] but rather the object of desire. The accumulation of nouns for the subject highlights by contrast the singular importance of the '*étoile*', whose brilliance seems undimmed by death: italicized, its symbolic power shines forth.

Before analysing the relation of the '*étoile*' to 'Je', of the object to the subject, of other to self, we should consider the position Nerval occupies with regard to romantic subjectivity. Without going as far as Fichte[6] in believing the world to be a product of the subjective imagination, Nerval 'reads' the world very much according to his personal history and feelings of loss and desire. The world of his dreams was, as he said, 'a second life'. And that totally subjective existence was at times privileged over existence in an external reality already heavily imbued with subjective meaning. Like Novalis, Nerval felt that 'the mysteries of the spirit are within, or they are nowhere', so, paradoxically, by descending deep within the self one has the best chance of knowing the cosmos or Spirit without. Yet this knowledge or possession of the Other is not quite so straightforward, for – as this poem attests – the Other is lost to the self and the ensuing narrative is dedicated to her recapture. The entire Nervalian *œuvre* is, in fact, an effort to link together subject and object. There is another philosophical source which combines the withdrawal into the self exemplified in Nerval's lyricism with a complex dialectic of exchange with another consciousness (the Other). This philosophical conception of the subject/object relation was developed by the philosopher to whom, as we have seen, Nerval himself refers in connection with *Les Chimères*: Hegel. In *The Phenomenology of the Spirit*, Hegel charts the path to achieving self-knowledge through a dialectic of withdrawing into the self (*Innerlichkeit*) and alienation (a feeling of otherness within consciousness: *Entfremdung*).[7]

In the first quatrain of the sonnet, we immediately notice that the most salient feature of the phrase 'Ma seule *étoile* est morte' is the italicized word at dead centre. This typographic embellishment and emphasis is also given to two terms in line 4: '*Soleil noir*' and '*Mélancolie*'. The former seems at first diametrically opposed to '*étoile*' (as the self is to the other), but a dead star could find no better synonym than a black Sun. Thus, the object is mirrored by an attribute of the 'Je'. The second italicized term that qualifies him, '*Mélancolie*', is a psychological state that is the direct consequence of loss of a loved one. This loss produces a loss of self-esteem (expressed by the connection of disinheritance in the image 'tour abolie') where the self feels impoverished on a grand scale. The isolation of the 'Je' is made more striking by the dashes that set apart 'le veuf'. At this death or loss, feelings of love and desire are withdrawn into the ego, and an identification of the ego with the lost object is established. Indeed, 'the ego wishes to incorporate this object into itself'.[8] In the sonnet, Nerval has constructed this very incorporation. Not only by embedding the object in the incantations of the 'Je', but by embedding the star in his starry lute ('*étoile*', 'consTELLé') has he managed this. What is more, the next appearance of the object (in quatrain 2, line 1), 'toi', is itself incorporated into '*éToile*', which is incorporated into a possession of the 'Je'. So the textual song, figured in the starry lute, presents a joining together of subject and object even as the '*étoile*' is lost and the 'Je' remains inconsolable and melancholic. (This would appear paradoxical were it not for the explanation of melancholia given above: incorporation of the lost object into the self creates a sense of impoverishment directed against the self. Truly to triumph in joining with the object, the 'Je' must triumph over death.) Finally, the alliterative series of 'm's' ties object to subject: '*ma*'...'*morte*'...'*mon*'... 'Mélancolie'; it also confirms the connection proposed between melancholia and the loved one's death. An early indication that the text will work to overcome the irreversible barrier of death is found in the use Nerval makes of three different techniques of versification: alliteration, interior rhyme and enjambement.[9] The alliteration that surrounds 'seule étoile' seems to frame it and the dash that follows cuts it off from the rest of the quatrain. But this closure of the frame and of death opens out again with the interior rhyme of 'morte'/'Porte', for 'Porte' literally carries the verse into the next line by the technique of enjambement, and hence opens a door in death into the next thought-image.

> 5 Dans la nuit du tombeau, toi qui m'as consolé,

A contradiction immediately greets us in the opening verse of the second quatrain: if the loved one has consoled the 'Je', how can he profess to the title of 'l'inconsolé'? And that even in the arms of death? 'Consolé' is clearly a negation of the previous term but strangely, this antithesis does not serve to annul it, and we will see why in the final tercet. At this juncture in our reading we can only wonder how Nerval has managed to make two antithetical terms exist simultaneously in a shimmering presence that threatens to disappear at any moment (like a dying star). If 'consolé' echoes 'constellé', it is not simply because of the rhyme: *sol* (sun) is also a star (*stella*) and thus harkens back not only to '*Soleil*' (*solé*), but to '*étoile*' as well. '*Soleil*-toi(le)' was already there in 'seule étoile'! So, if the loved one is the agent of consolation, the means of bringing consolation is to appeal to the qualities that already exist in the 'je' (luth constellé, '*Soleil*'). But, as we have seen, these qualities are attributes of the object ('*étoile*') that the subject has incorporated unconsciously.[10] True consolation will come about only when the 'luth' is transformed into a 'lyre' capable of overcoming the finality of death.

'Toi', the '*étoile*', consoled the 'Je' by radiating a kind of sunlight out of death's night, and thus the sunny images that immediately follow are not in opposition to what has gone before, but instead emerge out of the first quatrain. What was at first lost in shadow has been brought forth into the light by close attention to the echoes in the text. It is as though dark ('seule *étoile*') and light ('soleil-toi') were seen in rapid alternation, thanks to the handling of sonorities in the poem.

> 6 Rends-moi le Pausilippe et la mer d'Italie,
> 7 La *fleur* qui plaisait tant à mon cœur désolé,
> 8 Et la treille où le pampre à la rose s'allie.

The subject's supplication – to give him back something he once had and has somehow lost – employs the vocative for the first time in the sonnet. The vocative directly addresses the Other, 'Toi', and therefore carries a sense of immediacy and is a heightened expression of the personal, emotional outcry of the self. It is quintessentially lyrical in tone. The three images seem disparate, but are all to be found in nature (unlike what has gone before). Despite its place in the natural world, the flower also belongs to the realm of symbols that characterized the first quatrain. If we compare the two italicized words in the field of the Other, '*étoile*' and '*fleur*', their antithetical nature becomes clear: the star is celestial and the flower springs forth from the earth. These two poles are constantly evoked in Nerval's writing, as indeed they are in all romantic writing; but in Nerval they are consistently associated with a 'choice' between two women. The divergent qualities attributed to the loved one in the quatrains may already have struck the reader as strange: a dead star in the night of the tomb who bears the gift of sun-drenched seascapes and earthy promise. Yet, even if these natural objects have helped in the past to make loss less acute, 'cœur désolé' indicates that 'consolation' has as yet to heal the absence felt so deeply by the subject.

In contrast to the first quatrain, here we find an evenly distributed series of 'couples': 'toi'/'moi'; 'le Pausilippe'/'la mer d'Italie'; 'la *fleur*'/'mon cœur'; 'le pampre'/'la rose'. What is more, they are all composed of a feminine and a masculine element. And the final verse gives us an image of their union: 'la treille où le pampre à la rose s'allie'. This quatrain, then, puts forth a new mode of joining with the object: an alliance that is an intertwining and alternation rather than the mode of incorporation we saw at work in the first quatrain. In line 7, the poetic device of interior rhyme (*'fleur'*/'cœur') ties subject and object together, whereas in line 8 another man-made device ('la treille') intertwines the two natural objects.

But let us not forget that these things – and their union – are lost. That is the cause of the split in the 'Je' so clearly presented in line 9 of the first tercet.

> 9   Suis-je Amour ou Phébus? ... Lusignan ou Biron?

Here the vocative seems less destined for 'Toi' than for either the reader or the subject himself. In the latter case, the self would then be taken as object. That is indeed what has been implied all along in this travail of construing the self through poetry. With the use of the interrogative, Nerval has made the task explicit (the self asks itself whether it is this persona or that one).

We can readily see that the splitting of the self into disparate entities ('Amour ou Phébus', 'Lusignan ou Biron') is the only way 'Je' has of discovering an identity. But, already in the first line of the text, 'Je' is an object to himself in the experience of regarding himself. This self-reflection or *Innerlichkeit* already divides the subject into a 'Je' who acts and a 'Je' who watches himself act or be. In seeking affirmation from the Other (who has become radically

Other through death), though, 'Je' is faced with a silence. Yet in the past (quatrain 2) the Other has offered the recognition he seeks. The desire for recognition from the Other in order to affirm one's identity causes alienation, and we see the result in line 9 of the first tercet. This is evidence of the self-fragmenting nature of the self's relationship to others.

That the 'Je' still remains ignorant of his identity is seen in the question form. The lyric quest for pure subjectivity is in fact only at mid-point.

> 9 Suis-je Amour ou Phébus? ... Lusignan ou Biron?
> 10 Mon front est rouge encor du baiser de la reine;
> 11 J'ai rêvé dans la grotte où nage la syrène ...

The idea of a gap that marks the search for self-identity is empha-sized by the three *points de suspension*; but this punctuation is not as radical an abyss as were the dashes in the first quatrain. Similarly, the dash that recreated the effect of acute loss (after 'seule *étoile* est morte') is modified, and an effect of suspension – an absence accompanied by a sense of expectation – replaces it.

Amour (Eros, the god of love), and Phébus (Apollo, the god of light) relate directly to the problems of identity raised earlier: love and light ... or rather, their absence. Lusignan and Biron, on the other hand, relate to the two feminine figures named in the tercet: 'la reine' and 'la syrène'. If the 'Je' is Amour or Phébus, he reclaims his right to possession of love or light by virtue of his own self-identity; if he is Lusignan or Biron, he can claim a (past) recognition by the Other. The 'fée' is glossed in the Eluard manuscript of the poem[11] as Mélusine, with whom Lusignan was in love according to the medieval legend. And one of the possible personae represented by Biron, Lord Byron (the same manuscript spells the name with a 'y'), loved the sister of a queen.

Even though the quatrains presented an initial opacity we were able to penetrate their tomb-like, stony obscurity. One of the factors that helped us to follow the 'Je's' 'path' or quest was the narrative quality of these verses. However, the first tercet offers no logical progression whatsoever. Line 9, as I have just shown, is not a total break from the 'story' of the quatrains. In fact, it is simply a reversal. From 'Je suis' Nerval shifts to 'Suis-je?', from 'ténébreux' and 'veuf' to 'Phébus' and 'Amour'. An identity first annulled is precariously preserved by the interrogative.

But what of the next two lines? The lack of logical connection here would not be so striking were it not for the narrative line in the quatrains. Because of this lack, the images in lines 10 and 11 offer a fine example of what Freud called primary process thinking, that is, thought-images that emerge unaltered from the unconscious.[12] What remains with the reader is not a string of words but an indelible image. (These sorts of images appear frequently in Nerval and caused those determined explorers of the unconscious, the Surrealists, to claim him as a precursor.)

The romantics undertook the exploration of the psyche in the form of the dream narrative, the supernatural, the confession, and their discoveries were extraordinarily intuitive forerunners to the findings of psychoanalysis.[13] This sonnet partakes of the same mysterious atmosphere as one finds in dream narratives and in supernatural tales, as the title *Chimera* suggests. The descent into the unconscious depths, the repository of myth, is often metaphorized as the descent into the Underworld, and this is precisely where the final tercet of 'El Desdichado' is set.[14] It is of course logical that the search for one's identity should entail a plumbing of the unconscious. The alienated discourse of the 'Je', 'I am X, Y, or Z', implies that the 'Je' has somehow lost contact with his true self and must seek it 'underneath' these fictions of the ego. None the less, the way the 'Je' imagines himself to be is only fictional in part; the personae we invent to imagine and describe ourselves always carry keys to the self. By seeking the meaning shared by these identities, by analysing the way the 'Je' is separated or connected to the Other, one arrives at the true self. In other words, by studying the poem in these ways, the self should emerge. It appears that the reader pieces together meaning in precisely the same way as the 'Je' re-constructs his identity.

> Mon front est rouge encor du baiser de la reine;
> J'ai rêvé dans la grotte où nage la syrène …

For the first time there is a palpable connection between subject and object, one that has been preserved, and whose image is distinctly erotic. This is a far cry from the abstract tie created by the linguistic tricks of verse lines 3 and 4 in quatrain 1. And, like the continuation of the past kiss through the persistent presence of its imprint, the mermaid continues to swim in the grotto where the 'Je' has dreamed. This eternal present is typical of primary process thinking, as is the impression that these lines are clearly governed by the pleasure principle and are unmodified by censorship. The act of dreaming, brought in at this moment of the text, confirms the idea that we are dealing with primary process thinking, since the dream-work is its privileged site. Thus, this verse marks the moment where unconscious desires are allowed to emerge and play a part in the constitution of the self. Surely the resolution of identity that immediately follows derives in part from this breakthrough.

If we were to go outside this particular sonnet, we would find a myriad of allusions to queens and sirens in Nerval which would encourage us to posit various interpretations. Yet even within the confines of the text, one can venture some remarks about the nature of these two feminine figures. Both are highly eroticized, and both are the stuff of which legends and myth are made, hence the stuff of which dreams are made. Reading these lines aloud brings out their dream-like, incantatory mystery, the almost eternal quality of these images of desire.

Since the name Lusignan is traditionally connected to the mermaid Mélusine (see note 11), if the subject is Lusignan, he is no longer 'veuf', for the 'syrène', contrary to the 'étoile', is not dead.

But there is another reason why the image of the siren swimming provides a solution to the problem of isolation, separation and loss the poet has been describing. The siren not only swims, but sings. It can be said that the lines in the sonnet that 'sing', or that are more melodic, are those that 'flow'. An analysis of rhythm in the text reveals an almost perfect alternation of flowing and staccato lines of verse. Because of the dashes, the first line is hesitant, fragmented and staccato. Because of the articulated 'e' in Prince, and the melding together of '... taine à la Tour abolie' created by the alternation of 't' and 'l' tied together by the 'a' sound, the second line flows. The third line leans toward the staccato due to the number of monosyllabic words it contains, the emphatic consonants in the second hemistich ('luTH ConSTellé'), and the break created by the dash. However, the first hemistich is mellifluous with its evenly placed 'l's', 'm's' and 'é' sounds, and the enjambement makes it flow into the next line of verse. Therefore a tension exists in this line between fragmentation and a flowing together that defeats fragmentation. This battle pushes us to examine the content of line 3 in the light of two opposing forces. Surely they are the death of the loved one and the starry lute. The lute 'lutte contre la mort'. Finally, the fourth line has a very pronounced flowing quality. Quatrain 2 begins with the staccato rhythms of the emphatic consonants d, t and k, and these are repeated in line 7. Line 8, on the other hand, is the most melodic line in the quatrains, thanks to the vowel sounds that fuse with the 'l's' ('où le', 'à la'), and the articulated 'e' that fuses with the following word ('rose s'allie').

The tercets are somewhat more complex, but they too observe a pattern of alternation. The rhythm of the first two lines of verse is broken in tercet 1, while the final line is arguably one of the most melodic, incantatory alexandrines in all of French poetry. In tercet 2, the alternation accelerates: the first hemistich in lines 12 and 13 is staccato, while the second flows. On the contrary, the first hemistich of line 14 flows, while the second is emphatic and staccato.

What conclusion can be drawn from this alternation? Does song, like the mermaid, need a flowing, watery element? Analysis of the content of the verses whose rhythm is flowing and unfragmented will partially answer that question. 'Et la treille où le pampre à la rose s'allie' speaks of connection, the coming together of the flower and the vine. 'J'ai rêvé dans la grotte où nage la syrène': the poet has dreamed and perhaps created his poem out of the dream of the siren's song and undulating, flowing movement. In addition, the object of desire is not cut off from the subject, for she exists in the present. But, whereas the erotic feeling for the mermaid is soothing and pleasurable, the red mark of the queen's kiss indicates a more violent *eros*: hence the contrasting rhythms. Similarly, 'traversé l'Achéron' concerns water flowing and the subject's association with this element. Certainly, sighs should be gentle and harmonious, while cries should be rendered in the broken way we hear them in the poem. (The contrast between euphonious and staccato rhythms has already been established in tercet 1 as a difference in the self's relation to the object of desire.) I will leave 'sur la lyre d'Orphée' for the conclusion, because it ties together everything I have been saying up until now.

Clearly, the fragmented self seeks an identity which would encompass and tie together these others in the self. He also seeks fusion with the object of desire. The self is fragmentary, and this is why broken rhythms must continually make themselves felt in the sonnet. But there *is* fusion of the disparate selves, and of the self with the object, through poetry. The poet modulates/alternates both rhythms, both ways of being, both feminine figures – the earthly and the celestial – both 'songs' – fading sighs and strident cries – on the lyre of Orpheus. Elsewhere, Nerval cites a refrain from Gluck's opera *Orfeo ed Euridice*. The refrain comes from the air Orpheus sings to cajole the Shades of the Underworld into letting him retrieve Eurydice from the dead. The sweet sounds from the repetitive plucking of his lute lay down a soothing, incantatory melody over which alternate the soft, flowing melody of his plea and the punctuating outcries of the 'Shades and Larvae', obstacles to his recovery of the object of desire.[15] If this aria was Nerval's inspiration for the last tercet of 'El Desdichado', then another layer of meaning may be added to the staccato rhythms he modulates throughout the poem: they represent an obstacle to the fusion of subject and object described in the verse lines that 'flow'.

> 12 Et j'ai deux fois vainqueur traversé l'Achéron:
> 13 Modulant tour à tour sur la lyre d'Orphée
> 14 Les soupirs de la sainte et les cris de la fée.

The importance of the lyre in the final tercet cannot be underestimated. Lyric poetry is not only an expression of subjectivity as we have analysed it here, but also (as the word suggests) meant to be sung or lending itself to song. Hence the triumphant conclusion to the quest is not only the negation of the finality of death, and the reconciliation of the diverse personae of the 'Je' with the self; it is also the mastery of the lyric form itself. The struggle of melodic rhythm over broken rhythms may be seen in this light as well. Here too Nerval's text is intimately tied to his personal story. Among all the French romantics, it was he who best understood and most treasured and promoted the folk-song, having collected and published the *Chansons et vieilles ballades du Valois*.[16] He also wrote lyric pieces either set to music or imitative of music: romances, songs, verses for opera.

In fact, a connection can be established between two earlier incarnations of the 'Je' and lyric poetry or song: the Prince of Aquitaine evokes Guillaume IX, Duke of Aquitaine, who wrote the first love-poems of courtly literature in France (played on the lute by troubadours); and Biron/Byron evokes the lyric poet Lord Byron. The master of the lyric is the only persona named who is capable of bringing together the fragments (the various 'I's') of the self.

Yet the legend of Orpheus itself speaks of fragmentation: his body was torn to bits by ecstatic maenads. This *corps morcelé* is a startling physical enactment of the self in bits laid out by the poem, and at the same time it provides a visual representation of the fragmented rhythms that emanate from the lyric poet's song. So, if the persona of Orpheus allows the 'Je' to piece together the fragments of his identity through poetry, it also implies the inevitable return of fragmentation brought about by desire.

The modulation of flowing and fragmented rhythms has a corollary: expansion and containment. The verse lines that flow give the impression of expansion (seen most clearly in those with enjambement), while the verse lines that are broken up give the sense of containment (seen most clearly in the framing of '– le veuf, –' and 'morte –'). The key images are the stony enclosure of the tomb and the flowing of water. Isolation and containment here might signify artistic sterility, the absence of poetic power. Certainly the water image is directly connected with poetic power: the poet is victorious in twice crossing the Achéron. He defeats the containment not only of space but of time and death ('la nuit du tombeau'). The subtle shifts in the text from past to present should be read in this light. Instead of the recollections of the poet's past which lead back to the present position of the 'I' which one encounters in most romantic lyric poetry, Nerval works out a complex alternation of present and past. The other image of stone in the sonnet, 'tour abolie', is not so much one of containment as one of disintegration (the metaphoric antithesis of the new-found integration of the self at the end of the sonnet). Here again, it is the poet's song that takes up this negative quality and transforms it into a positive force: 'modulant *tour* à *tour*'.

Indeed, the strict, rigorous confines of the classical sonnet form itself is an example of containment; but we have seen how Nerval intertwines words, sounds and concepts to make the sonnet a vertiginous place of movement, metamorphosis and infinite expansion. Through poetry, or song, he makes what is entombed come out into the light. The fourteen lines of the sonnet might appear to us now as the seven courses of the double-strung lute.[17] Through a seemingly narcissistic reflectiveness and an introjection of the object (both enclosures) in the quatrains, he makes the self emerge in exemplary romantic ex-pression.

Hegel wrote that consciousness was transformed into pure subjectivity when, certain of its Self, it discovered itself in its own discourse. That is what happens in the final tercet of 'El Desdichado', where the alternating discourses of flowing together and fragmentation are discovered in the persona of the lyric poet, Orpheus. The ultimate identity of the 'Je', Orphée, contains an otherness with which he can feel at home; this otherness is the 'fée' in 'Or-fée'. In his final role of poet, and only then, does the subject consciously possess the object and the golden rays (*or*) of the sun she promised. This is an *Aufhebung*[18] of the moment in quatrain 1 where the starry lute contained the 'étoile', yet failed to provide consolation. Now the victorious lyric voice of Orpheus contains the 'fée', a feminine figure very closely aligned in the imagination with the siren (who also contains in herself the 'reine': 'sy-rène'). The lyric poet recognizes himself at last: in the very model for his art (Orpheus, master of the lyre) and for his desire (Orpheus, whose quest is the retrieval of the lost, beloved other).

NOTES

1 Gérard de Nerval, 'A Alexandre Dumas', preface to the 1854 edition of *Les Filles du feu*, followed by *Les Chimères* in *Œuvres* (Paris, 1974), Vol. 1, pp. 158–9. The word 'scarcely' is ironic, since one would be hard put to find texts more opaque than these two.

2 Nerval suffered from delusions of grandeur and from schizophrenia. His stays in psychiatric hospitals or clinics took place in 1840–1, 1851, twice in 1853 and in 1854. In 1853, he suffered aphasia (loss of speech), loss of his ability to write, and loss of identity. Aspects of this crisis may

be found in 'El Desdichado', published for the first time later that year (10 December in *Le Mousquetaire*).

3 On the Eluard manuscript of 'El Desdichado', the sonnet is in fact entitled 'Le Destin'. The version of 'El Desdichado' reproduced in the present study is the one published in the 1854 edition of *Les Filles du feu*. See Marie-Jeanne Durry, *Gérard de Nerval et le mythe* (Paris, 1956) for a detailed study of specific mythic figures in Nerval's work.

4 Psychoanalysis attempts to work backward in one's personal story to recover meaning out of the names and events that surround these gaps (the gaps represent material repressed from conscious memory). None the less even the most insistent 'descent' into the unconscious will leave some gaps intact.

5 The word 'subject' is used here to mean the thinking being, the individual person, and is placed in opposition to 'object'.

6 Johann Gottlieb Fichte, an early German romantic philosopher whose ideas (particularly in *Wissenschaftlehre*, 1794) were developed in Schelling and Hegel. See Fichte, *Science of Knowledge, with the First and Second Introductions*, translated and edited by Peter Heath and John Lachs (New York, 1970).

7 G. W. F. Hegel, *Phänomenologie des Geistes* (Berlin, 1832; first published in 1807).

8 Freud, 'Mourning and Melancholia' (1917), in *Sigmund Freud: Collected Papers*, translation supervised by Joan Rivière (New York, 1949–50), Vol. 4, p. 160. Freud wrote that melancholia, an abrogation of interest in the outside world, is the only narcissistic neurosis. That is why the 'Je' has to go beyond the initial stage of self-mirroring to reach the Other, and therefore give up the lute of melancholia for Orpheus's lyre. In the nineteenth century, however, when this poem was written, melancholia was perceived as a form of psychosis.

9 Enjambement is 'the overflowing of a clause begun in the one line into the next line'. The wording of this definition is found in L. E. Kastner's *A History of French Versification* (Oxford, 1903).

10 Another subtle form of incorporation is created by the repetition of consonants from le TéNéBreux in la Nuit du TomBeau: the subject places himself in the object's death. This helps us to see that the subject's dark, shadowy character is a function of this death.

11 The 'fée' (fairy) Mélusine, half-serpent and half-woman, cried out when Lusignan saw her in her bath. The figure of Mélusine, therefore, connects the 'fée' to the mermaid ('la syrène'). The home of the illustrious Biron family is the Périgord (Aquitaine), and this figure therefore harkens back to 'le Prince d'Aquitaine'. Nerval also manages

to tie the mythological persona of Phoebus to the Aquitaine in a letter written to Georges Sand from the psychiatric clinic signed 'Gaston Phoebus D'Aquitaine' (and dated 22 Novembre 77 353, ère nouvelle). *Œuvres*, Vol. 1, pp. 1106–8. Thus, the bi-polarity of the Medieval (Prince d'Aquitaine, Lusignan, Biron, sirène, sainte, fée) and the Ancient (Amour, Phébus, Orphée) is subtly effaced and two different realms tied together.

12 Primary process is, according to Freud, constituted by those forms of representation that prevail in the unconscious, where psychic energy is unbound, free to become invested in any zone that allows for its discharge, thereby producing pleasure. Like this energy, the forms of representation in the unconscious operate for the benefit of the pleasure principle and not the reality principle (whose energy is bound by censorship, and associations under the control of the Ego). These forms of expression violate linguistic laws of syntax and semantics. See Freud, *The Interpretation of Dreams* (1900) and *The Unconscious* (1915) in *Sigmund Freud, Collected Papers*.

Another aspect of the resurgence of the unconscious here is the red imprint of the queen's kiss on the subject's forehead, which might be analysed as Oedipal desire, since he is the 'Prince', not the King. The image of the 'tour abolie' would then be seen as phallic symbol and as punishment for the Prince's desire.

13 Freud of course acknowledged this debt (in particular to Goethe, Schiller and E. T. A. Hoffmann).

14 'La Descente aux Enfers' is a recurrent theme in Nerval; it appears, for example, in *Aurélia, Voyage en Orient*, and in the 'Preface' to Nerval's translation of *Faust*.

15 In a letter to George Bell dated 31 May 1854 Nerval writes,
> J'ai trop chanté dans les ténèbres:
> Laissez-vous toucher par mes pleurs
> Ombres, larves, spectres terribles!

Nerval, *Œuvres*, Vol. 1, p. 1141.

16 See *Chansons et légendes du Valois*, in *Les Filles du feu*, 1854 edition. Other versions of this study had already been published, the earliest among them being *Vieilles Ballades françaises* in *La Sylphide*, 10 July 1842. Paul Bénichou has written on the importance of folk-song in *Nerval et la chanson folklorique* (Paris, 1970).

17 The idea of the seven double strings of the lute has been mentioned by Anita Grossvogel in *Le Pouvoir du nom: Essai sur G. de Nerval* (Paris, 1972). She also notes the presence of 'or' and 'fée' in the name Orphée, and referring to the entire *œuvre* writes: 'De Narcisse, il était devenu

Orphée, celui qui a l'or de la fée, de Lorely … l'or enfin de la mort' (p. 152).

18 *Aufheben*, the verb Hegel had recourse to so often in order to describe the dialectical process in his philosophy, means (paradoxically) to cancel or annul, preserve, and transcend in a higher coming-together.

6

UNDER-READING AT NOON:
LECONTE DE LISLE'S 'MIDI'

Mary Ann Caws

Midi, roi des étés, épandu sur la plaine,
    Tombe en nappes d'argent des hauteurs du ciel bleu.
Tout se tait. L'air flamboie et brûle sans haleine;
    La terre est assoupie en sa robe de feu.

5 L'étendue est immense, et les champs n'ont point d'ombre,
    Et la source est tarie où buvaient les troupeaux;
La lointaine forêt, dont la lisière est sombre,
    Dort là-bas, immobile, en un pesant repos.

Seuls, les grands blés mûris, tels qu'une mer dorée,
10 Se déroulent au loin, dédaigneux du sommeil;
Pacifiques enfants de la terre sacrée,
    Ils épuisent sans peur la coupe du soleil.

Parfois, comme un soupir de leur âme brûlante,
    Du sein des épis lourds qui murmurent entre eux,
15 Une ondulation majestueuse et lente
    S'éveille, et va mourir à l'horizon poudreux.

Non loin, quelques bœufs blancs, couchés parmi les herbes,
    Bavent avec lenteur sur leurs fanons épais,
Et suivent de leurs yeux languissants et superbes
20 Le songe intérieur qu'ils n'achèvent jamais.

Homme, si, le cœur plein de joie ou d'amertume,
    Tu passais vers midi dans les champs radieux,
Fuis! La nature est vide et le soleil consume:
    Rien n'est vivant ici, rien n'est triste ou joyeux.

25   Mais si, désabusé des larmes et du rire,
      Altéré de l'oubli de ce monde agité,
    Tu veux, ne sachant plus pardonner ou maudire,
      Goûter une suprême et morne volupté,

    Viens! Le soleil te parle en paroles sublimes;
30   Dans sa flamme implacable absorbe-toi sans fin;
    Et retourne à pas lents vers les cités infimes,
      Le cœur trempé sept fois dans le néant divin.

***

It may well be that, as we tend to overstate, we tend to over-read. Ideological passions may make thundering rhetoricians of us all: thunder is more eloquent than low-voiced suggestion, and more instantly of interest. But suggestions may be equally insistent, low voices equally persistent in the long run, and understatement ultimately no less convincing than over-. It depends on what is, or seems to be, called for.

Leconte de Lisle, inscribing himself in a tradition of stoic, severe and antique-voiced poetry, might seem to call for a response along the lines of overstatement. His deliberately radiant and almost silent 'Midi' (*Poèmes antiques*, 1852) with its sweep of landscape burnt by the sun and drenched in the heavy water of oriento-philosophic thought,

>... La nature est vide et le soleil consume:
>Rien n'est vivant ici, rien n'est triste ou joyeux...

is sermonizing in tone (a sort of 'Man, look ye and do thou' approach), and lofty in leaning. It might seem to demand exactly the sort of treatment that a treatise might, arguably not what a poem demands. But it stands, within the corpus of Leconte de Lisle's work, together with the tropical langour of some of the best *Poèmes barbares*, as his most notable achievement, and, incomparably more complicated than the most complicated of them, as the summit of his neo-classic, super-stoic and yet sensual temperament. The very lively tensions of the poem disprove the statement that 'nothing is living here' and lend to the text a kind of presentness that even the 'divine nothingness' on which it ends does not cancel out, rather throwing it into retrospective relief. I will want, if not precisely to argue, then to illustrate what kind of relief a quiet, 'under-' reading can bring to such an unlikely presentation of presentness.

Specifically, in this poem, we are arrested by its rather bizarre *detail*.[1] For there is something about those white oxen lying there right in the grass at the centre of that poem that sneaks up on the unwary mind and stays there. There are not a lot of white oxen lying about in French verse or in any European writing, I think, and these are likely to radiate a particular appeal for the present reader, precisely because they do not mesh with the normalized landscape of French poetry, in which the sacred cows have tended to be other.

They are, equally, quite unlike the jaguars and snakes, the panthers and bulls and wolves and vultures in the rest of Leconte de Lisle's poetry – all of them underlining the pagan wildness and brute force, either sinuous or leaping, of the 'barbarous' part of nature, the part that ends up loudly, if I may put it like that. For a striking example on the human and animal side, in the poem 'Le Cœur de Hialmar', the dying warrior, even as he requests his heart to be ripped out by a crow who will carry it to his 'fiancée' like a noble tribute to valour, knows he will end up seated, and gloriously, in the sun:

> Moi, je meurs. Mon esprit coule par vingt blessures.
> J'ai fait mon temps. Buvez, ô loups, mon sang vermeil,
> Jeune, brave, riant, libre et sans flétrissures,
> Je vais m'asseoir parmi les Dieux, dans le soleil!

By contrast these odd white beasts are just lying and looking; they would seem to resemble a *punctum* in the concept of photography that Roland Barthes refers to in his *Chambre claire*: they form the sort of instant perception that stands out as memorable, apparently not fitting in with the scheme of things.[2]

So it is that we might want to talk about that text and its obsessive detail as important, paradigmatic and problematic. In short, what is to be done with a poem we intuit as interesting, but on our own readerly terms? Its terms are quite other. It already presents itself as high in tone, solemn in outlook, and careful in shape – were a reading simply to repeat those characteristics, in a sort of agreeing echo, it would be tantamount to an acceptance of imitation as the fine art of criticism. It would put nothing in crisis – something which criticism is bound to do, according, once again, to Barthes[3] and to the etymology of the word; it would make no allowance either for the sense of freedom or for the sense of humour which might be seen as two of the other criteria necessary to an adequate response in the present to such a text – unless it is to be considered readable only in the past, a dead-weight manifestation of a philosophy which in all probability we neither espouse nor particularly care about.

When we try to deal with its more apparent profile, we are bound to take up Large Issues, such as the following: being about Being (but what great poems are not?) and being lit in the high mode, it is also, and perhaps even more, about Nothingness. When you write about nothingness and high noon at once, where are the shadows to be placed, and what is put in relief, against this dazzling backdrop? What sort of visual resolution is aimed at, along with the philosophic? Where does the reader or observer stand, in what light, and what is the role of such sunlight and such sparse shade? Is that observer, too, doomed, with the 'Man' addressed by the solemn speaker of the text, to move back to the deathly cities with slow footsteps after the sublime solar absorption he discovers at the close and, also, in the heart of the poem – this oblivion called nothingness, but called, no less, divine? How does the 'heart' of the one summoned in the narration respond to the heart of the poem? Where do we go from this antiqued language, towards what more living texts, and how will this one have mattered?

Responding, then, to the overstatement of such questions as these, I want, rather paradoxically, to risk the low-key climate of understatement, even in this poem of sublime philosophical summons, and to use it as an illustration of what I am here calling under-reading, and then under-writing. It is the notion of taking what seems to lie just (or deeper) below the surface as equal in value to what appears, and, more particularly, of *stressing* – in the sense of metrical stress, both in the interpretation and the styling of the presentation – those details that seem crucial to the reading of that underlayer.

The suggestions I will sketch out as possible replies to those questions will be just that, sketchy and mere mentionings of answers. They will, for example, point to where those shadows are and leave them, will suggest a description of the landscape and an attendant seascape and move on. They will deal with the topic

briefly, and not gravely, and – what is graver still – they will often
rely upon a re-hearing of the words themselves, reading *under* the
evidence to a wealth of suggestion they will call upon, but not
always spell out. They will not examine Leconte de Lisle's possible
intentional[4] or conscious use of this undertext, since we cannot
know it; but not to know that should not rule out, I would claim,
our own multiple-possibility of response. This I am calling under-
reading, and I want to dwell upon its justification no longer than
upon those strange and wonderful white oxen: it is simply there.[5]

The poem makes a strong beginning statement of two syllables,
which will not recur until the close, already having been sufficiently
said: 'Midi'. And defined, already also, after its initial undefined and
internally-rhymed isolation before, first, a comma, and then its
luminous definition: 'roi des étés', set off, again, in commas, before
the expansion: 'épandu' . . . The long opening to the poem is dramatically stretched out with pauses that can only be heard as majestic:

Midi, roi des étés, épandu . . .

Midi indeed. Strongly there, illuminating everything to come,
royally summering in original and, as it were, pre-conscious splendour, before spreading out into the plains of belated consciousness.
The very dazzlement of the start places this reign under the sign of
present being: the verb 'is' echoes notably in this and the succeeding
stanza, as the sound 'est', thus:

étés
épandu
tait
étendue
est immense
et les
et la
blés
épuisent . . . épis
s'éveille, etc.

The poem is slanted towards this being, even as it is paradoxically
imbued with silence ('Tout se tait', 'la source est tarie'). Visibly, the
nearby springs are dried up, those from which, presumably, some

flocks of safely-grazing beasts used to drink; the 'source ... tarie' and the total noon-struck silence are put in parallel, that silence falling directly after the fullness of the silver-clothed drench of light, and striking hard. Here the punctuation serves to strike the point:

Tout se tait. L'air flamboie et brûle sans haleine;

The silence is strengthened both – at the level of the spoken – by the twice-sounded 't' and – at the level of the written – by the four-fold visible signs of silence ('t–t–t–t'), like four corners of a roof over it, for dwelling in. It is markedly set apart for a full arrest by the sentence, directly there in the middle of the line. That very silence is rendered more drastic by what follows, the breathlessness of the burning air, coming to a half-stop in the semi-colon for a half-arrest before the heaviness of the earth somnolent in its fiery dress. These full stops, making a mid-line crisis, should be enough to persuade the most hardened non-reader of punctuation of its importance, and even of its possible delights.

Readers of romanticism, for example, love to linger over such lines as the following from Wordsworth's 'Lines written a few miles above Tintern Abbey':

> ... For nature then
> (The coarser pleasures of my boyish days,
> And their glad animal movements all gone by,)
> To me was all in all. I cannot paint   (ll. 73–6)

Held in mid-flight before the announcement of the inability to render, and after the parenthetic bulge which so wonderfully swells the sentiment ('For nature then was all in all to me'), the plenitude of the all-in-all stops right there, nostalgically but necessarily, contained within those parentheses.

Such mastery of containing and stopping recurs, in like manner, in the later and no less celebrated lines in that justly celebrated poem about that 'still, sad music of humanity',

> Not harsh nor grating, though of ample power
> To chasten and subdue. And I have felt
> A presence ...   (ll. 92–4)

'Subdue' had to find its full stop just there, in the centre, and the feeling of presence had to begin directly after, visible because precisely *not* at the normal end of the line. Punctuation is about making things, important things, visible as well as audible, and making that point against what the eye sees, the ear hears, as 'normal', therefore, invisible and inaudible.

In the foreground here of 'Midi', there is only glaring light and fullness; speech is not needed, nor are flowing things. The gilded sea far away is present only by suggestion in the distant field of wheat, those sheaves marked themselves as solitary, set off, like the initial 'Midi', by an initial sheltering comma, and then a following one, before the spread out into simile:

> Seuls, les grands blés mûris, tels qu'une mer dorée,
> Se déroulent au loin ...

Now this extraordinarily strong usage of the initial comma to set off the subject in heroic splendour is a frequent device, as is its *textualizing* of the important. It is reminiscent of other settings-apart of loneness, for example one of the strong beginnings of a *laisse* in *La Chanson de Roland*:

> Roland, tout seul, par les champs s'en va donc ...

The same suspension in space is visible for the name, and then for the verbal restatement of the solitude, before the line spreads out into the landscape and the action.

The unfolding is set into the distance, like the liquid source seen as maternal and as at least half-adored: 'une mère (a)dorée,' from which what lingers is again that sound of being: 'est'. Motherness is not suppressed, nor is being, but both are removed here, as a natural part of the engendering landscape, complete with faraway dark-edged forest:

> La lointaine forêt, dont la lisière est sombre

So the darkness is held at eye's length, not permitted within the stretch of our near space in its radiant immensity:

> L'étendue est immense, et les champs n'ont point d'ombre

Only in the distance is there nourishment, there where the sacrality of the earth and the shining sea nourish, from the very goldenest bowl of the sun, the calm and wheat-maned children of the far-flung text:

> Pacifiques enfants de la terre sacrée,
> Ils épuisent sans peur la coupe du soleil.

Maternality is clearly placed at this distance, but even there a full-breasted fling is allowed:

> Parfois, comme un soupir ...
> Du sein des épis lourds ...
> Une ondulation majestueuse et lente
> S'éveille, et va mourir ...

The majestically motherly response to the initial reign of the royal noon is set up as distant to near, as wet to dry, as waving to still, as murmuring to silent – and as dying, to drowsing and to dead:

> Midi ...
> Tombe ...
> La terre est assoupie ...

For the initial fall is readable as *tomb*, and the shower of dry silver ('Tombe en nappes d'argent') is already installed as the predecessor of the gilded sea ('une mer dorée'), under that full cup of the sun heralded as fearless. The wheat in the distance holds in itself no fear of this fall into the too-early tomb, where the nourishment is set out on tablecloths already incorporating the silver cutlery into the whole cloth ('nappes d'argent').

So an enormously full scenic contrast is established between two scenes of death and plenty: the near-dry brightness and the distant (over)flow of the sun's inexhaustible cup; the double statement 'Ils *épuisent* sans peur' plays at once on the exhausting of the resources, but without actual fear of exhausting them, and on the presence and fullness of the notion and gesture of dipping: ('est' or then 'et' and 'puisent'). The strong marking of the fearlessness ('sans peur') seems to apply to the constancy of the distant source, which will not dry up, unlike the one close by. Dip in the distance, seems to be the motto, but be warned that even that motherly undulatory nourishment is headed for the horizon of death.

The laying out of that landscape/seascape in its binary split between near and far occupies the first four stanzas of this eight-stanzaed text, playing hard, if quietly, on its oppositional strengths. As far as the mind can reach: the description ends with the horizon.

'Not far', begins the second round, as if in a middle distance between that too-bright too-near too-dry field and that too-far scene of plenty.

> Non loin, quelques bœufs blancs, couchés parmi les herbes,
> Bavent avec lenteur sur leurs fanons épais . . .

As if iconicized and emblematized, the oxen – white and sacred, in this neo-Indian philosophical setting – repose with all the marks of slowness (redundantly, they slowly dribble – what would a quick dribbling be? and their dewlaps are, just as redundantly, heavy), placed right in the centre of the poem. Chewing their cud, they never finish their interior dream – of course not, for the completion of a dream has no place in this static inscape of a meditative text, watched over and through by these languid eyes of the deified figures, non-recurring and no less obsessive.

That they should be the guardians of the nirvana scene, that they should be, in a sense, our guides to a solar dreaming, is what distinguishes, in my view, this languid and strangely profound poem from 'Le Cœur de Hialmar' quoted above. That warrior, eyes bleeding, sword broken, heart readied for ripping out by the summoned crow, sees himself as young and meriting the sun's glory by his past heroism; he needs no guide, for he has himself and a battle-glorious past. Nothing in that poem haunts me, or seems to remain unexplained. Here, on the contrary, the long and wide landscape lengthily precedes, in the waving of its distant wheat, this brief picture of slowness and interior, unfinished dream, which itself announces the final three-stanzaed sermon in praise of absorption and oblivion and alteration. It is a question not of the single heroic stance but of a general humanity needing, in a subtle sense, both supervision and sublime word, both exactly *impersonal*. The superbly impersonal, those splendid white oxen provide:

> Et suivent de leurs yeux languissants et superbes
> Le songe intérieur qu'ils n'achèvent jamais.

For their 'yeux languissants et superbes' set the model for the necessary slowness and unengagedness, for detachment, incompletion and interiority. Supremely other, they mark the transition from outer to inner, from nature to humanity – from the wheat to the passer-by – and from the real to the 'divin'.

The final address, taking up the three concluding stanzas, reads, in its exact binary and oppositional structuring, as an imperative invitation to decision:

> Homme, si ...
> Fuis!
> Mais si ...
> Viens!

It is really, as stated, a case of either/or, of 'fuir' or 'venir'. Those given over to living, those capable of feeling, must flee the emptiness at noontide. For here, two stanzas before the end, the only complete recall of the initial reigning 'Midi' makes itself heard and harkened to: such sunlight does not pour out nourishment, as from the preceding 'coupe', but rather consumes, cuts off, *coupe* in the other, inferred sense. The golden bowl here is self-consuming and other-destroying:

> Rien n'est vivant ici, rien n'est ...

The echoing being, that 'est' which dominated the first stanzas, is clearly marked here with the sign of nullity. Self-absorption, endless, like that non-completed interior dream, is the only possible result of this Nietzschean noontime in which no dwelling is allowed.

In *Thus Spake Zarathustra*, the noon passage strikes an unforgettable note:

Hush! Hush! Hath not the world now become perfect? What hath happened unto me?

As a delicate wind danceth invisibly upon parqueted seas, light, feather-light, so – danceth sleep upon me.

No eye doth it close to me, it leaveth my soul awake. Light is it, verily, feather-light.

It persuadeth me, I know not how, it toucheth me inwardly with a caressing hand, it constraineth me. Yea, it constraineth me, so that my soul stretcheth itself out: –

– How long and weary it becometh, my strange soul! Hath a seventh-day evening come to it precisely at noontide? Hath it already wandered too long, blissfully, among good and ripe things?

It stretcheth itself out long – longer! it lieth still, my strange soul. Too many good things hath it already tasted; this golden sadness oppresseth it, it distorteth its mouth.

... O happiness! O happiness! Wilt thou perhaps sing, O my soul? Thou liest in the grass. But this is the secret, solemn hour, when no shepherd playeth his pipe.

Take care! Hot noontide sleepeth on the fields. Do not sing! Hush! The world is perfect.[6]

The steps now taken are as slow as that oxen-dribble, as heavy as those jowls, upon the return from the divine sevenfold immersion in nothingness:

> Et retourne à pas lents vers les cités infimes,
> Le cœur trempé sept fois dans le néant divin.

And yet. And yet. This sunlit immersion tale – suffused as it is with the feeling of myth – concerns itself, evidently, with regeneration through fire ('dans sa flamme implacable'), as for a phoenix, and through a no less regenerative magical liquid ('le cœur trempé'), as for a heart. All along in the poem, the liquid images have been, however distanced, juxtaposed with the fiery ones, from the sea to the goblet dipped into (the 'puiser' suggested by its contrary, the 'épuisement'), from the undulation to the slow saliva, down to this final seven-time submersion in nothing, the latter however qualified in an ambiguous fashion at the poem's closure, remarkably returning to the opening set. For here in the concluding word 'divin' the beginning word 'midi' finds a half-recall in the initial syllable 'di', as if the text were to turn upon itself, spinning intoxicated with nirvana and the suggestion, in the last syllable, of an appropriate liquid: 'vin'. This is the sort of under-writing that can form a part of interpretation, enriching by present reading the writings of the past, providing the consequences are not overstated.

Now the continual absorption recommended ('absorbe-toi sans fin') promises to yield a voluptuousness as supreme as the sun vocabulary is sublime – the narration is self-intoxicated, high upon itself and the singular stress of its monosyllabic command system: 'fuis!'/'viens!'

What might have been seen as textual burn-out and dry-out is thus suffused with all the passionate possibilities of nothingness sensed as the regenerative point, as a renewing liquid sacralized, baptismal in force. So strong is the sense of regeneration that the sevenfold immersion ('trempé sept fois') can be re-read (under-read as I say here), as a definite deictic: 'cette fois', this time, and we know we will survive this time (im)personally, dipped in that sacred potion, even though we might have to return, textually, to those cities we left at the start.

But what of the position of the one speaking, summoning us to choose between a fullness of feeling and an emptiness of soul ('ne sachant plus pardonner ou maudire'), to flee the scene or absorb ourselves in it like those sacred cows? This voice was neutral at the outset, impersonalized throughout the scene until the concluding sermonizing: 'Man...' Lofty and moralizing, it talks on even after the return of the wanderer to the city, after the sublime speaking of the sun, endless in its self-absorption, as emblematic as those cows lying in the grass in the centre of the text.

This is a poem of return, marked by a motionless textuality, issuing a stoic summons, invoking the presence of a wanderer toward and through the flame, to be finally given his regenerative draught from the limitless, equally female source of nothing: but a nothing which would be divine. 'Cette fois...' moves, in this time of re-reading, re-generative as re-generating, far past the traditional infinity-longing of 'sept fois' to a space of presence as of presentation, right in front of us, here, now and always. We too can drink from that 'néant' in which birth ('né/nait') is so clearly included, in which it can be under-read, this time around.

Others[7] have drunk at that source, making something from nothingness. Rimbaud's resplendent prose poem 'Aube' seems to share the Nietzschean joy of Zarathustra, in the same pagan space, but more specifically it seems to write our 'Midi' of twenty years earlier backwards, from its initial dawn of summer,

J'ai embrassé l'aube d'été

to its final awakening at noontide after the fall:

<blockquote>
L'aube et l'enfant tombèrent au bas du bois.
Au réveil il était midi.
</blockquote>

Re-read in this later light, Leconte de Lisle's noon as king of summer gives way to dawn and his plural to Rimbaud's singular ('roi des étés'/'l'aube d'été') – the cosmic yields, now twenty years later, to the specific. Yet the double expression 'tombe' remains as a marker of the fall and the death included in his stoic text, moving as it does from 'midi' in the fields to a return to city life, regeneration equated with regression, whereas Rimbaud's pagan rewriting and unmoralizing reawakening moves from constructed richness to natural light.

Rimbaud's move restores, in a sense, exactly what the static iconicization of the white oxen ruminating heavily in the centre of Leconte de Lisle's poem might have been thought to diminish: life. That is something to chew the cud over, to dribble slowly down: the 'lenteur' of the latter act is matched, finally, by the slow steps taken back towards the city. 'Midi' moves towards a retrogressive closure, towards return. The poem 'Aube' starts earlier in the day, and moves forwards, towards a real sunlight, in a real, if past, summer time: 'il était midi'. Noon as Leconte de Lisle's initially negativizing, royally immobilizing king of summers and of silence has prepared the way for, has spread out the cloth for, has been, with its oddly superb animal guides towards the interior, the source for, that supreme sense of noon rendered positive, out in the open.

NOTES

1 See Naomi Schor, *Reading in Detail* (New York, 1987).

2 Roland Barthes, *La Chambre claire: Note sur la photographie* (Paris, 1980).

3 Roland Barthes, writing on the idea of criticism and of teaching itself as being in crisis at the time of the events of 1968, and just after, was critically persuasive. See, for example, his 'Writers, Intellectuals, Teachers', in Stephen Heath's translation, reprinted many times, and recently in *A Barthes Reader*, ed. Susan Sontag (New York, 1982), pp. 378–403. Here he worries about teaching and speaking as being on the side of the Law, and as practising such exercises as the 'reduction of the text', whereas, on the one hand, the writer's message cannot be summarized, and on the other, the look of the student spoken to punctures the discourse.

Barthes's emphasis in the text as independent of the biography of its author, as having its own life, in the much-noted theory of 'the death of the author', and his clearly-stated evocation of the evolution in criticism, 'From Work to Text' (reprinted in Josue Harari, ed., *Textual Strategies: Perspectives in Post-Structuralist Criticism* (Ithaca, NY,

1979), pp. 73–81) freed much contemporary criticism from the heavy weight of the kind of author-ity that would say: 'What is it that Hugo meant here?' and the like. The *body* of one author's writings is not any longer thought, in general, to be necessarily a determinant of the way we should see each piece of that writing. Nor is it thought that we all see alike: heaven be praised.

4 The narrow approach to intentionality – as distinct from the approach I recommend in my reading of this poem and others – is well summed up in E. D. Hirsch, *Validity in Interpretation* (New Haven, NJ, 1967). Against the arguments that would allege, for example, a changing meaning of the text, even for the author, Hirsch makes clear his point of view, based on a distinction between the terms of 'meaning' and 'significance':

Meaning is that which is represented by a text; it is what the author meant by his use of a particular sign sequence; it is what the signs represent. *Significance*, on the other hand, names a relationship: between the meaning and a person and a conception, with a situation, indeed anything imaginable. (p. 8)

Meaning, he continues, is not what changes, but the relationship – therefore, the significance. On this view, such attitudes as those expressed by W. K. Wimsatt and Monroe Beardsley, *The Verbal Icon: Studies in the Meaning of Poetry* (Lexington, 1954), are making a confusion between intention and effectiveness, with no real application to verbal meaning. Something which is to be differentiated from 'meaning' as Hirsch intends it is 'public meaning', that is, the conception arrived at from the outside of what was originally written. The aim would be, according to Hirsch, a *re-cognitive* interpretation, the term taken from Emilio Betti (*Teoria generale della interpretazione* (Milan, 1955), pp. 343–432), where the critic would re-cognize what the author had originally 'cognized'. For the intention of the poem itself, where the reader is enjoined to refrain from applying any standards or approaches 'external' to the poem, see such critics as I. A. Richards, in his *Practical Criticism: A Study in Literary Judgement* (New York, 1956; repr. from 1929), p. 195: 'The aim of the poem comes first, and is the sole justification of its means. We may quarrel, frequently we must, with the aim of the poem, but we have first to ascertain what it is. We cannot legitimately judge its means by external standards ... Which have no relevance to its success in doing what it set out to do, or, if we like, in becoming what in the end it has become.' Or, more succinctly still, 'the whole state of mind, the mental condition, which in another sense *is* the poem' (p. 195).

5 My under-readings of the 'sous-texte' of Antonin Artaud in several of his more obsessive works – 'L'Enclume des forces' perhaps more than any others – appeared in English as 'Antonin Artaud: Suppression and Sub-Text', in Mary Ann Caws, ed., *About French Poetry from Dada to Tel Quel* (Detroit, 1974), pp. 254–72, and, in a slightly different version, in French as 'Suppression et sous-texte: une re-lecture d'Antonin Artaud', in *Le Siècle éclaté: dada, surréalisme et avant-gardes*, 2 (*Théorie/Tableau/Texte*, 1978), pp. 175–98.

6 Friedrich Nietzsche, *Thus Spake Zarathustra*, in *The Philosophy of Nietzsche* (New York, 1954), pp. 308–9.

7 For starters, Paul Claudel's high-flown, lyric, and extraordinary play, in the eyes of most critics his masterpiece, *Partage de midi*, and Paul Valéry's 'Cimetière marin', with its central passage about high noon. There is, of course, a multitude of others.

7

INTERTEXTUALITY AND INTERPRETATION: BAUDELAIRE'S 'CORRESPONDANCES'

Jonathan Culler

La Nature est un temple où de vivants piliers
Laissent parfois sortir de confuses paroles;
L'homme y passe à travers des forêts de symboles
Qui l'observent avec des regards familiers.

5   Comme de longs échos qui de loin se confondent
Dans une ténébreuse et profonde unité
Vaste comme la nuit et comme la clarté,
Les parfums, les couleurs et les sons se répondent.

Il est des parfums frais comme des chairs d'enfants,
10 Doux comme les hautbois, verts comme les prairies,
– Et d'autres, corrompus, riches et triomphants,

Ayant l'expansion des choses infinies,
Comme l'ambre, le musc, le benjoin et l'encens,
Qui chantent les transports de l'esprit et des sens.

✳✳✳

'Correspondances' from *Les Fleurs du Mal* (1857) has long been a
central document for the study of Baudelaire's poetics. Jean
Pommier used it as the key to *La Mystique de Baudelaire*. Cherix's
Commentaire des Fleurs du Mal identifies it as 'la pièce maîtresse de
la doctrine esthétique de Baudelaire', and Lloyd Austin says of his
study of *L'Univers poétique de Baudelaire* that 'ce livre part de la
doctrine des correspondances. Les meilleures critiques Baudelairiens
n'ont pas manqué d'accorder une importance capitale à l'ensemble
des théories que Baudelaire a constitué autour de ce mot.'[1]

Briefly and schematically, 'Correspondances' has been an important poem for three reasons. First, because its definition of our
encounter with the world as a passage through 'des forêts de
symboles' has seemed aesthetically productive: the world as a forest
of signs accessible to poets and visionaries. 'Correspondances' seems
to be the economical enunciation of principles of aesthetic signification that are at work in Baudelaire's *œuvre*, as it explores
correspondences between *le mal* and *la beauté* or *la boue* et *l'or*, for
example.

Second, the poem is important because it echoes numerous
statements of Baudelaire's prose writings – about *correspondances*,
analogie universelle – and in so doing works to confirm the
possibility of a correspondence between poems and prose accounts
of aesthetic principles. If critics make much of 'Correspondances', it
is partly because criticism relies on the possibility of a correspondence between poems and poetics. As a poem based on what Lloyd
Austin calls 'la doctrine des correspondances', 'Correspondances'
confirms the vital possibility of a close, signifying relation between
poems and critical statements.

Third, but most important for our purposes, 'Correspondances' is
essential to any attempt to situate Baudelaire because of its echoes of
a range of romantic sources, not to speak of the echoes of it in the
later poetic tradition. This theme of correspondences, writes
Antoine Adam, 'formait depuis le début du siècle le support prin-
cipale du romantisme'.[2] Treating Baudelaire as the founder of
modern poetry, Marcel Raymond makes this poem the point of
departure for the trajectory summed up by his title, *De Baudelaire
au surréalisme*. More recently, Paul de Man writes of 'Correspondances' that 'it, and it alone, contains, implies, produces, generates,
permits (or whatever aberrant verbal metaphor one wishes to
choose) the entire possibility of the lyric'.[3]

'Correspondances' is thus an exemplary case of intertextuality
and a fine instrument for considering the claim that a text is an
assimilation and transformation of other texts and its meaning a
function of its relation to other texts. In undertaking a reading of
this poem, I am interested in elucidating the stakes of intertextual
readings, the investments in the multifarious discussions of this
poem and the methodological issues they raise.[4] A good deal of the

scholarly energy devoted to this poem has worked to constitute an intextual space for it that includes passages from Swedenborg, Schelling, Mme de Stael, Hoffmann, Balzac, Esquiros, Sainte-Beuve, l'Abbé Constant and Gautier, not to mention Hugo and Lamartine.[5] The first quatrain, in particular, is seen as echoing a romantic topos: the visible forms of the universe are signs of an invisible spiritual reality. This is the idea of vertical correspondence: relations between material signifiers and spiritual signifieds or what Baudelaire calls 'cet admirable, cet immortel instinct du beau qui nous fait considérer la terre et ses spectacles comme un aperçu, comme une correspondance du ciel'.[6] Baudelaire's contemporary and acquaintance Alphonse-Louis Constant had in 1845 published a poem entitled 'Les Correspondances':

> Formé de visibles paroles,
> Ce monde est le songe de Dieu;
> Son verbe en choisit les symboles,
> L'esprit les remplit de son feu ...[7]

But more pertinent sources are to be found in better poets. The opening verse of 'Correspondances', 'La Nature est un temple', echoes such formulations in the poetry of Hugo and Lamartine. Here is Hugo:

> C'est Dieu qui remplit tout. Le monde, c'est son temple.
> Œuvre vivante, où tout l'écoute et le contemple!
> Tout lui parle et le chante.[8]

Here is Lamartine:

> Dieu caché, disais tu, la nature est ton temple!
> L'esprit te voit partout quand notre œil la contemple.[9]

The spirit is necessary here, for the eye does not suffice:

> Nature! firmament! l'œil en vain vous contemple;
> Hélas! sans voir le dieu, l'homme admire le temple.[10]

And again:

> L'univers est le temple, et la terre est l'autel.
> ... Mais ce temple est sans voix. Où sont les saints concerts?
> ... Tout se tait: mon cœur seul parle dans ce silence.
> La voix de l'univers, c'est mon intelligence.[11]

These sources sketch two possibilities, each of which involves an authoritative, established relation of signification: in the first case, everything actively signifies God – singing him aloud. In the second case, the signs are there but silent; their meaning must be grasped by the spirit or enunciated by the poetic intelligence. Now 'Correspondances' echoes these passages, but there is a question about the meaning of such echoes or correspondences. It is not clear that Baudelaire's signs are similar to Lamartine's and Hugo's. The absence of God is not the issue, though this is a striking difference from the romantic sources, so much as the way Baudelaire's signs function intermittently. In his temple living pillars 'laissent *parfois* sortir de confuses paroles'. It is as though in compromising between Hugo's version, in which everything speaks and sings, and Lamartine's version, where 'Tout se tait', Baudelaire had let things speak *sometimes*, giving us, if not a compromise that parodies the alternatives, at least an undermining of the continuous, authoritative signifying relation that seemed the basis of any 'doctrine' of correspondences.

There is clearly a correspondence between Baudelaire's poem and others which articulate the figure of nature as temple, but in that very relation Baudelaire's echo seems to disrupt the one-to-one correspondence between natural sign and spiritual meaning that the others promote. While commentators often identify as the underlying image Chateaubriand's comparison of the forest to a cathedral ('nous allons chercher ces forêts, berceau de la religion, ces forêts dont l'ombre, les bruits et le silence sont remplis de prodiges'[12]), if there is a forest here its prototype might rather be Hugo's in 'A Albert Dürer': 'Une forêt pour toi, c'est un monde hideux', where one can find 'Pendre à tous les rameaux de confuses pensées'. The relation between 'confuses pensées' and Baudelaire's 'confuses paroles' suggests a connection between the two passages. Hugo's dramatizes the exotic eeriness of a forest world in which 'Rien n'est tout à fait mort ni tout à fait vivant', and where

> ... sur vous qui passez et l'avez réveillée,
> Mainte chimère étrange à la gorge écaillée,
> D'un arbre entre ses doigts serrant les larges nœuds,
> Du fond d'un antre obscur fixe un œil lumineux.[13]

He concludes with a literalized image of confused speech: like you, Dürer, I have never wandered in the woods without hearing

> Et rire, et se parler dans l'ombre à demi-voix,
> Les chênes monstrueux qui remplissent les bois.

But this Hugolian intertext, by its very similarities, makes clear how comparatively uninterested Baudelaire is in exploiting the grotesque picturesqueness of a world of spirits imprisoned in matter. Though the living pillars in Baudelaire's forests of symbols do, like Hugo's, look at the passer-by ('l'observent avec des regards familiers'), stress falls not on the piercing eye, as in Hugo or in Nerval's 'Vers dorés' – 'Crains, dans le mur aveugle, un regard qui t'épie' – but on the familiarity of the look. Paul de Man even suggests that *Nature* here means 'the world' and, for Baudelaire, the crowd, whose members are the living pillars emitting confused speech and observing one with familiar looks; 'forêts de symboles', de Man writes, describes 'the rhetorical dimension in which we constantly dwell'.[14]

Baudelaire's inflection of the traditional scene towards words, symbols and familiarity recalls a poetic forest from the fourth canto of Dante's *Inferno*, which Baudelaire quotes in the *Salon de 1846*: 'nous traversions la forêt, l'épaisse forêt d'esprits, veux-je dire' (II, 437). Discussing Delacroix, Baudelaire cites this passage at surprising length, no doubt because it tells of the young poet being received as an equal by the company of great poets. 'Forêts d'esprits' reminds us that 'Correspondances' does not necessarily place us in a forest at all: we are told that man passes not through forests that are symbolic but through forests of symbols. *Forest* may be a figure not of nature but of enumeration and confusion. In the *Salon de 1859* Baudelaire evokes the possibility of being 'perdu dans une forêt d'originalités' (II, 608), and forests of symbols may well evoke, above all, the eerie condition of the poet who, arriving on the scene after romanticism, finds that the world is indeed a forest of symbols, marked by prior poetic discourse. The wind in the trees is already a symbol but a confused one, since it has borne different meanings. As Sainte-Beuve put it, 'Lamartine avait pris les *cieux*, Victor Hugo avait pris la *terre* et plus que la terre. Laprade avait pris les *forêts* ... Que restait-il?'[15] Baudelaire finds himself passing through 'des forêts de symboles', which, as though brought to life by the apostrophes and personifications of prior poetry, 'l'observent avec des regards familiers'.

Baudelaire's scenario in this quatrain presents two activities: living pillars 'laissent parfois sortir de confuses paroles' and forests of symbols observe man with 'des regards familiers'. What is striking, in the intertextual context, is how each of these two formulations and the combination of the two transform the clarity of individual sources into an indeterminate rhetoricity. Some precursors declare that all nature speaks; others have it silently signify; but Baudelaire first raises doubts about whether nature engages in wilful speech or whether something like confused words simply emerge, as pillars *'laissent* parfois *sortir'*; Baudelaire then presents symbols that instead of signifying, being read, or bearing meaning, as the sources would lead one to expect, *observe* the passer-by. They do not even fix one with an 'œil lumineux' as in Hugo, so as to make it clear that one should attend to them. Rather they install the passer-by in that familiar modern condition of seeing people in crowds whom one does not exactly recognize but who look at one in a way that seems to betoken familiarity, leading one to wonder: Do I know them? Do they know me? Does that look mean something? The question of whether a *regard familier* bespeaks a relation or not is a problem about whether particular forms or appearances are signifying elements, whether they do bear meaning. It is the problem of signification par excellence. It is also the problem of intertextuality: the difficulty of deciding whether a proposed source which has a familiar look is indeed relevant, significant, connected. An intertextually attentive criticism can scarcely, then, simply maintain, as Baudelairian criticism has often sought to, that this poem affirms the so-called doctrine of vertical correspondences. Echoes scarcely amount to affirmation, especially 'de longs echos qui de loin se confondent' and which thus pose the problem of signification.

In recent years, readings of the sonnet have shifted attention from the vertical correspondences to the so-called horizontal correspondences of the remaining quatrain and tercets. Leo Bersani writes,

In fact, the metaphysical suggestiveness of the first four verses is *simply dropped* in the second and third stanzas. We move from vertical transcendence to horizontal 'unity'. 'Les parfums, les couleurs et les sons se répondent': that is, stimuli ordinarily associated with one of our senses can produce sensations 'belonging' to another sense. Baudelaire asserts, and in the third stanza illustrates, the reality of these analogies (certain perfumes, for example, are 'green as fields'). 'Correspondances' does present itself as a doctrinaire poem and the doctrine which the poem espouses and vaguely outlines has much less to do with symbolism in Nature than with a metaphorical unity within Nature. Comparisons using the word *comme* occur six times in the two middle stanzas, and we might think of this as a stylistic demonstration of those 'echoes' of a distant likeness which the poet asks us to hear in each of our experiences.[16]

Baudelaire's assertion in an essay on Eugène Delacroix that 'tout l'univers visible n'est qu'un magasin d'images et de signes' (II, 627 and 750) and his notion of a 'clavier de correspondances' on which the artist plays (II, 577) suggest that the poet's task might be to construct melodies out of the metaphorical equivalences between sensations belonging to the different senses, of the sort listed in the first tercet. 'Chez les excellents poètes', he writes in an essay on Hugo, 'il n'y a pas de métaphore, de comparaison ou d'épithète qui ne soit d'une adaptation mathématiquement exacte dans la circonstance actuelle, parce que ces comparaisons, ces métaphores et ces épithètes sont puisées dans l'inépuisable fonds de l'*universelle analogie*, et qu'elles ne peuvent être puisées ailleurs' (II, 133). The last four lines of the sonnet then move from tropes that relate one sensory experience to another to the more general claim that certain sensations effect a spiritualization – explicitly thematize the movement beyond sense suggested by synaesthesias: they 'chantent les transports de l'esprit et des sens'.

We have here, it seems, a notable poetic adumbration of a symbolist aesthetics, but such a reading of this 'doctrinaire poem' depends on an understanding of another set of intertextual relations, correspondences between the verse text and various prose texts which it echoes: the theoretical statements about analogies, correspondences, colours, smells and sounds. Here a problem arises. Antoine Adam writes,

Il est notable, pourtant, que s'il existe un texte de Baudelaire qui offre des analogies de pensée et d'expression avec le sonnet, c'est bien moins le *Salon de 1846* que l'article sur *L'Exposition Universelle de 1855*. Le mot de *correspondance* s'y trouve, et dans une phrase qui est comme le commentaire du sonnet; le professeur d'esthétique est un barbare 'qui a oublié la couleur du ciel, la forme du végétal, le mouvement et l'odeur de l'animalité, et dont les doigts crispés, paralysés par la plume, ne peuvent plus courir avec agilité sur l'immense clavier des correspondances'.

One might note the initial complication that the passage of aesthetic writing which Adam calls *'comme* un *comme*ntaire du sonnet'* is about the inability of a professor of aesthetics to play with and appreciate correspondences. When the piece of aesthetic writing that offers the best 'analogie de pensée et d'expression avec le sonnet' concerns the incompatibility of works of art and aesthetic doctrine, this at least raises a question about the relation of correspondence critics must take for granted in discussing a *doctrine* of correspondences.

The prose text continues more explicitly to address this question. 'Tout le monde conçoit sans peine que si les hommes chargés d'exprimer le beau se conformaient aux règles des professeurs-jurés, le beau lui-même disparaîtrait de la terre, puisque tous les types, toutes les idées, toutes les sensations se confondraient dans une vaste unité, monotone et impersonnelle, immense comme l'ennui et le néant' (II, 578). There are striking echoes here.

Prose	Poem
Se confondrait	se confondent
dans une vaste unité	dans une ténébreuse et profonde unité
vaste unité, immense	unité vaste comme la nuit
comme l'ennui	

There is an exchange of letters involved ('l'ennui', 'la nuit'), if not a correspondence. Antoine Adam, however, declares categorically that 'la ténébreuse et profonde unité dont parle le sonnet est *sans rapport* avec l'unité monotone et impersonnelle dont parle l'article sur l'Exposition universelle'.

The critic's position here is not an altogether comfortable one. To claim that these two sorts of unity are unrelated is to reject as irrelevant what Adam admits are among the strongest echoes in the Baudelairian corpus and thus to put in question the critical project of developing interpretations of the poems by finding prose passages that echo them. Adam denies the correspondence between these passages in order to maintain the doctrine of correspondences: 'A cette réalité métaphysique des "correspondances", il croit de la façon la plus ferme, et il est inconcevable qu'on ait pu soutenir le contraire.' In order to maintain the inconceivable position – to contest the absolute firmness of Baudelaire's commitment to the metaphysical doctrine – one must insist on the correspondence between these texts, the relevance to one another of the echoing descriptions of unity.

The problem both in the poem and in the critical reading of its relation to prose texts is that of 'échos qui de loin se confondent', a problem about the signifying status of resemblances, about whether patterns we detect are meaningful or not. Sometimes we treat such questions as a matter of inferring the intention of a speaker or an author, but in many cases the signification we are interested in is precisely one that an author may not control. It is unlikely that Baudelaire meant one formulation to echo the other, but the fact that he uses very similar words echoing in his memory may be significant; the prose passage seems to observe us with a *regard familier*. The term *echo* plays an important role in literary studies; we speak of an author or a work echoing others or of one part of a work echoing another doubtless because it evokes a range of phenomena: an impersonal mechanical process which may not involve considerations of meaning at all, an intentional act of meaningful repetition, and an unintentional event (an 'unconscious echo') which may nevertheless be meaningful. The term thus poses and leaves open the issue of signification. Baudelaire's poem strikingly proposes the echo as the model for signifying correspondences, suggesting that smells, sounds and colours echo or answer one another in much the same way as these two passages do.

Adam maintains that 'Aux yeux de l'écrivain, la ténébreuse et vaste unité entrevue par les poètes est la source de toute vérité, mais la vaste unité des esprits systématiques n'est qu'ennui et néant.' Can we distinguish the good unity of poets from the bad unity of systematizers? In some of Baudelaire's prose texts, as in the prior texts of the tradition, the unity of the world and thus the echoing of its elements comes from its divine origin, from its creator. E. T. A. Hoffmann, whom Baudelaire cites in the *Salon de 1846*, writes, 'je trouve une analogie et une réunion intime entre les couleurs, les sons et les parfums. Il me semble que toutes ces choses ont été engendrées par un même rayon de lumière' (II, 425). In a critical article, 'Richard Wagner et *Tannhäuser* à Paris', Baudelaire himself writes in the manner of a systematizer:

Le lecteur sait quel but nous poursuivons: démontrer que la véritable musique suggère des idées analogues dans des cerveaux différents ... ce qui serait vraiment surprenant, c'est que le son ne put pas suggérer la couleur, que les couleurs ne pussent pas donner l'idée d'une mélodie, et que le son et la couleur fussent impropres à traduire des idées, les choses s'étant toujours exprimées par une analogie réciproque, depuis le jour où Dieu a proféré le monde comme une complexe et indivisible totalité.

He then cites the two quatrains of 'Correspondances' as illustration and without further comment, although they do not derive analogies of sensation from a divine act of creation. In fact, the poem here is more cagey than the prose systematizations, linking unity not to an origin or creator but to the position of a perceiver: echoes blend into a unity when they are heard from far away, the perceptual distance making it difficult to distinguish, and the verb used to describe this blending, 'se confondent', suggests also that they are confused with each other. The unity itself is described as 'vaste comme la nuit et comme la clarté' – perhaps the proverbial *nuit où tous les chats sont noirs* (night and luminosity share the property of making it difficult to distinguish).

In the contrast between the unity of poets and the unity of systematizers, the sonnet, in its linking of unity to an effacement of differences, articulates the more sceptical truth. But in fact, the distinction between a poetic and systematizing unity cannot be correlated with a distinction between poetry and prose, for there are two prose texts whose descriptions echo that of the sonnet: *L'Exposition universelle*, where unity results when professors forget the distinctiveness of each idea, type and sensation and these 'se confondent', and the *Salon de 1846*, which, citing Hoffmann on correspondences, describes the unity of nature as follows: 'et comme la vapeur de la saison, hiver ou été, baigne, adoucit, ou engloutit les contours, la nature ressemble à un tonton qui, mû par une vitesse accélérée, nous apparaît gris, bien qu'il résume en lui toutes les couleurs' (II, 423). Here the unity of nature is produced by a specific mechanism for effacing difference: the top whose colours blur as it spins is comparable to echoes that blend sounds when heard from afar. The distinction we discover, then, separates accounts of unity that reveal a tropological mechanism from those that do not, and here Baudelaire's sonnet can be set against the systematizing assertions of an originary unity, raising a question about the status of echoes, which is also a question about poetic representation and intertextual relations.

The second quatrain introduces the tercets by announcing that smells, colours and sounds 'se répondent', answer each other. Given that the sonnet treats the 'ténébreuse et profonde unité' not as an origin but a result of the effacement of differences, what does it tell us about these synaesthesias? Curiously, when we ask about the basis of the echoing relation between smells, colours and sounds, we find that the relevant lines are made convincing by verbal echoes or relays, whether semantic or phonological:

> Il est des parfums frais comme des chairs d'enfants,
> Doux comme les hautbois, verts commes les prairies ...

The idea of a 'parfum frais' is made more plausible by the repetition of 'r' and 'f', which link the two words and then reappear in 'chairs d'enfants'. 'Chairs' connects with 'doux' by a pun ('chère') that is close to the surface in 'chairs d'enfants' ('chères enfants'); 'doux' in the sense of 'sweet' is certainly a possible property of 'ce qu'on boit', which lies concealed in the 'hautbois' said to be soft and sweet, and the 'bois' of 'hautbois', this time in its meaning of 'wood', further helps to justify 'verts', in 'verts comme des prairies', where 'verts' itself is echoed in the first syllable of 'prairies'. Rather than focus on associations between sensations themselves, as in sources such as Hoffmann, for whom 'l'odeur des soucis [marigolds] bruns et rouges' makes him hear 'les sons graves et profonds du hautbois' (II, 425), the poem links synaesthesia with verbal art by asserting links between sensations that seem to rely on verbal echoes.[17] But the tercets also distinguish the regular, specifiable relations between sweet or innocent smells and the corresponding sounds and colours from the indeterminate signifying possibilities of corrupt, rich and triumphant smells.

Why smells, one wants to know? If the point is, as Bersani claims, to assert the metaphorical unity of the universe, to present a stylistic demonstration of 'the echoes of a distant likeness which the poet asks us to hear in each of our experiences', why should smells have been selected as the case in point? Poe writes in his *Marginalia*, 'I believe that odors have an altogether idiosyncratic force, in affecting us through association, a force differing essentially from that of objects addressing the touch, the taste, the sight, or the hearing'.[18] Of all sensations, smells are the most inextricably linked with tropological, specifically metonymical operations (the substitution of cause for effect or the naming of something by what is contiguous to it). Other sensations may have literal names. Smells mnemonically generate chains of metonymical associations: to name a smell is metonymically to describe its cause or the circumstances in which one first smelled it (unlike colours, which have names of their own), so that smells hold the attention to reorient it towards what surrounds them – for example, in the poetic (discursive and descriptive) movement evoked in Baudelaire's 'La Chevelure', in the prose poem 'Une hémisphère dans une chevelure', or in 'Parfum exotique':

> Quand les deux yeux fermés, en un soir chaud d'automne,
> Je respire l'odeur de ton sein chaleureux,
> Je vois se dérouler des rivages heureux
> Qu'éblouissent les feux d'un soleil monotone.   (I, 25)

Smell, poor in literal names for sensations, joins the mnemonic power of recognition to the discursive exfoliation of a metonymical imagination.

I have outlined two kinds of intertextual explorations whose methodological compatibility should not be taken for granted but which do, taken together, generate a plausible reading of the poem. The first places the sonnet in the intertextual space of possible sources, a persistent prior discourse about nature and temples, and treats the poem as an ironic repetition or transformation of this language – accentuating its difference from what it echoes. The poem undermines the transcendental claims it cites and modifies. The second approach (for the second quatrain), emphasizing verbal echoes or repetitions within the Baudelairian corpus, makes the so-called doctrine of horizontal correspondences more textual and tropological. Bringing thematically distinct texts closer to each other, suggesting that in their repetition they infect one another, showing that unity might be viewed as a tropological effect, foregrounding the ambiguity of 'se confondent', one reinstates 'Correspondances' as an *art poétique*.

Combining these procedures, which seem to work in different directions and on different principles, nevertheless generates a reading of the poem according to which the ironic treatment of doctrines in the first two quatrains sets the stage for the assertion in the tercets of tropological relations which, as I have claimed, are cast in terms that suggest, on the one hand, that supposedly natural or inherent equivalences of sensory qualities may depend on verbal links, and, on the other, that what is most valued is the process (epitomized by smell) of expansion and metonymical extrapolation from sensation – 'transports de l'esprit et des sens'. 'Correspondances', often thought to declare that the natural is a sign of the divine, in fact celebrates the poetic process whereby, for example, the smell of hair evokes or generates a hemisphere.

Such a reading, exploiting intertextual relations, preserves the status of *Correspondances* as a key, doctrinal poem and makes it a crucial poem for any literary history seeking to integrate Baudelaire in a story of post-Enlightenment poetry. In fact, this reading makes sense of the odd status the poem has had, as at once the culmination of the romantic doctrine of vertical correspondences and the adumbration of a symbolist aesthetic and point of departure for surrealism. It treats the poem as bringing echoing romantic doctrine but, with an ironic twist, sending it off in a new direction: through its ironic repetition, it makes correspondence no longer a one-to-one divinely sanctioned relation but rather a metonymical exfoliation such as is set off by the recognition of a smell. The romantic line runs into this poem; the modernist line runs out of it. The change from one line to another takes place at the Baudelaire correspondence.

Now this is a plausible and in many ways satisfying reading, but there are objections that could be raised to it. The first bears on the notion that this poem is a Baudelairian *art poétique*. As Sandro Genovali notes, there are surprisingly few synaesthesias in Baudelaire – 'des parfums verts' is not a common sort of image but actually very rare.[19] Quite a few poems, such as 'Les Bijoux', talk

about synaesthesia – 'j'aime à la fureur / Les choses où le son se mêle
à la lumière' – but it is not a major poetic technique. If 'Correspondances' is about poetry, it is not describing Baudelaire's poetic
technique. Indeed, one might well ask, if, as 'Correspondances'
asserts, smells are fresh, soft, green, rich, corrupt or triumphant,
what follows? The poem offers encouragement to the producers of
'scratch and sniff' books but no explicit pointers for poets.

The answer to this valid objection might be that Baudelaire is not
interested in synaesthesia, as the first tercet suggests, so much as in
sensations as stimuli to reverie, memory, imagination: smells 'Ayant
l'expansion des choses infinies'. This exfoliation is both a subject of
poetry and the process of poetic production, and in taking 'Correspondances' as an *art poétique* for *Les Fleurs du Mal*, one can
bracket the first two lines of the tercets while concentrating on the
last four. But there is an odd problem here: in a curious change of
register, the second tercet tells us that these other smells do not
simply evoke luxury and corruption with a power of infinite expansion; they sing the 'transports', the ecstasy and displacement, of the
mind and the senses. The poem leaves us, finally, not in a universe of
interconnected properties and sensations, 'l'inépuisable fonds de
l'*universelle analogie*', but with smells singing. What are we to
make of these singing smells, especially smells which sing about the
ecstasies and displacements of human minds and senses? This is an
eerie universe indeed, when smells do not even address human
beings but sing *about* them. Although the verb 'chantent' inclines
critics to take 'Correspondances' as a poem about poetry, the little
allegory in which it figures resists easy translation into an *art
poétique*.

The third objection bears on the interpretation of the tercets as
glorifying tropological relations – specifically on such claims as Leo
Bersani's that comparisons using the word *comme* demonstrate the
relations we are invited to perceive in nature. Paul de Man notes of
the final *comme* in the poem – 'Et d'autres, comme l'ambre, le musc,
le benjoin et l'encens' – 'Ce comme n'est pas un comme comme les
autres.' It is not comparative, bringing together different sorts of
sensations, bridging gaps in a metaphorical transfer of properties or
fusion involving analogy (as in 'des parfums frais comme des chairs
d'enfants'). It is a *comme* of enumeration – smells *such as* a, b, c –

opening a list which can continue without getting us anywhere else.[20]

Considered from the perspective of the thesis or of the symbolist ideology of the text, such a use of 'comme' is aberrant ... Instead of analogy, we have enumeration, and an enumeration which never moves beyond the confines of a set of particulars ... the enumeration could be continued at will without ceasing to be a repetition, without ceasing to be an obsession rather than a metamorphosis, let alone a rebirth ... what could be more perverse or corruptive for a metaphor aspiring to transcendental totality than remaining stuck in an enumeration that never goes anywhere? ... Enumerative repetition disrupts the chain of tropological substitution at the crucial moment when the poem promises, by way of these very substitutions, to reconcile the pleasures of the mind with those of the senses and to unite aesthetics with epistemology. That the very word on which these substitutions depend would just then lose its syntactical and semantic univocity is too striking a coincidence not to be, like pure chance, beyond the control of author and reader.

This shift to a *comme* of enumeration does disrupt the synthesis that takes the tercets as a celebration of the tropological productivity of poetic imagination and memory (poetry as the exploitation of a 'clavier de correspondances'). And for de Man it gives rise to no new synthesis – no integrative reading. 'Correspondances' is for him a poem of radical unintelligibility, which is translated into intelligibility by another poem of Baudelaire's, 'Obsession':

> Grands bois, vous m'effrayez comme des cathédrales;
> Vous hurlez comme l'orgue; et dans nos cœurs maudits,
> Chambres d'éternel deuil où vibrent de vieux râles,
> Répondent les échos de vos *De profondis*.
>
> Je te hais, Océan! tes bonds et tes tumultes,
> Mon esprit les retrouve en lui; ce rire amer
> De l'homme vaincu, plein de sanglots et d'insultes,
> Je l'entends dans le rire énorme de la mer.
>
> Comme tu me plairais, ô nuit! sans ces étoiles,
> Dont la lumière parle un langage connu!
> Car je cherche le vide, le noir, et le nu!
>
> Mais les ténèbres sont elles-mêmes des toiles
> Où vivent, jaillissant de mon œil par milliers,
> Des êtres disparus aux regards familiers.   (I, 75)

'Obsession' is linked with 'Correspondances' by the opening image which makes nature a temple, by the echoes which answer in line 4, and by the 'regards familiers' of the final line. It is about correspondences, but correspondences between man and nature. While 'Correspondances' consists of a series of mysterious declarative sentences in the third person about nature, man, and smells, 'Obsession', full of exclamations and apostrophes[21] to elements of nature, brings about two changes. First, as the title indicates, it translates the concerns of 'Correspondances' into a psychological register. Second, its anthropomorphisms and figures of address establish a specular relationship between man and nature, assuring the intelligibility of the universe and man's relation to it, whether this relation be a happy or unhappy one. The surrealistic speech of live columns in 'Correspondances' is naturalized in 'Obsession' into the frightening but natural roar of the wind among the trees ('Vous hurlez comme l'orgue'), which resounds in the echo chambers of our hearts as groans that answer, echoing what becomes in the process of circulation an all too human '*De profondis*'. And in place of the bizarre singing smells with which 'Correspondances' concludes – smells singing *about* minds and senses rather than to them – 'Obsession' makes nature speak *to* human subjects.

'Obsession' transforms the question of the signifying status of elements of the world into the problem of the relation between inside and outside. Thus, while 'Correspondances' asserts that there are equivalences between smells, colours and sounds, without situating them in relation to a human subject, 'Obsession' sets up a relation between inside and outside which is such that qualities, like echoes, can be passed back and forth and poses the question of whether patterns are projected from outside to inside ('tes bonds et tes tumultes, / Mon esprit les retrouve en lui') or from inside to outside ('Mais les ténèbres sont elles-mêmes des toiles / Où vivent, jaillissant de mon œil par milliers, / Des êtres disparus aux regards familiers'). Either way, there is correspondence. Whereas 'Correspondances', describing a world in which living pillars sometimes give off confused speech and forests of symbols observe man with a familiar look, raises a question about the signification of appearances and their relation to man, 'Obsession' resolves that question, presenting all too cosy a world, in which 'la lumière parle un langage connu', and even darkness is but a screen on which the dead are projected. In place of the 'regards familiers' of 'Correspondances', whose significative status is uncertain, the 'regards familiers' of 'Obsession' are clearly identified as a psychological projection of the subject, the product of an obsession.

'Obsession' translates 'Correspondances' into lyric intelligibility through figures of apostrophe (address) and prosopopoeia (the endowing of the inanimate with speech), which establish an I–you relation with the woods, ocean and night. The ambiguousness of living pillars and familiar looks in 'Correspondances' is transformed here into a clear anthropomorphism, 'a conceit by which human consciousness is projected or transferred into the natural world'.[22] Here, the anthropomorphized nature asserts the reciprocal relation between man and nature, which may be the source of anguish, even torture, but at least assures one's vital place in the universe.

'Obsession' is a lyrical reading or translation into lyric intelligibility of 'Correspondances'. 'Correspondances' itself, with its stutter of enumeration and puzzling figures, takes on significance through its intertextual relation, as that which gets translated into lyrical intelligibility. Intertextual study helps one perceive in relationships a circulation of meaning and identify the distinctiveness of 'Correspondances': a certain unintelligibility which poems and critics work to make intelligible.[23] Meaning, we can see, is not a property of an individual text but exists in the relation between texts, depending on contrasts and on echoes whose displaced repetitions offer material for interpretation. De Man describes reading as

a process of translation or 'transport' that incessantly circulates between the two texts. There are always at least two texts, regardless of whether they are actually written out or not; the relationship between the two sonnets, obligingly provided by Baudelaire for the benefit, no doubt, of future teachers invited to speak on the nature of the lyric, is an inherent characteristic of any text.[24]

'There are always two texts' means that no text is unequivocally what we take it to be; rather, it is divided, caught up in a repetition that presents its 'doctrine', shall we say, as an echo of other formulations, affected by that echoing. But since the signifying status of echoes or repetitions is problematical, this intertextual perspective is not a method for finding correct interpretations so much as a recognition that to interpret is to translate echoes or patterns into meaning.

A criticism focussed on intertextual relations discovers echoes whose significative status is uncertain, but finds that a way of discussing such echoes is to claim for them a critical, ironic force which can work in both directions, infecting what is repeated, as when the 'doctrine' of horizontal correspondences is questioned by repetition in the essay on the *Exposition universelle*. To associate the force of echo and repetition with irony is entirely plausible, for irony is above all a figure of repetition that puts in question the precise force and status of what is repeated. Irony is a capacious concept used in literary studies for designating problematical relationships. So one might be tempted to take 'Correspondances' as an ironic demystification of 'Obsession' that exposes its way of producing a cosy, intelligible universe. But to call something ironic is also a recuperative strategy, a way precisely of making intelligible what intertextual relations have enabled one to identify as resistance, repetition, unintelligibility. Since criticism works for intelligibility, it cannot altogether avoid this recuperative imposition, but the critical, intertextual reader should be alert to the recuperative process, aware that the solution of irony may dissolve the resistance that drives a poem. 'Correspondances', with its exploration of the problem of echoes and their signifying status, can encourage vigilance and embody resistance for the intertextual reader.

NOTES

1 Lloyd Austin, *L'Univers poétique de Baudelaire* (Paris, 1956), p. 51.
2 Antoine Adam, ed., *Les Fleurs du Mal* (Paris, 1961), p. 271. All further references to Adam are to his notes to this poem, pp. 270–7.
3 Paul de Man, *The Rhetoric of Romanticism* (New York, 1984), pp. 261–2. For a resourceful discussion which seeks to explain and justify the stranger claims of this essay, see Kevin Newmark, 'Paul de Man's History,' in *Reading de Man Reading*, ed. W. Godzich and L. Waters (Minneapolis, 1988).
4 For discussion of intertextuality, see Julia Kristeva, *Semiotiké* (Paris, 1969), p. 146 and *passim*; *La Révolution du langage poétique* (Paris, 1974), pp. 337–58 and 385–90; and Michael Riffaterre, *The Semiotics*

of Poetry (Bloomington, Indiana, 1978). I use 'Correspondances' to discuss a different question – whether criticism should think of interpretations as data to be explained or as the goal of literary study – in 'Interpretations as Data or Goals', in a special issue of *Poetics Today*, ed. Paul Hernadi, 9, 2 (1988).

5 For parallels other than those I cite, see the notes to *Les Fleurs du Mal*, ed. Jacques Crépet et Georges Blin (Paris, 1942) as well as those to the Garnier edition by Antoine Adam and the Pléiade edition by Claude Pichois cited below. Other valuable discussions are to be found in Austin, *L'Univers poétique de Baudelaire*; Jean Pommier, *La Mystique de Baudelaire* (Geneva, 1967) and F. W. Leakey, *Baudelaire and Nature* (Manchester, 1969).

6 Charles Baudelaire, 'Notes nouvelles sur Edgar Poe', in *Œuvres complètes*, ed. Claude Pichois (Paris, 1975), Vol. iI, p. 334. References to this edition will henceforth be placed in the text.

7 Cited in Baudelaire, *Œuvres complètes*, ed. Pichois, Vol. I, p. 840.

8 Victor Hugo, 'Pan', *Les Feuilles d'automne* xxxviii, in *Poésies* (Paris, 1972), Vol. I, p. 345.

9 Alphonse de Lamartine, 'L'Immortalité', *Méditations*, ed. F. Letessier (Paris, 1968), Vol. I. v, p. 20.

10 Lamartine, 'Dieu', *Méditations*, Vol. I. xxxiv, p. 111, ll. 133–4.

11 Lamartine, 'La Prière', *Méditations*, Vol. I, xix, pp. 68–9. As F. W. Leakey points out (*Baudelaire and Nature*, p. 199), the metrical structure of Baudelaire's opening line forbids the reader to pause after 'temple' and moves onward to 'piliers' and 'Laissent': 'La Nature est un tem/ple où de vivants piliers'. The sources, by contrast, isolate as doctrinal assertions the phrases involving temples.

12 Chateaubriand, *Le Génie du Christianisme*, *Œuvres complètes* (Paris, 1861), Vol. II, p. 12. Another passage (III, 8) compares the architecture of cathedrals to forests.

13 Hugo, 'A Albert Dürer', *Les Voix intérieures* (1837), Vol. X, p. 390.

14 De Man, *Rhetoric of Romanticism*, p. 246.

15 Quoted in Baudelaire, *Œuvres complètes*, Vol. I, p. 790.

16 Leo Bersani, *Baudelaire and Freud* (Berkeley, CA, 1979), p. 32.

17 Baudelaire is quoting a French translation. The German original concerns a dark red carnation which evokes the sound of a basset horn! See Leakey, *Baudelaire and Nature*, p. 212n.

18 Edgar Allan Poe, *Essays and Reviews* (New York, 1984), p. 1133.

19 Sandro Genovali, *Baudelaire, o della dissonanza* (Florence, 1971), pp. 137–47.

20 de Man, *Rhetoric of Romanticism*, pp. 249. De Man notes that one might also take this *comme* as comparing amber, musk, benjamin and incense with infinite things. However, even this involves the syntax of enumeration: 'infinite things, *such as* amber, musk ...' If one produces a syntax of comparison – 'and other smells having the expansion of infinite things, as amber, musk, etc. do' – then the sentence compares other smells with these four smells, returning us to an effect of enumeration.

21 Apostrophe is the figure of addressing something that is not a real listener, such as an inanimate object or a person who is absent.

22 *Ibid.*, p. 89.

23 'Correspondances' thus represents what de Man elsewhere calls the materiality of language, which is then made intellegible by figuration, much as the physical sounds are made intelligible by being read as an echo, which can then be interpreted. For discussion of this complicated problem, see Jonathan Culler, 'Reading Lyric', *Yale French Studies*, 69 (1985), pp. 98–106, and de Man, 'Hypogram and Inscription', in *The Resistance to Theory* (Minneapolis, 1986).

24 De Man, *The Rhetoric of Romanticism*, pp. 260–1.

8

QUESTIONS OF METAPHOR: GAUTIER'S 'LA NUE'

Christopher Prendergast

A l'horizon monte une nue,
Sculptant sa forme dans l'azur:
On dirait une vierge nue
Emergeant d'un lac au flot pur.

5   Debout dans sa conque nacrée,
Elle vogue sur le bleu clair,
Comme une Aphrodite éthérée,
Faite de l'écume de l'air;

On voit onder en molles poses
10   Son torse au contour incertain,
Et l'aurore répand des roses
Sur son épaule de satin.

Ses blancheurs de marbre et de neige
Se fondent amoureusement
15   Comme, au clair-obscur du Corrège,
Le corps d'Antiope dormant.

Elle plane dans la lumière
Plus haut que l'Alpe ou l'Apennin;
Reflet de la beauté première,
20   Sœur de «l'éternel féminin.»

A son corps, en vain retenue,
Sur l'aile de la passion,
Mon âme vole à cette nue
Et l'embrasse comme Ixion.

25 La raison dit: «Vague fumée,
Où l'on croit voir ce qu'on rêva,
Ombre au gré du vent déformée,
Bulle qui crève et qui s'en va!»

Le sentiment répond: «Qu'importe!
30 Qu'est-ce après tout que la beauté,
Spectre charmant qu'un souffle emporte
Et qui n'est rien, ayant été!

«A l'Idéal ouvre ton âme;
Mets dans ton cœur beaucoup de ciel,
35 Aime une nue, aime une femme,
Mais aime! – C'est l'essentiel!»

✳✳✳

Suppose that, on the analogy with 'la petite', 'la vieille', etc., but in ignorance of the fact that there are constraints (in usage if not by grammatical rule) on the analogical extension of the use of adjectives as nouns, we were to 'mis'-read the title of Gautier's poem as signifying a naked woman instead of a cloud; or alternatively, that we were to claim, in more knowing fashion, that Gautier has engineered an ambiguity by wilfully suspending these constraints in favour of the conventions of poetic licence. But suppose we go further still, and start to see or represent clouds in the natural world *as* naked women. Whereas the former might seem merely incorrect or illicit, the latter might appear as bizarre, eccentric or even mad. Yet this is exactly what the lyric subject of Gautier's poem does, and the poetic embodiment of that act of 'perception' raises the central question of 'La Nue', or, more accurately, is the question raised by 'La Nue' itself: the question of metaphor, the ground and the legitimacy of metaphorical representation.

Metaphor, it is commonly said – and notably by the nineteenth-century poets themselves – is the very life-blood of poetry, 'the life-principle of poetry, the poet's chief test and glory'.[1] But what, in that otherwise banal metaphorical celebration of metaphor, is the meaning here of the word 'test'? Or, more generally, in what senses might we regard metaphor as a test for the poet? Does it mean that metaphor is the instrument by which the poet tests something or other – for example, the adequacy of received or 'normal' ways of describing reality in the interests of supplying new perceptual access to the world? Or does it mean that metaphor is a test of the poet himself, in the sense of a challenge to his powers of inventiveness (the notion that the aesthetic and cognitive power of metaphor is in direct proportion to its 'novel' or 'striking' qualities)? Or is it a test of the poet in the radically different sense that the felicitous choice of metaphor calls on resources and criteria of judgement – intuitively deployed but perhaps rationally formalizable – concerning the 'appropriateness' of the metaphorical representation to what it represents, thus implying some set of limits on what will count as a successful metaphor or even as a metaphor *tout court*? Or, finally, is it to be construed as a test in a quite different sense still, beyond what plausibly appears to be intended by the above quotation: the idea that metaphor is less a 'life-principle' than a kind of poison, as that against which the poet pits his strength in a relation of resistance, seeking for some moment of pure unmediated 'presence' behind the eternal, endlessly interpretable cycle of substitutes, surrogates and indirections?[2]

These questions, in one form or another, have come to obsess modern critical theory, largely as a preoccupation with the 'ground' – linguistic, epistemological, ontological – of the operations of the figural. But if they are questions for modern critical theory (indeed in a form by now so complex that, if we are to pursue the questions in these terms, we are unlikely to be staying for an answer), they are also questions for the body of verse with which this volume of essays is concerned. We routinely, and in many respects rightly, think of nineteenth-century poetic theory and practice as based unambiguously on an affirmation of metaphor, as the privileged instrument of that equally privileged faculty, the Imagination (the 'reine des facultés', as Baudelaire described it). But alongside celebration, there is also anxiety, a worry about being taken over by what Mallarmé was to call the 'démon de l'analogie'. For, since virtually anything in the world can be compared with anything else, what 'authorizes' a proposed metaphorical likeness, what guarantees that it has any significant perceptual or intellectual content whatsoever, as distinct from being merely the arbitrary and ungrounded figment of the individual mind? What – in the characteristic worry of Coleridge and Baudelaire – prevents the degeneration of metaphorical representation into mere 'fancy', or, more alarmingly, its coalescence with delirium and hallucination?

What may seem more surprising is that in certain respects these are also questions for Gautier. The received view of the place of Gautier in the development of nineteenth-century poetry promotes a quite different version of his significance, and, in particular, as singularly inhospitable to the large and weighty philosophical questions that surround the issue of metaphor.[3] One of my further purposes in this essay therefore will be to argue, through a reading of 'La Nue', for a reassessment of Gautier's poetry in terms that seek to rescue it from what has become the largely unexamined orthodoxy within which it is usually discussed. This, broadly, is the view of Gautier as the champion of a particular notion of 'art for art's sake', according to which the poet appears as a kind of literary artisan moulding his poem in the artistic *atelier* as a delicately crafted artifact; for whom the making of the poem is strictly analogous to the skilled artisan's making of jewelry – whence of course the connotations of the title of the collection to which 'La Nue' belongs (*Emaux et camées*),[4] the idea of the poem as a perfected 'cameo', from which both intensity of feeling and complexity of argument have been banished because their intrusion is seen as potentially threatening to the integrity of the perfected work. This is the version of Gautier which in turn leads into the now fashionable view of his poetry as essentially the work of a 'minor' poet, inventive in the sense of technical resourcefulness and ingenuity, but in the last analysis emotionally and intellectually sterile. In the following analysis of 'La Nue', I want to challenge this view by suggesting that Gautier's 'formalism' or 'aestheticism', his apparent severance of poetry from purely emotive, referential or utilitarian purposes, in fact constitutes the grounds of his main achievement; what Gautier offers us is a sophisticated, ambiguously poised inquiry into both the conditions of art and the terms of its relation to life.

I also want to suggest that, in respect of 'La Nue', this large claim is inseparable from the specific question of Gautier's use of, and attitude towards, metaphor. In these terms – and to put the matter in summary form – the argument comprises three major levels or stages. First, I give a straightforward description of the various metaphorical articulations of 'La Nue' (in this regard I initially treat metaphor and simile as synonymous, although towards the end I shall take up the view that there are significant differences between the two forms). Secondly, I consider the ways in which, in this poem, metaphor is crucially linked to desire, the notion that it is from the projections of human desire on to the natural world that the poem's metaphorical elaborations principally derive. Thirdly, and most important of all, I consider the poem as containing a commentary, a reflection, on its own metaphorical constructions. This commentary takes two distinct forms: one is implicit, tacitly developed in the texture of the writing itself; the other is explicit, and is marked by the intervention in stanza 7 of the voice of reason, which intrudes to question and censure the activity of the metaphoring imagination.

Furthermore, to these two forms correspond two distinct purposes. The first involves what is sometimes called 'foregrounding': the attempt to foreground the metaphorical workings of the text, in the sense of 'showing', demonstrating the *labour* that has gone into the production of the poetic artifact. This, for Gautier, is the area of the pleasure of the text, which consists not, as the emotional and psychological pattern of the poem would suggest, in the drive of desire towards possession of its object, but in the recognition of the ways in which that 'object' has been constructed by the rhetorical manoeuvres of art. The poem visibly takes pleasure in laying bare and putting on display the 'art' in the art, the forms and conditions of an aesthetically controlled work of fantasy on the world. On the other hand, this self-reflexiveness also becomes a self-questioning. From stanza 7 onwards the poem manifests (but also qualifies) a certain scepticism, even an anxiety concerning the *product* of the poetic labour. In acknowledging that the work of art is nothing other than a work of the imagination, Gautier enters certain doubts and queries as to the validity of the perceptions built into figurative accounts of the natural world. The problem of metaphor, from the point of view of reason (the point of view represented in stanza 7) concerns its intellectual (and ethical) reliability, and is directly connected with the investment of desire in the natural world. Do the likenesses perceived by the imagination and consecrated by metaphor have any rational 'grounding', are they epistemologically secure, or is their anthropomorphic character epistemologically ruinous? Does not metaphor clothe Nature in false garb ('dressing' and 'undressing', as themselves metaphors, are central to many of Gautier's poetic representations of Nature, and I shall return to this at the end) in order to accommodate the fictions of desire, fictions that are not only intellectually empty, but also ethically dangerous in that they blur the dividing line between self and other?[5] This, of course, is the point at which Gautier's reservations about metaphor join with that more general worry about figurative language which occupies the romantic mind as a whole. However, as we shall see, the terms of Gautier's 'reply' to these questions in 'La Nue' are of an unusually paradoxical sort, such that it is virtually impossible to tell by the end of the poem what exactly Gautier's stance is on the issues that it raises.

'La Nue' is 'about' a cloud, but the interest shown by the poet towards the cloud is not that of the detached observer of the natural world. 'La Nue' is not primarily a descriptive poem. For the cloud formation interests only by virtue of its mobile and mutable qualities, its capacity to turn into other 'forms', or rather by virtue of the capacity of the perceiving subject to transform it.[6] More specifically, the cloud arouses interest to the extent that it generates or attracts metaphor. In the course of the poem the cloud undergoes four major metaphorical transformations. The fourth of these occurs in stanza 7, and has a rather paradoxical status (I shall return to this at a later stage). The first three are all connected with an idea of femininity; they take the form of three female figures, the general import of which is explicitly resumed in the quotation in stanza 5, '"l'éternel féminin"'. The three female figures are, respectively, the 'vierge nue' of stanza 1, Aphrodite, the goddess of love, in stanza 2, and, in stanza 4, another figure from classical mythology, Antiope, or, more precisely, the figure of Antiope as represented in a painting by the Renaissance artist, Correggio.[7]

These three representations of the cloud as three female bodies are motivated by an interest that is clearly erotic in character. They are instances of the way desire 'appropriates' the forms of the natural world to its own ends and needs, and illustrations of the way the metaphoring imagination acts as an instrument of desiring fantasy (more precisely, as an instance of male desiring fantasy for which the female is the object, and this fact bears strongly on some of the more general cultural and ethical issues raised by the poem). Metaphor here is thus the medium through which desire fashions its fantasmatic objects from the objects of the material world. The fantasy circulates freely throughout the poem (until temporarily checked by the censorship of reason), but is at its most active in the elaboration of the reference to Aphrodite: the erotic connotations of 'onder en mille poses', suggestive of both sexual receptiveness and sexual allure; the hint of sexual ambivalence in 'contours incertains'; the sensuality of the image of the dawn sun making Aphrodite's skin flush red (although the presence of the artificial substance, satin, indeed the wilful preciosity of the whole image of sunrise scattering roses on satin, is already a marker of a certain 'aesthetic' distancing of desire from its object); finally, the highly erotic image of 'melting' at the beginning of stanza 4 ('Ses blancheurs de marbre et de neige/Se fondent amoureusement'); indeed, even metrical factors arguably contribute, in the second of those two lines, to the sexual atmospherics of the poem: Gautier's famous octosyllabic line – 'that most mercurial and mobile of lines'[8] – could be scanned here as giving the rhythm 2/6 ('Se fond/ent amoureusement'), with a convergence, in the second measure, of metrical energy and erotic energy on the key word 'amoureusement'.

This description of the terms of 'La Nue' – its recourse to metaphor in the representation of nature and the libidinal investment of the poetic subject in these metaphorical transformations – will make it sound a poem amenable to a perfectly straightforward analysis. Indeed it will make it sound simply trite, as a fantasy uncritically trafficking in the literary clichés and stereotypes of nineteenth-century 'neo-paganism'. What, however, makes the poem more complex and demanding derives from the way it pursues a reflection on the conditions of that fantasy, on the 'constructed' nature of its objects. Moreover, the clearest indication of this reflexive aspect of the poem comes paradoxically (the poem is full of paradoxes) at the culminating moment of its celebration of its various feminine incarnations. In the last two lines of stanza 5, the various metaphorical representations of the cloud are gathered up in a further image, as a 'reflection' of primordial feminine beauty: 'Reflet de la beauté première'. The term 'première' has edenesque echoes, female 'nakedness' in its original, natural state prior to the Fall into self-awareness and guilt. Yet the evocation of that massively over-subscribed stereotype is then followed, in the last line of the stanza, by the self-consciously literary allusion to what is a highly familiar literary stereotype: 'Sœur de "l'éternel féminin"'. The Eternal Feminine is, of course, one of the most commonly recycled romantic images of woman (deriving largely from a simplified reading of Goethe's *Faust*). The fact that it appears in 'La Nue' in *quotation marks* is a sign of the poem's ironic sense of the image's bookish origins and stereotyped character. The quotation marks are a sign that the text itself 'knows' what it is doing, of its ability to distance and examine the metaphorical constructs it produces. If this is desiring fantasy at work, it is fantasy which can identify its stereotypes *as* stereotypes; which, having invoked (albeit in the refracted form of an image, a 'reflet') a culturally embedded notion of female 'naturalness', at the same time refuses any complicity with the naturalizing rhetoric which elsewhere in the period informs the presentation of that image.

I want now to pursue in more detail this self-examining dimension of the poem by concentrating in particular on three key points or moments of the text: first, the figuring of the cloud as naked virgin and as Aphrodite in stanzas 1 and 2; secondly, the reference to Antiope and Correggio's painting in stanza 4; thirdly, the figurative representation of the poet himself in stanza 6 (the subject rather than the object of desire), where the comparison involves yet another mythological character, Ixion.

Given that the poem is ostensibly a 'nature' poem (a skyscape), it is significant that its first metaphorical moment should turn on a specifically artistic image: the transition from cloud to naked virgin is mediated by the analogy likening the cloud to a sculptor ('Sculptant sa forme...'). Imagery drawn from the plastic arts is, of course, a commonplace of Gautier's poetic procedures.[9] But its particular interest here concerns the way it gives the terms of a *double* metaphorical articulation: the cloud is compared to a sculptor, sculpting a 'form' which is then compared to a naked woman (the 'vierge nue'). In other words, the cloud, in its metaphorical guise as sculptor, is staged as producing its own metaphorical representation. Thus, already in the first stanza we have an image of an image-making process; the cloud sculpts, metaphorically, its own metaphor, or, in more general terms, the text tropes its own troping activity. It is less a question of art imitating nature than of nature imitating art, as a kind of reverse or counter-mimesis whose strategies of figurative construction are deliberately being put on display.

Similar considerations arise in connection with the subsequent metaphorical developments of the poem. For example, in respect of the comparison with Aphrodite in stanza 2, what exactly is being compared to what? What, syntactically, is the referent of the pronoun 'Elle' in line two? Either it refers back, in the first stanza, to the 'nue' of line one (the cloud), or it refers to the 'vierge nue' of line two. In terms of narrative plausibility, we are more likely to opt for the latter, and this in turn carries implications for how we interpret the place of Aphrodite in the figurative economy of the poem. Aphrodite is not so much a secondary metaphorical transformation of the inaugural term (cloud), as a transformation of the naked virgin. But, since 'vierge nue' is itself metaphor, then Aphrodite appears not just as figure ('comme Aphrodite...'), but as the figure of a figure, the metaphor of a metaphor.

A more complex instance of this doubling or refracting of the figurative discourse of the poem is the reference to the body of Antiope in the painting by Correggio. This is the third term in the successive metamorphosing of the cloud into a female persona. It connects in an obvious way with the erotic interests of the poem (in the mythological story Antiope is visited by Zeus in the guise of a satyr). But in Gautier's poem the allusion to Antiope is not just to a character from ancient myth, but also to a representation of that character in a Renaissance painting. And the superimposition of the aesthetic reference on the narrative reference again complicates in significant ways the question of what precisely is 'imaging' what in the poem. Pictorial allusion in Gautier's poetry (like sculptural allusion) is normally accounted for in terms of Gautier's adherence to the doctrine of *transposition d'art*, whereby the poem is seen as an attempt at creating impressionistic verbal 'equivalents' of a painting. It would not be difficult to analyse 'La Nue' from the point of view of its presumed painterly qualities: the profusion of colour terms; the characteristic nominal syntax of 'blancheurs de marbre et de neige', where the noun 'blancheurs', in focussing attention on the quality of the object rather than the object itself, effects a blurring of object-contour analogous to the displacement of attention from object to quality in the Impressionist painters (or indeed the *chiaro-scuro* of Correggio); the ambiguity of 'poses', at once the erotic poses of a mistress and the poses of an artist's model in the studio.

Yet it is that very ambiguity which suggests that more work is being done here by pictorial allusion than is implied by the mimetic doctrine of *transposition d'art*. It would doubtless be stretching the conventions of poetic licence to breaking point to ambiguate the title of the poem so as to see in it also the sense of 'nude'.[10] But with the introduction of Correggio's Antiope, it is precisely that connotation which is activated, as part of the double framing of the female body as an object of aesthetic interest as well as an object of erotic interest: in the Greek myth the sleeping body of Antiope arouses the sexual attention of Zeus; in Correggio's painting, although the theme of the original story is reproduced, she is also an example of an artistic study in the nude. And that doubling or splitting of the reference to Antiope points to the inadequacy of the purely mimetic or impressionistic reading. It is not that the poem images, or imitates, Correggio's painting; it is rather that the painting is used to image, or allegorize, the poem. Its value within the economy of the poem is less impressionistic than rhetorical; it functions as analogy, and turns on the word 'comme': Correggio's painting is *like* the cloud–naked virgin–Aphrodite, in the sense of being a further metaphorical representation. The pictorial 'framing' of the object of desire duplicates and repeats, at yet another level, the process of figuration itself, and accordingly inserts a distance between the appropriating gestures of the poem and its knowledge of the 'artificial' means whereby that appropriation is accomplished. The work of the poem at this juncture is to re-present the object of desire in terms of other works of art, as a re-troping of that object at yet a further remove. The artfulness of Gautier's poem, we may say, here shades into artiness, but in order to remind us that what we are confronted with are *representations* and their necessarily mediated character.

We are similarly reminded of the role of mediation even at that moment of the poem when, in stanza 6, its metaphorical incarnations appear to produce a powerful discharge of emotional energy. Here the centre of attention shifts from the object of desire to its subject, or rather to the urgent movement of desire towards possession of its object ('Mon âme vole à cette nue / Et l'embrasse comme Ixion'). Yet that apparently direct movement is in fact impeded by the intervention of further ambiguities in which the very notions of 'subject' and 'object' are themselves equivocated. For example, what does the subject 'embrace'? Which of the two homophones of the first stanza applies in the line 'Mon âme vole à cette nue' (assuming we can plausibly substantivize the adjective 'nue' as naked woman)? If we refer back to 'corps' in line one, we are still with the idea of the naked virgin (the figurative object of desire). If, however, we refer forwards to the simile 'comme Ixion' (in the classical myth Ixion chases a cloud), we are back with the idea of clouds (the literal or 'original' object). But even if we read it in the latter sense, this in no way signifies a return of the text to its founding 'referent' in the natural world. On the contrary, the poem is still working entirely at the figurative level, but is doing so in ways that radically ambiguate the question as to what is figuring what. In the first place, the allusion to Ixion is itself metaphor, or simile, used to figure the desire of the poet ('*comme* Ixion'). Secondly, and more important, we should recall the story of Ixion itself: it recounts Ixion's sexual pursuit of the goddess Hera and her deception of him by disguising herself as a cloud in a cloud-formation; Ixion embraces a cloud in the belief that he is possessing Hera. Thus, in the myth, the clouds act as a displacement or deflection of desire from its original object (the body of Hera) on to a substitute. In other words, stanza 6 operates a *reversal* of the chain of representations: instead of, as in stanza 2, a cloud represented as a goddess (Aphrodite), we have, tacitly, a goddess represented as a cloud. The poem thus blurs the relation between what is figure and what is figured, what is 'original' and what is 'substitution'. It is rather like a chain or spiral in which figures are repeated, doubled, turned back on themselves, as a series of mirror-images where ultimately what is being foregrounded for the attention of the reader is the figuring process itself. At the moment of anticipated consummation, of the fusion of subject and object, the poem blocks that anticipation by again reminding us that the play of the erotic imagination is an irreducibly mediated one, that it never once leaves the domain of 'figure'.

There is, however, one further aspect to the story of Ixion, which opens on to the remaining part of the poem. Hera's evasion of

Ixion's desire entails a deception. Ixion mistakes one thing for another. And, in that reference to the theme of misperception and misinterpretation, it is possible to read an implicitly *critical* allegory of the metaphoring imagination itself. Despite the poem's delight in displaying its own artifices, there remains a tension, a worry, about the status of the metaphorical substitutions. It is that worry which results in the transition to stanza 7, where the censorious voice of reason intervenes to dismiss the constructions of the imagination as empty chimeras. This is the point at which Gautier's poem echoes that more general romantic anxiety concerning the intellectual and cognitive security of metaphorical representation. It resurrects that 'spectre' (stanza 8) which haunts the romantic mind in the form of the question: what legitimates a perceived metaphorical likeness as anything other than the figment of the individual psyche? The playfulness of the poem gives way to anxious and irritated scepticism. The cloud is now but a 'vague fumée', and its transformations by the desiring imagination merely unreal, insubstantial and evanescent phantoms. The poem retreats from its earlier commitments, notably through the weakening force of '*croit* voir', stressing the purely subjective work of the imagination, with a strong implication of delusion, the blurring of the frontiers between reality and dream ('ce qu'on rêva').

The criticism of imagination by reason is not, however, the last word of the poem. Indeed no sooner are its objections raised, than they are dismissed by the 'reply' of sentiment in stanzas 8 and 9. Yet in stanza 8 the terms of that reply are somewhat curious, and are in part the source of ambiguities in the otherwise far more enthusiastically affirmative final stanza. For sentiment's reply is nonchalantly low-key. It not only bypasses, rather than refutes, the problems raised by reason; it tacitly concedes as much as it salvages from reason's attack. Thus, the aesthetic category of the 'beautiful' is reaffirmed, but at the same time qualified and reduced ('Qu'est-ce après tout que la beauté?'); it certainly no longer occupies the literally 'elevated' position assigned to beauty in stanza 5. Beauty is now the 'spectre charmant'; it charms, seduces, but as mere spectre, unreal and above all ephemeral (a notion captured in the logical and grammatical play of 'n'est rien, ayant été'). The emphasis, at this juncture, on the ephemerality of the products of the imagination would seem to involve a movement away from the poet's commit-ment to his own creation. It is, however, the moment of a paradox that, retrospectively, casts its net back over the whole of the poem, and it turns precisely on the question of metaphor and simile.

I have so far proceeded as if there were no substantial difference between these two figures. But many accounts argue that metaphor is a stronger and more committed version of analogy than simile; metaphor is absolutist in the analogical transfer it proposes; the link maintained by simile, on the other hand, implies a connection that is more provisional and temporary from the perceiving subject's point of view.[11] In other words, the distinction between metaphor and simile is in part a temporal distinction: the perceptions organized by metaphor are unconditional and atemporal; those organized by simile are more non-committal and ephemeral, closer to being a matter of 'passing fancy'; simile, on this view, is like the 'bulle qui crève et qui s'en va'; it is that which 'n'est rien, ayant été'. Here, however, is the area within 'La Nue' of Gautier's brilliant paradox. For, in the figurative representations of both cloud and poet up to stanza 7, the controlling device is that of simile; the terms of the analogical relations are governed by the word 'comme' (or, in the first stanza, by the phrase 'on dirait'). Pure metaphor, at least in any concentrated form, makes its first appearance in the dialogue between reason and sentiment. Whence the paradox: reason, scep-tical of metaphor, voices its criticism in terms that are consistently metaphorical ('vague fumée', 'Ombre au gré du vent déformée', 'Bulle qui crève'), while sentiment replies in kind, using metaphor in the very act of downgrading it ('spectre charmant'); or, to put this another way, the cloud now becomes a metaphor for the emptiness and insubstantiality of metaphor.[12]

Quite what the general implications of this paradox might be remains highly uncertain, though they are clearly of the sort that has preoccupied a great deal of modern literary theory. Within the poem itself, however, the paradox does have implications that directly affect our reading of the last stanza. Stanza 9 seems to be the decisive rejection of the strictures brought by rational criticism to both poetry and desire. It reads as a passionately didactic exhortation to keep desire alive and in circulation, irrespective of any sceptical inquiries that might surround its 'object'. Indeed the question of the 'object' is here dismissed as virtually irrelevant to the concerns of the desiring subject. In the insistent repetition of the verb 'aime', the third instance is without object, suggesting that it is the condition of desiring as such, intransitively, that is the important value for the poem. In other words, here the poem seems to effect a retrieval of the idealizing impulse in terms that steer close to the spirit of romantic solipsism, where ego is all and other is nothing; we might note in particular the reifying implications of the throwaway juxtaposition of 'femme' with 'nue', suggesting that, in the last analysis, the difference, for the desiring subject, between human object and natural object is negligible. Thus, if reason wishes to raise questions in connection with the reality of the object-world, that is the problem of reason and not of imagination (and doubly so by virtue of the imprisoning bad faith of reason, compelled to speak itself in the forked tongue of metaphor).

Yet, at the very moment the poem appears to collapse into uncritical panegyric, it once again equivocates its own positions, plays ambiguously with its own devices and strategies. Thus, metaphor is still in business, and moreover in the mode of the imperative ('Mets beaucoup de ciel dans ton cœur'). But the injunction to put lots of heaven into our hearts has an obvious connotation of the trite and the incongruous. There is a possible irony here; or more accurately, in the juxtaposition of 'cœur/ciel', a possible zeugma, another figure of speech, but one which ironically figures the incongruity of the metaphor. There is a similarly odd note in the sound patterning of the stanza. We find, as elsewhere in the poem, much internal echo: 'une nue' as anagrams of each other; liminal rhyme ('mets/mais'); the phonemic resemblance of 'âme' and 'aime', reinforcing the idea of the unity of desire, spirituality and ideality. The sound echoes could then be construed as resemblances lying parallel to and reinforcing the resemblances proposed by metaphor. There is, however, a jarring note, a dislocation, in the terminal rhymes of lines one and three: 'âme' and 'femme' are near rhymes, mis-hits. Given Gautier's technical virtuosity (he would have endorsed everything that Banville had to say on the subject of rhyme), it would be wrong to see this as a mere 'slip' of the versifier; indeed, although the rhyme words are mis-matched in terms of contemporary pronunciation, the rhyme is authorized by the history of poetic convention.[13] The question, therefore, is how we interpret the awkwardness, the tension between what convention permits and pronunciation denies. Is it an oblique way of sabotaging the poem, the introduction of a disruptive dissonance into its harmonics (the notion of 'harmony', it will be recalled, is central to much nineteenth-century thinking about both poetry and the imagination)? Or alternatively, is it an awkwardness deliberately engineered to remind us yet again of the 'artificing' character of poetry? Is it another reminder, in the negative mode of the unfinished, of the work, the 'labour' of making poetry?

It is doubtful that the poem itself supplies grounds for deciding that question. But to the extent that it draws the mind back to the principle of artifice, it can be interestingly linked to the more general questions I raised at the beginning concerning the meaning of Gautier's 'aestheticism'. This link – along with some necessarily provisional conclusions – can be made by returning to the paradoxes of Gautier's treatment of the theme of the naked body, and their context in a much wider nineteenth-century opposition between the rival claims of nature and art or, in the pertinent metaphorical contrast, between the 'naked' and the 'dressed'. Representations of nature in the metaphors of 'clothing' and 'dress', along with their counterparts, nature as 'undressed' or 'naked', are a poetic commonplace. Their interest lies in the connection with a question of a more general order. For these particular metaphors of dressing and undressing are direct illustrations (or a metaphorical *mise en abime*) of a function often ascribed to figurative language as a whole: the notion of figures of speech as 'adornment', as the 'clothing' of nature in the garments of artifice. This notion is a recurring topic in writing about rhetoric from the ancients onwards, and is often used to articulate a profound mistrust of the ornamental strategies of rhetorical discourse: metaphor, as the garb poetry puts on nature, is a source of concealment, falsification and decadence. Figurative discourse entails a dis-figuring or de-naturing of nature, whereas true discourse (simple, unadorned) removes that false covering to restore nature to its pristine, undressed or 'naked' state.[14]

This is an idea that will be found everywhere in the nineteenth century, even in the work of that inveterate hater of nature and high priest of artifice, Baudelaire (in the poem 'A une mendiante rousse', the play of figurative language around the beggar girl is dramatized as a verbal clothing of her person, as so much false finery, which is then 'stripped' as the poem turns against its own metaphorical procedures in the effort to see the girl in her unadorned 'pauvre nudité'). There is, however, an acute difficulty with this opposition between the dressed and the naked: it is the paradox whereby the critic of metaphor expresses his criticism in the very terms which are the object of suspicion and censure. For to describe metaphor as false garb is not only to describe it as false; it is also to describe it metaphorically. In exactly the same way, the enterprise of retrieving for poetry the 'nakedness' of nature comes up against the problem that 'naked' in this context is itself a figure of speech.

It is part of the lesson of Gautier that he remains constantly alert to this paradox. In those of his poems where the motifs of 'dressing' and 'undressing' nature are most actively at work ('La Fleur qui fait le printemps', 'Camélia et pâquerette'), there seems to be at moments a certain nostalgia for an unmetaphored, rhetorically 'unclouded' mode of perception and representation. But a more at- tentive reading of these poems will show how in fact such nostalgia is displaced and even parodied by a subtle form of self-referring irony. In 'La Nue' the paradox of nakedness and the myth of naturalness are exposed by virtue of the fact that its major terms are never presented as anything other than figurative. The poem is obsessed with images of the naked body, but since the naked body here is all metaphor, mere trope, it can hardly furnish the ground of a putative recovery of the natural world in its 'naked' immediacy. This is the play of Gautier's poem, but also the sign of its seriousness. It illustrates, finally, the intellectual sophistication of Gautier's aestheticism. This involves not, as in the familiar reductive cliché, the refusal of life in the name of art, but rather the breaking down of the false antinomy of life and art. The argument of 'La Nue' is that the very 'life' of desire is in, and only in, the cultural forms and rhetorical conventions by which both the 'subject' and 'object' of desire are constituted. It is an argument the nineteenth century often forgot or chose to ignore, and nowhere perhaps more insistently than in the movement of 'neo-paganism' with which Gautier is so often associated. But, to the extent that nineteenth-century neo- paganism seeks to recover the unself-conscious spontaneity deemed to reside in the spirit of the ancient Greeks, Gautier's poem, in self-consciously foregrounding its own artifices, arguably seeks to free us from the seductions of that hopelessly nostalgic myth. It tells us in the terms of poetry what Walter Pater (a great admirer of Gautier) tells us in the terms of criticism: that 'freedom', for the modern mind, consists not in the escape from artifice into the illusion of unself-conscious wholeness, but in *recognizing* the character of the artifice, seeing clearly and fully the seams and joints of what we make and what makes us.[15]

NOTES

1 C. Day Lewis, *The Poetic Image* (London, 1947), p. 17.
2 *Cf.* J. Culler, 'Commentary', *New Literary History*, 6 (1974), pp. 219–29.
3 *Cf.* C Gothot-Mersch, ed., Gautier, *Emaux et camées* (Paris, 1981), p. 13: 'Peu de métaphores, les mots sont employés dans leur sens propre, ils sont précis, et souvent techniques.'
4 Editions of *Emaux et camées* in Gautier's lifetime appeared in 1852, 1853, 1858, 1863, 1866 and 1872. To each new edition Gautier added new poems; 'La Nue' was written for the 1866 edition; its relative 'lateness' might explain in part its high degree of self-consciousness.
5 Since the questions about metaphor that I am pursuing here are specified by being asked in the context of 'La Nue', it may appear that I am confusing claims about metaphor in general with more restricted claims about the particular *kind* of metaphor characteristic of this poem (anthropomorphic and geared to the movements of desire). For example, not all metaphors are anthropomorphic in the strict sense of representing the non-human in terms of the human. Paul de Man, discussing anthropomorphism as 'a conceit by which human consciousness is projected or transferred onto the natural world', poses it as a special case of figural discourse, involving not just an art of the trope but also a strong psychological 'identification', a freezing or essentializing of identities in the human and natural worlds: 'Anthropomorphism freezes the infinite chain of tropological substitutions and propositions into one single assertion or essence' (*The Rhetoric of Romanticism* (New York, 1984), pp. 89, 241). Would this then mean that those metaphors which do not fall into this class are not 'insecure', or, if so, for different reasons? But, in a broader sense, arguably all metaphor is anthropomorphic, or at least anthropocentric, in that its operations blur self/

154

other distinctions; on this view, the explicitly anthropomorphic character of Gautier's metaphors in 'La Nue' simply renders more salient a disposition of metaphor in general. The more problematic claim, I think, concerns the linking of metaphor with *desire*. Clearly, metaphor can rest on a wide range of affective and intellectual responses to the world, including curiosity, playfulness, fear, etc., as well as desire. The psychological ground of a poem which presents clouds as, say, buildings or mountains (Hugo's 'Soleils couchants') may well be quite different from poems which see clouds as naked women.

6 Clouds are of course a central topos in romantic poetry and painting, and, as Ruskin points out, are linked to the interest of the modern artist in the phenomenon of 'mutability' (*cf.* 'On Modern Landscape', in *The Genius of John Ruskin*, ed. J. D. Rosenberg (London, 1980), p. 84).

7 The ostensible pictorial inspiration for 'La Nue' was in fact Botticelli's *Birth of Venus*. For a discussion of the importance of clouds in Correggio's painting, *cf.* Hubert Damisch, *Théorie du nuage, pour une histoire de la peinture* (Paris, 1972).

8 Clive Scott, *French Verse-art: A Study* (Cambridge, 1980). p. 42.

9 *Cf.* Russell S. King, 'Emaux et camées: sculpture et objets-paysages', *Europe*, 57, no. 601 (1979), pp. 84–9.

10 The term for 'nude', in the painterly sense, is of course 'le Nu', whether the subject of the painting is male or female.

11 For an interesting discussion of these distinctions, *cf.* Clive Scott, *A Question of Syllables* (Cambridge, 1986), pp. 61–2.

12 The notion that certain kinds of poetic representation are 'vague', do not give precise purchase on the real world, is indeed sometimes expressed in the (dead) metaphorical idea of having one's head in the clouds. When Lamartine brought out *Les Nouvelles Méditations poétiques* in 1823, Thiesse, editor of the *Revue Encyclopédique*, remarked that 'ce qui n'était que vague dans les premiers essais est obscur dans les seconds ... l'auteur se perd dans les nues' (cited in Mary Ellen Birkett, *Lamartine and the Poetics of Landscape* (Lexington, KY, 1982), p. 7). Mallarmé, on the other hand, will give to these associations the far stronger context of radical philosophical despair, linking the motifs of clouds, nakedness and the spectral ('hantise') to the human subject's impossible striving for a pure but elusive and unending Absolute: 'la trop lucide hantise de cette cime menaçante d'absolu, devinée dans le départ des nuées là-haut, fulgurante, nue, seule', 'Richard Wagner', *Œuvres complètes* (Paris, 1945), p. 546.

13 The rhyming of the vowel sounds of 'âme' and 'femme' survived changes in pronunciation (the two must have been homophonic in

Middle French), rather like the so-called *rime normande* (e.g. 'élever'/ 'hiver' in Baudelaire's 'La Cloche fêlée'). This kind of rhyme was authorized, therefore, not by current pronunciation but by poetic custom deriving from the history of rhyme itself; it was a matter of consecrated convention over-riding the phonetic demands of the ear. In these terms, the rhyme of 'âme' and 'femme' would not have struck the nineteenth-century reader as a 'slip' nor even – although this is less certain – as an approximation. On the other hand, in a poet of Gautier's teasing self-consciousness, it would not be implausible to see here a certain playing with the manifest discrepancy between convention and pronunciation, thus opening on to further perspectives of paradox and ambiguity. For instance, the discrepancy might be said to bear directly on the substantive ethical issues raised by the poem's treatment of the topic of metaphor; it invites us to reflect on how far sexual stereotyping was itself responsible for keeping certain rhymes in place long after there was very little phonetic justification for them.

14 *Cf.* T. Todorov, *Théories du symbole* (Paris, 1977).
15 *Cf.* Walter Pater, 'Style', in *Appreciations* (London, 1889). Consider in connection with the themes of Gautier's poem the following two passages, the first dealing with the relation between self-consciousness and 'freedom', the second with the relation between self-consciousness and metaphor:

> ... the attention of the writer [is] a pledge ... that the writer is dealing scrupulously with his instrument, and therefore indirectly with the reader himself also, that he has the *science* of the instrument he plays on, perhaps, after all, with a *freedom* which in such cases will be the freedom of a master. (p. 10, my italics)

> Still opposing the constant degradation of language by those who use it incorrectly, he [the lover of words] will not treat coloured glass as if it were clear; and, while half the world is using figure unconsciously, will be fully aware not only of all that latent figurative texture in speech, but of the vague, lazy, half-formed personification – a rhetoric, depressing, and worse than nothing, *because it has no really rhetorical motive* – which plays so large a part there, and, as in the case of more ostentatious ornament, scrupulously exact of it, syllable for syllable, its precise value. (p. 17, my italics)

9

TRAINING FOR MODERNITY: VERLAINE'S 'LE PAYSAGE DANS LE CADRE DES PORTIÈRES ...'

Ross Chambers

> Le paysage dans le cadre des portières
> Court furieusement, et des plaines entières
> Avec de l'eau, des blés, des arbres et du ciel
> Vont s'engouffrant parmi le tourbillon cruel
> 5 Où tombent les poteaux minces du télégraphe
> Dont les fils ont l'allure étrange d'un paraphe.
>
> Une odeur de charbon qui brûle et d'eau qui bout,
> Tout le bruit que feraient mille chaînes au bout
> Desquelles hurleraient mille géants qu'on fouette;
> 10 Et tout à coup des cris prolongés de chouette. –
>
> – Que me fait tout cela, puisque j'ai dans les yeux
> La blanche vision qui fait mon cœur joyeux,
> Puisque la douce voix pour moi murmure encore,
> Puisque le Nom si beau, si noble et si sonore
> 15 Se mêle, pur pivot de tout ce tournoiement,
> Au rhythme du wagon brutal, suavement.[1]

✱✱✱

How does one read a poem? Obviously, a poem would not be readable (as a poem) if one did not approach it with at least some vague pre-existing generic 'theory', a notion of what a 'poem' is or does. What I want to suggest is that what such an enabling theory enables us to read is however the way the poem *theorizes itself*, that is, specifies its own situation as poetic discourse.[2] It does so, generally, with respect to the tradition of pre-existing understanding of what 'poetry' is and does in which – but also against which – it exists.

In contemporary culture, the two major 'axioms' with which people approach poetry appear to be these. One, a poem belongs to the category of *interpretable discourse*; two, within that category, it belongs to the sub-category of *measured (or rhythmic) utterance*. Interpretability is, of course, or can be, a characteristic of all discourse, so we must specify that poetry belongs to the category of discourse that is conventionally regarded as interpretable. The ways in which it is interpretable – that is, in which its meaning(fulness) is understood not to coincide with 'what it says' – are innumerable: they range from various hypotheses of an 'unconscious' (psychoanalytic or socio-political[3]) to the view espoused by Michael Riffaterre that a text 'makes sense' only as an intertext, that is by reference to another text or texts.[4]

Under the heading of the 'measured' character of poetic discourse, one should think not only of phonetic characteristics such as metre (conventional or otherwise) and rhyme, but also of semantic and syntactic features that 'repeat', or *beat*, in the text, producing it as a manifestation of what Roman Jakobson defined as the 'poetic function' of language.[5] For example, in 'Le paysage dans le cadre ...', the relation between the two adverbs in – *ment* ('furieusement', l. 2; and 'suavement', l. 16) is phonetic (they rhyme), syntactic (they belong to the same 'part of speech') and semantic (the contrast in their meaning implies an underlying similarity). Since obviously all language is repetitive and so potentially 'measured' in this way, we must again say that poetry is discourse which we frame, as a matter of convention, as discourse whose measured quality *counts*.

How, then, does it count? My sense is that a dialectic is operative between the two axioms (of interpretability and measuredness). 'Measure' produces the textual material that a reader will want to interpret (e.g. one would hypothesize that the relation of 'furieusement' and 'suavement' is *poetically significant*). But which of the many, many items that measure discourse will I regard as being significant? Here, one must initially refer to the interpretive 'project' of the reader: the foreknowledge of what the poem is 'about' with which the reader comes to the text. Thus, if I have determined that the poem is 'about' a train journey and am interested in its attitude to the technological realities of the French nineteenth century, then I may or may not 'pick up' on the way it 'repeats' Dante in lines 12–15 (although I will probably want to take account of the generalized way cultural codes are activated to produce contrasting imagery of 'hell' and 'paradise'). If, on the other hand, I see the text in relation to the context of, say, nineteenth-century poetry about travel, I will want to check the poem's reminiscences of, say, the description of trains in Vigny's 'La Maison du berger' or Nerval's evocation of the effects of movement on perception in 'Le Réveil en voiture'. No reader is ever an interpretive *tabula rasa*: one always brings a certain 'encyclopaedia' of knowledge to one's reading, together with a pre-formed conception of what one will find in the text.

So each of my axioms *depends* on the other in an important way, so as to produce the poem as a verbal means of making meaning, a 'signifying practice' of a specific sort. The interpretive project selects the items of 'measuredness' that become objects of interpretation, and these in turn usually modify the initial project of interpretation, so that it will now select new objects of interpretation in a 'hermeneutic circle'[6] that is more like an enlarging spiral. This means, among other things, that a text of this kind cannot 'exist' autonomously (or it does so only as a kind of theoretical fiction): it becomes a text (a signifying apparatus as opposed to inert 'words-upon-a-page') only insofar as an act of reading produces it (makes it signify) in terms of an interpretive context.

Now, in everyday life, if I say: 'Please get up and open the window!' and you do so, one might say that you have conformed to the 'addressee role' implied by the second-person imperatives 'get up' and 'open'. But suppose that, instead of opening the window (or while opening it) you think 'Who is this person to be bossing me around?' or 'Why is he so obsessed with fresh air?' or even ' I like the rhythm of that phrase' ... Something interesting has happened: the 'original' discourse situation (with its addressee defined by the imperatives) is being bracketed, and taken as a kind of fiction, and you, as *interpreter of that fiction*, have begun to 'read' it – to interpret it as a *text*, thereby occupying a very different addressee position. In this relation to the discourse as text, the question has become something like: 'What does the production of this discourse mean to me?' 'What can I make of it?' There has been a shift from what I will call an 'illocutionary' communicative relationship to one in which the 'situation of the enunciation' and the interpretive relationship it implies have become prominent. All discourse situations have in them the potential for this double mode of 'address'; and the interpretability we attribute to literary discourse merely means that, in reading it, we habitually activate this characteristic.

Lyric poetry, however, is frequently described as the genre which most ostensibly produces a 'fictive' discourse-situation such that we are led, not to occupy the fictive addressee slot, but to interpret the discourse situation 'textually', that is to occupy the interpreter slot implied by the discourse as 'poem'.[7] Compare:

1　Please get up and open the window!

2　Shall I compare thee to a summer's day?

3　　Mon enfant, ma sœur,
　　Songe à la douceur
　　　D'aller là-bas vivre ensemble ... (etc.)

If we read these examples as poetic (and note that there is nothing inherently unpoetic about the first), we do not 'identify' with the fictive addressee (being asked to open the window, or undergoing hypothetical comparison to a summer's day, or being invited to share the pleasures of relocation). Rather we take the speech situation (the relation of an 'I' to a 'you') that is being produced in the poem as the object of our reading and look for ways of interpreting it.

That is why the figure of 'apostrophe' is sometimes taken to be particularly characteristic of the lyric as a genre.[8] In the classic definition of apostrophe, the speaking subject is described as 'turning away' from the matter at hand in order to address a personage who is thought of as 'absent'.[9] The interest thus lies in the *production through language* of an addressee who exists, as far as the reader is concerned, only as the discourse gives us to imagine that figure (skilled at window-opening, comparable to summery weather, appropriate as a travel-companion, etc.). What the classical analyses do not specify, however, is that the *subject* of the apostrophe (the 'speaker') is similarly produced, as far as the reader is concerned, only in and through the discourse we imagine that subject producing: it is someone powerful or lazy enough to expect someone else to get up and open the window, or dubious about the appropriateness of comparing someone to a summer's day, or the site of emotions both paternal and brotherly combined with a desire to relocate with an appropriate companion, etc.

To put it more technically, the subject of address and the addressee in the 'fictive' speech-situation – what I will call the 'illocutionary context'[10] of the poem – are produced entirely, as a relationship, through (a reading of) the 'predications' attributed to the 'speaker' as a grammatical subject ('I') addressing a 'you'. So the supposed 'turning away' of the discourse from the matter at hand is perhaps better described as a *'turning away' from the reader,*[11] on the part of the 'fictive' or 'illocutionary' discourse-situation, which thereby becomes interpretable.

The Verlaine poem is not strictly couched as apostrophe: it is more like a fictive monologue (introducing us into the 'mind' of the speaker); but it functions as a pseudo-apostrophe, since it is easy to surmise that the unattributed 'vision', 'voix' and 'Nom' of lines 12–15, described as they are in such flattering terms, are meant to be taken by some fictive addressee as 'la vision de toi', 'ta voix' and 'ton Nom si beau'. Indeed, this vagueness of attribution, combined with the capital letter of the word 'Nom', is itself a major element of the flattery, since it permits a degree of confusion between the implied addressee of the apostrophe (the absent 'person' being thought about by the subject) and a personage divine or semi-divine. And since the indications encode a feminine figure, I will say that the addressee of the pseudo-apostrophe is being produced as a kind of latter-day Beatrice, that is, among other things, a Muse, whose name has characteristics ('si beau, si noble et si sonore') that identify it with poetic discourse itself, or rather a certain traditional or classical conception of poetic discourse.[12] My hunch will be that here is being named the poetic tradition within which, but also against which, the poem is defining itself. But for now it is only necessary to note that what I have done was to *interpret* this illocutionary situation: I did not imagine that the 'Nom' named me, but understood myself as being on the one hand excluded from the discourse-situation (it has 'nothing to do with me') and on the other as being invited to *understand* it.

But texts do not become interpretable simply by 'turning away' in order to enact a fictive situation of address. They can control their reading in other and more positive ways. Notably, they have ways of *describing themselves as texts*, and, in so doing, of 'addressing' the reader. Or, to put it more technically, they produce 'figures' (metaphors, metonyms, etc.) that are readable as figures of the text within the text, that is, as self-representations or self-descriptions on the part of the text.

This is a tricky business, for many reasons. One is that such features of the text are normally part of the referential apparatus by which the 'illocutionary' situation is itself produced (here, the situation we are led to imagine of a man sitting in a speeding train and thinking of his beloved). It takes a *reader*, precisely, to perceive (from outside the fictive speech-situation) that these items have *potential relevance to the poem* itself, as a kind of writing. In the present case, the subject of the 'illocutionary' situation is responsible, for example, for the metaphoric transformation of the telegraph-lines into a 'paraphe' (a certain form of writing), and also for the contrast between the 'suavité' of his mental images and the 'rhythme du wagon brutal'.[13] It is for a reader, however, to perceive that such features might be applicable to the poem itself: perhaps it too has a 'brutal' rhythm (mingled with suaveness), perhaps it, too, as a form of writing, is somehow like a 'paraphe'? . . .

The implication, then, is that through its self-referentiality, each poem becomes its own *art poétique* – the *art poétique* being the genre that simultaneously describes poetry and enacts its description. This means that a principle of redundancy is operative between what the poem is (can be interpreted as) saying and what the poem is (can be perceived to be) doing – a principle not different in kind from the feature often regarded as characteristic of nineteenth-century poetry and variously described as 'sound echoing sense' or *harmonie vocalique*. But such redundancy does not necessarily imply simple identity: all sorts of 'dissonances' as well as all sorts of *harmonies* can be imagined between a poem's self-description and the poem's own perceived features, and that is where the reader's interpretive activity is most interestingly solicited.

If, as I suspect, the Verlaine poem is *describing its own originality* through terms like 'paraphe', the clash of adverbs such as 'furieusement' and 'suavement', and the relation it draws between 'le Nom si beau, si noble et si sonore' (as an indicator of traditional 'poeticity') and 'le rhythme du wagon brutal' (as a sign of poetic modernity), it is still up to us, as readers, to figure out *what specific features* of the poem such terms might be referring to, and hence the degree of accuracy of its self-referentiality. What follows is an attempt to illustrate schematically what might happen when a reader of 'Le Paysage dans le cadre ...' attempts in this way to interpret its self-figuration in the light of the poem, and the poem in the light of its self-figuration.

The thick upholstery we associate with 'Victorian' furniture was specifically invented because it was necessary to insulate the bourgeois body (and hence the bourgeois 'soul') from the rigours of train travel. We have to make a considerable effort of imagination, these days, to understand the assault on the sensibility that rail travellers experienced. In a horse-drawn coach, one moved along roads that closely conformed to the contours of the land, at speeds only slightly faster than a brisk walk; and one could observe every detail of the roadside. For entertainment on these long journeys there was conversation with one's fellow-travellers. In a train, one was whisked through cuttings and over embankments in a straight line that (in Europe) cut directly across the landforms; the foreground vision from the window ('dans le cadre des portières') became a blur and could not be watched for more than a few moments without fatigue and discomfort, so landscape broadened and flattened into a shifting, long-distance panorama. The intimacy of the coach-traveller with his/her surroundings disappeared; and in the train middle-class travellers felt, they said, like parcels being consigned in some kind of projectile from point A to point B. At the same time the noise was deafening and the atmosphere heavy with smells and soot; conversation was out of the question, not only because of the racket but also because there was little point in striking up acquaintances for so short a period of time. Travel became associated with reading; it quickly became one of the conventions of bourgeois travel that one bought a book or a magazine and isolated oneself in a 'world of words' from the alien and alienating, industrialized environment of the train. The working-class travellers in third and fourth class, with their drinking, smoking, singing and general congeniality, had their own forms of upholstery; but the first- and second-class passengers, isolated in their own observations, thoughts and reading, were thrown onto the resources of their individual selves.[14]

So it is not surprising, perhaps, that the bourgeois subject felt battered, fatigued and weakened – or at least under assault – or that literature might come to play the role of symbolic upholstery in a cruelly industrialized world (for which the bourgeoisie as a class was largely responsible). Not that upholstery fully protects one from the jolts of movement, 'le rhythme du wagon brutal'; on the contrary, it transmits them to the body, but in a softened way, 'suavement'. My initial hunch will be, in any case, that in Verlaine's poem, poetry is being presented, by virtue of its traditional values (beauty, nobility, sonorousness) as an element of *suavité* in a brutal world of noise that signifies the modern, a world whose brutality it simultaneously accepts, accommodates and transmits. Or, in more spatial and kinetic terms, it provides an element of stability, like upholstery, in a world of furious movement, a safe centre in the 'tourbillon' or the 'tournoiement' that surrounds it. It does not exclude the new and violent environment of modernity, but it cushions the jolts.

The poem does not mention upholstery; but the way it imagines a centring that simultaneously permits the mingling of the 'suave' and the 'brutal' is in the notion of a pivot. The 'Nom si beau' that provides the elements of *suavité*, and on which the subject's thoughts are centred, is simultaneously the device that permits a fusion of 'brutality' and *suavité*. The pivot, as centre, is pure ('pur pivot de tout ce tournoiement') – and yet, curiously, it is not pure, for the softness, sweetness, musicality etc. that are associated with this purity at the stable centre of things are simultaneously mingled, and by means of the pivot, with 'le rhythme du wagon brutal'. We can recognize here a characteristic trick of the imagination in reconciling contradictory desires, and conclude that, if the poem is theorizing itself as a kind of pivot, it suggests that we should look at it as a mode of naming (and of naming a subject) that functions in something like the self-contradictory way that is attributed here to the pivot. That is, we should look at it on the one hand as the production of a privileged centre in the whirling world, but on the other as a site of mixing, where the *suavité* is mixed with the brutality of the 'tourbillon'. My specific hypothesis will in fact be that centring will prove characteristic of the poem viewed in terms of

the fictive speech-situation or 'illocutionary context' that it produces. However, the mixing and mingling will be to the fore, I
assume, in the mode of 'textual' self-referentiality that relates reader
to text. Here, perhaps, the 'subject' will be less a self-enclosed 'I' and
more like an 'eye' (and a nose and ears), and so identified with the
sensory perception that mingles 'self' with 'world', and blurs the
boundaries that make the 'pivot' thinkable as pure.

Since the poem – it seems – is producing the 'pivot' as the crucial
metaphor that governs its own self-theorizing, it is natural to ask: is
there a pivot in the poem? As soon as we look, we discover that there
are two. An artifice of punctuation – the rather unusual double dash
at the end of line 10 and beginning of line 11 (which some editors
normalize to a single dash) – marks one pivotal moment in the
poem, corresponding to a change of mental focus (from externally
directed to internally directed), and a parallel change of mood. The
other is at the mathematical centre of the poem (ll. 8–9), where there
is a very strong enjambment: only the conventional metrical break at
the end of the alexandrine line interrupts the long 24-syllable phrase
with its concatenation of relative clauses ('... que feraient ... au
bout/Desquelles ... qu'on fouette') that seems to measure out the
length of a chain (or perhaps a whip?) ... So one notices immediately
how, in each case, the poem (ironically) enacts its own pivot(s) as a
'nothing'. Marked as the space between two dashes, it is a negative
entity defined entirely by the *turning* of the verse[15] and by the *turn* of
the poem as it swings in focus and mood: such a pivot 'centres' the
poem and steadies it only by facilitating its 'tournoiement'. Or, even
more alarmingly, the pivot is an entirely artificial and conventionally
induced pause (the metrical break) in a chain that 'continues' right
through the pause, a chain of phrases that (speaking syntactically) is
a rather 'tormented' one, and whose 'suffering' the pivot does
nothing to allay. I will return to this second pivot later, but we can
note already that the 'purity' the poem attributes to the salutary
pivot in the world of speed, noise and torment, is a rather illusory
one: it is the purity of a 'nothing' that is virtually inseparable from
what surrounds it.

But the first pivot can be understood as that which permits the
poem, nevertheless, to centre itself in its 'illocutionary' functioning
and hence to produce itself as a discourse anchored in an individual

subject ('je') and addressed to another individual subject (the implied 'tu'). The key to understanding its function is the phrase 'Que me fait tout cela' (l. 11) as an expression of *indifference* for the dynamized, blurred 'tourbillon' of the visual landscape and the howling, clanking, malodorous environment of the subject's other senses – in short, for the 'sound and fury' (*cf.* 'bruit' and 'fur-ieusement') of the hellish onslaught on his being. In declaring himself 'indifferent' to it all, he affirms his *difference* from it.

We can notice, however, that what makes the visual landscape itself so alarming is that movement produces in it an effect of *indifferentiation*. Its elements are described in broadly generic terms ('des plaines entières'), as if there was no time to notice particular-izing details before the whole was swallowed into the 'gouffre', and with a partitive syntax ('de l'eau, des blés, des arbres et du ciel') that reduces landscape to its constituent matter, as it all swirls into the same all-engulfing abyss that swallows up the telegraph-poles. And what of the subject himself? It is significant that the 'je' has so far not manifested himself as a discursive subject, and will make his appearance in the text only after the turn of the poem on its pivotal dashes at lines 10–11 and with the subject's expression of indiffer-ence ('Que me fait tout cela'). In the whole first part of the poem, he has been virtually identified with the swirling landscape and so, it seems, likely to disappear into the same gulf of indifferentiation as the plains, fields, trees, telegraph-poles, etc. themselves. Indeed, his danger seems to increase as the poem develops, for if at first the 'portières' provide a protective separation between observer and landscape, and simultaneously a device of aesthetic framing, the olfactory and auditory experience of lines 7–10, by contrast with this visual distancing, obviously enters right into the compartment with the traveller. After the first line, the only manifestation one can detect of the traveller's individual subjectivity is in the metaphoriz-ing activity that gives the telegraph-lines 'l'allure étrange d'un paraphe' and turns train smells and train noises into a hell where giants are endlessly whipped and screech-owls call.

Indifferentiation affects the structure of these verses, too. As the landscape falls into the gulf, so the lines, constantly run-on (separa-tion of subject and verb in ll. 1–2 and ll. 2–3–4) or syntactically extended (by the relative clauses of ll. 5 and 6), seem to be losing their individual identity as alexandrines and to be caught in the same falling motion that blurs water, wheat-fields, trees and sky. This undifferentiated syntax and run-on metrical structure reaches a peak in the lines that discuss the noise and odour of the train (i.e. the moment of greatest threat of indifferentiation for the subject). A single 'sentence' is formed of a paratactic chain of noun-phrases, in which the only connective is 'et' and the nouns are themselves extended by chains of possessives ('une odeur de charbon ... et d'eau', 'des cris prolongés de chouette') and/or by repetitive concatenations of relative clauses ('charbon qui brûle ... eau qui bout', 'le bruit que feraient ... au bout/Desquelles ... qu'on fouette'). Such a monstrous sentence is endlessly flexible: it could go on for ever, like the suffering of the titans under the whip or the 'cris *prolongés*' of the locomotive–'chouette'. At the same time, our sense of the integrity of the alexandrine metre is subverted, not only by enjambment, but also by very flexible internal caesurae.[16]

But the quatrain of lines 7–10 does not only intensify the 'danger' of the landscape by bringing it into the compartment; it also introduces a complementary theme. If that of the landscape description is indifferentiation (a form of entropy, as the breaking down of distinctions), it is entropy as the threat of *disorder* that forms the theme of these four lines (interestingly, 'entropy' is a notion we owe to the science of thermodynamics, which developed initially as a theory of the energetics of the steam engine). Noise is a pollution of the auditory environment as the odour of soot and steam pollutes the air, and if desire for 'order' is a mark of bourgeois life (it was an important political slogan of the Second Empire), we can begin to understand that the thematics of suffering expressed by the chained giants under the whip derives from increased disorder experienced by the subject as a threatened *loss of control*. (Nineteenth-century train travellers were as uncomfortably aware of the possibility of catastrophe, through derailment or collision, as are twentieth-century air travellers.) And, of course, the poetic discourse demonstrates its own version of 'noise' and 'disorder' here by such 'clumsinesses' as weak rhyme ('bout' and 'bout'), prominent repetitions ('qui brûle ... qui bout', 'feraient mille chaînes ... hurleraient mille géants') and intrusive alliterations and assonances ('brûle ... bout ... bruit ... bout,' 'que feraient ... qu'on fouette,' 'tout à coup') – all rhetorical features that are meaningful to the extent that they violate the rules of classical taste, as that which is 'beau', 'noble' and 'sonore'.

Finally, the quatrain develops the metaphor of 's'engouffrant' (l. 4) into a full-fledged inferno: a hell that has classical features (tormented giants, fire and steam, screeching night-birds) but is essentially a modern one, not simply because it metaphorizes industrial experience but also because it represents an assault on the order and control of the 'autonomous' subject, here threatened with an indifferentiation of its own, through being engulfed in the all-engulfing world of disorder. As visual blurring and sensory pollution, 'hell' is that which threatens the 'purity' of the self.

That is why the insistent appearance of the linguistic subject in lines 11–13 ('Que *me* fait . . .'; j'ai dans les yeux'; '*mon* cœur'; 'pour *moi*') – insistent especially by contrast with the only 'spectral' presence of that subject in the previous lines – is so significant. What constitutes the 'pivot' of the poem in its 'illocutionary' context is a firm affirmation of subjecthood on the part of the threatened subject of the earlier lines. This appearance in the poem of the word 'je' (and related forms) is at least as significant as the images of the other to which the subject now attributes his salvation (the 'blanche vision', the 'douce voix', the 'Nom si beau'). Indeed, it is observable that these images are significant only insofar as they positively affect the subject: the vision 'fait mon cœur joyeux', the voice murmurs 'pour moi', the Name introduces *suavité* into the 'rhythme du wagon brutal'. Their function, then, is to strengthen him in his 'indifference' to the threatening world that surrounds him, and so to act as a kind of protective agent or cushioning against that world.

But consequently, the retreat of the subject into the mental world where his imagination furnishes comforting and centring imagery is replete with ironies. First, the subject constructs himself as an autonomous and stable identity only by a kind of appropriation of an *other*, the vision of whom protects him against the nightmarish visual world as her 'douce voix' contrasts with the shrieks and howls of the train, while her noble and sonorous Name (with all the permanence and centrality suggested by the capital letter) reassures him after the strange mobility of a landscape which 'court furieusement' and of the 'paraphe' formed by the telegraph-lines, with their 'allure étrange' ('allure' derives from the verb 'aller'). That this other on whom the subject's identity depends is a woman (a fact deducible, as I have suggested, from the codes used to describe her) might suggest to us, of course, a whole commentary on the *place*(ment) of middle-class women in the nineteenth century: idealized and idolized as a bolster, or cushioning, for a male ego significantly threatened by the harsh conditions of capitalist modernity, they were made to occupy a place of stability that functioned, for them, as a confinement. But also, we can now better understand the ambivalence of a 'monologue' that is simultaneously a 'pseudo-apostrophe': does the subject centre on 'je' or on 'tu'? and if the true centre is in the other, what does that do to the subject's apparent centring on his own self?

The other main irony arises from the fact that the subject defends himself against the threat of indifferentiation by a *declaration of indifference*. To be 'indifferent' to the industrialized environment is, for him, the condition of self-salvation by appropriation of the feminized world of *blancheur, douceur*, beauty, nobility ... etc., and of course purity, the world he sets up as opposed to it. But this is at the same time an acknowledgement of the power of that indifferentiating environment created by industrialization, of its power to swallow up individual subjects in its gulf and make them 'indifferent' too. And we can notice that the irony of a subject escaping indifferentiation by an affirmation of self as the site of indifference (that is, by repeating and prolonging the indifferentiation) is inscribed also in the *facture* of the poem itself. For we are now, theoretically, in a centred world of purity and sonorousness, and not surprisingly the structure of the alexandrines has become much more regular while the syntax, with its thrice repeated 'puisque' (ll. 11, 13, 14), has acquired an armature of logic and rationality. But perhaps the very repetitiousness of the 'puisque' conveys some sense of anxiety; for it is noticeable that the techniques we observed in the opening description have nevertheless carried over into this section. There are new enjambments (ll. 11–12 and 14–15), new systems of verbal assonance ('joyeux ... voix ... pour moi'; 'murmure'; 'sonore; 'tout ce tournoiement'), and – yes – in the last two lines, a new disordering of the alexandrine structure through the strong punctuation that introduces non-metrical pauses (after the third syllable of l. 15 and the eighth of l. 16).

True, our experience of poetic redundancy induces us now to *interpret* these effects differently: the enjambments function to express the *solidarity* of the subject's mind ('j'ai dans les yeux') and 'la blanche vision' that occupies it, or the *mingling* of the 'Nom si beau, si noble et si sonore' with the 'rhythme du wagon brutal'. The assonances are expressive of the sonority and musical sweetness of the beloved's voice, as opposed to the noise of the train; while the breaking up of the individual alexandrines of lines 15–16 produces an evident effect of symmetry and so of stabilization ... But, in the context of the whole poem, these differing effects can be seen to be produced by techniques that nevertheless tend toward indifferentiation (assonance and enjambment) and disorder (enjambment and internal disturbance of the alexandrine). Like the subject's indifference, the beloved's visual and sonorous representation, and the cries of the 'chouette' (mentioned, significantly, just before the poem 'turns'), these effects introduce a *prolongation* of the atmosphere of the first section into the final section of the poem. The poem talks reassuringly of a *suavité* mingling with the brutality of the train; but it enacts itself as brutality carried over into its own production of *suavité*. So there is a blur in this second part of the poem – has the subject defined himself, or not, by indifferentiation? has he centred himself, or centred on the other? has the poem enacted a change in mood or a continuation of the initial situation? – that corresponds to the blurring of identity through partial identification of subject and object (observer and environment) in the early part, and so puts in doubt the salvation 'je' seems to claim.

Notice, then, that my initial expectation about the poem in its 'illocutionary' context has had to be somewhat modified as a result of my reading. The 'pivot' produced a centred subject, as predicted, but ironized that subject in such a way that we were led to see the poem *prolonging* itself as well as *turning* on its pivot. The pivot functioned, therefore, not only as a centring moment but also as a mere connective, something like what in railroad engineering is called a 'tie' – an image suggested visually by those two dashes. In turning to the second pivot in the poem, which I hypothesize as the centre point of the poem in its 'textual' function, I will therefore want to bear in mind – or test the hypothesis – that this pivot may function not simply as an agency of mingling (as I first posited) but more specifically – as is now suggested – as a *connective* in the poem conceived as a linear series.

Can a pivot functioning as a 'tie' produce mingling? If so, how? And what are the implications for subjecthood of such a conception of the pivotal function in discourse? We have seen that the function of the pivot as a centralizing mechanism has been to comfort the subject in its own sense of autonomous identity. But we have also seen that 'centred' subject centring itself in the Name of another, and thus becoming the site of a blurred or 'mingled' identity ('je' + 'tu'). And clearly, the process of seeking one's own identity in another('s) Name has the potential of dissolving that identity into an endless chain of language (for where does the identity of the other reside, except in the Name of yet another?, and so on). So a subject may be more like a link in a chain, a 'tie', than a central 'pivot'.

Occurring as it does in the middle of the indivisible syntactic unit 'au bout/Desquelles', the second pivot, although it is, in metric terms, at the exact centrepoint of the poem, has very clearly the function of a 'tie' in the linear series of verses; and where the centring vision is described as 'blanche' and the pivot as 'pur', the linear pivot is not described, but produced in the poem, as a purely rhythmic entity, 'blank' and 'pure' in its own way. As the tie in the track produces the characteristic clickety-clack of train wheels, the pivot here is a component – indispensable albeit well-nigh indiscernible – of the 'rhythme du wagon brutal'. But the metaphor produced in the poem for such a linear rhythm, 'tied' together at regular intervals by a marker that divides it into repetitive segments, is not in fact that of the tie, but of the telegraph-poles (whose slenderness is commented on), and of the telegraph-lines that resemble a form of writing, a 'paraphe'.

One of the things the poem is doing at its central pivot is putting ends together, putting lines *bout à bout*. The perverse rhyming of the word 'bout' in two different senses (ll. 7–8), combined with the fact that the word 'bout' (meaning 'end') occurs not at the end of anything but, to the contrary, at the pivotal point in the poem and simultaneously in the middle of a sentence that is constructed (as we have seen) as a concatenation of end-to-end phrases, tells us, I think, two things. It tells us to look in the poem for a linear construction joining identical (or undifferentiated) segments end-to-end by 'pure', 'blank' pivots (as, for example, in all the cases of enjambment, but also as in the way the second part of the poem repeats and prolongs, in significant and ironic ways, its first part). But it tells us also to look for some difference in the linear structure, a movement or development, for example, or perhaps simply a change (like the 'change' between 'bout' in l. 7 and 'bout' in l. 8), that would be a change-in-similarity (corresponding to the similarity-in-change produced by the poem's *prolongement*).

Such a change, or development, if we take the two equal segments produced in the poem and placed end-to-end by its pivot at lines 8–9, might be the one that enables the 'tourbillon cruel' of line 4 to become something considerably less threatening, although still incorporating the 'same' dizzying turning motion, when it is described in line 15 as 'tout ce tournoiement'. What has produced the change? Presumably the admixture (or mingling) of *suavité* that has come with the thought of the 'blanche vision', the 'douce voix' and the 'Nom si beau'. But what provoked *that* thought was itself the direness and extremity of the suffering described at and around the central pivotal point of the poem: the odours, noise and torture of the giants which we have already read as expressive of the subject's own 'hell', threatened as he is with indifferentiation. In other words, the passage from 'tourbillon' to 'tournoiement' hinges or pivots on (is mediated by) a word ('tourment') which is not explicitly used but is irresistibly evoked by the poem, as a 'pure', 'blank' pivot at its centre.[17] 'Tournoiement' combines the 'tour-' of 'tourbillon' (and 'tourment') with the '-ment' of 'furieusement' and 'suavement' (and 'tourment' again), plus perhaps the '-oi' of 'la ... voix pour moi ...': in this respect, the movement of the poem depends on a word which, like a pivot, occurs centrally, but does so like a tie, in a way that is indiscernible although indispensable. And – like the relation of 'furieusement' and 'suavement' – the relation of 'tourbillon' and 'tournoiement' describes the two halves of the poem as similar but changed. The poem charges through its central pivot, as if it was scarcely there; and yet, it turns on it too. Where we were forced to notice of the pivot at ll. 10–11 that, although the poem turns on it, it also serves as a mere point of prolongation, here we make the complementary observation that the pivot at ll. 8–9 functions as a 'prolonging' tie, on which the poem nevertheless turns. In that sense, it is the operator of the desirable mingling (incorporating an element of *suavité* into the brutality) that the poem craves.

But this combination of similarity and movement, of linearity and change, that describes the poem's structure, is also exactly what the two lines (5–6) devoted to the telegraph describe. The regular and rapid 'fall' of the slim poles is a metaphor for a poem constructed in linear fashion (line by line, segment by segment) but 'speeded up' (notably by enjambment) in such a way that its segments 'fall' into each other and mingle, so as to form something recognizable as a mode of writing (having 'l'allure étrange d'un paraphe'). And the fact that they are telegraph-poles suggests that such a poetic model is being produced as a characteristically 'modern' one.

The 'telegraph' is the industrialized form of writing and communication that corresponds to the industrialized mode of travel that is the railroad. The two inventions, historically speaking, implied and supported each other; and the reason the telegraph-lines ran parallel to the track was that the railway could not operate without such a signalling system. Is the poem perhaps describing itself as *running parallel* to the railway experience it is describing, and part of the same system, rather than directly modelling itself on the train? Notice too that the 'tele-graph' is long-distance writing, a mode of speedy communication across space that corresponds to the speedy transportation the train made possible; and we can think in this connection of the 'hurry' in the poem's enjambed lines, but also of the relevance to literature (as a discourse that does not know its audience) of modern inventions – of which the telegraph was the ancestor – that permit 'telecommunication', i.e. communication without contact. Finally, it is surely significant that the telegraph relies on abbreviated messages and on the employment of a 'code': the poem is perhaps instructing us that, in order to read it as its distant audience, we need to learn its own speeded-up code, so that it can be read as a telegraphic message about the conditions of modernity.

But the telegraph, as a figure of the poem's 'rhythme ... brutal', resolves into a 'paraphe', with its 'allure étrange', i.e. into a figure of movement in writing or even the writing of movement. Dictionaries tell us that 'paraphe' can be translated as 'initials' (it is an abbreviated signature), and in this sense it stands in obvious (similarity and) contrast with the word 'Nom' of line 14. Incomplete, cursive and hasty, where the Name is complete, whole and stable, the 'paraphe' is a *series of letters* (it is linear), whereas the Name is a single (centred) *word*. Moreover, a 'paraphe' is usually a kind of rapid scrawl or squiggle, a cursory gesture in the direction of writing a name, that is neither a full signature nor even a legible series of letters. It is the *coded* representation of a name – itself symbolic of subjecthood and identity – but *speeded up* and blurred together, so that the name has become all but indecipherable, and the writing takes on a graphic visibility of its own. Finally a 'paraphe' (etymologically akin to *paragraph*, a 'writing beside') is, like the telegraph with respect to the train, a writing that is marginal(ized). It could be described, then, as an adaptation to the signature, as the writing of identity, of the principle of the (abbreviated, coded, speeded up, depersonalized) telegraph, running alongside the train-tracks. A poem that describes itself as the *naming* of a subject is very different, then, from a poem that describes itself as a 'paraphe', whose subject may be only dimly discernible in the blur of writing. The Verlaine poem, however, does both.

For the brutality of the 'paraphe' is not incompatible with the *suavité* of the Name. A 'paraphe' is always recognizable, and has legal status, as characteristic of an individual person, and hence as a kind of signature. It is just that the subject is present in the 'paraphe' much like the 'pivot' that ties together two enjambed lines of poetry, or two lengths of rail: it 'falls away' into the engulfing movement like the telegraph-poles on which the 'paraphe' of the lines is strung. Such a subject is an indispensable principle of continuity and rhythm (holding the rails or the segments of 'paraphe' together), but is virtually indistinguishable from what 'runs' by in linear series and falls into nothingness. We have seen that, but for the distance implied by the 'cadre des portières', something similar is true of the observer in the train with respect to the fleeting landscape. Just so, the subject disappears into a 'paraphe' whose characteristic 'rhythm' still, somehow, *names* that subject.

So the 'paraphe' mingles something of the *suavité* of the Name it alludes to with the brutality of the 'rhythme du wagon' that it figures, and which is so threatening to the subject. As a result, a kind of complementarity can now be seen between the poem in its 'illocutionary' (centred) mode and the (linear) 'textuality' figured by the 'paraphe'. As fictive speech act, the poem centres the subject but ironically undermines that centring in a number of ways; in its self-representation as linear writing, the poem disperses the subject, but still produces it as readable in the 'signature' – however abbreviated and cursory – that is its writing. Thus the linearity of the poem, imaged by the chains and whips at its pivotal *centre*, allows for a certain centring of identity, while the circularity, evoked specifically (as 'tourbillon' and 'tournoiement') at the two extremes of its linear, *bout à bout* structure, undermines the centring by reinscribing it in a linear system. As a result, the poem exists as an unresolved tension – and a kind of blur – between two systems: the 'illocutionary' system that seeks a centre in the world dynamized as a 'tourbillon' or a 'tournoiement', but leads instead into the 'textual' system in which the linear motion of headlong speed produces an effect of falling away that nevertheless still forms a 'paraphe', a form of signature in which a Name and a subject remain readable, and centring can therefore still be attempted ... In short the blurring of identity that is the poem's 'subject' (in more senses of that word than one) is produced as a *blur in the poem*, since the text centres, *simultaneously*, on two different 'pivots' that do not coincide: the pivot of its linearity at lines 8–9 and the pivot of its 'tournoiement' at lines 10–11.[18]

Or perhaps, rather than a blur, it would be more appropriate to speak of a vertigo or dizziness, of the 'falling' sensation that is alluded to here by the poem's combination of headlong speed and whirling landscape, of linearity and turning. For vertigo is the sensation of falling *without falling down*, of falling without a stop – and the poem, as an unresolved tension and hence an endless exchange, in both directions, between its two reciprocally complementary discursive systems, similarly cannot 'fall', but cannot stop falling. It enacts in this way what is certainly the major dilemma of modern literary sensibility: the non-coincidence of the subject with itself, resulting from an inability either to believe or not to believe in the autonomy of the human 'self'.[19] In miming the dizzying sensation of train travel, the poem simultaneously situates itself, and produces for us its own significance, as a discursive exemplification of the vertigo of being modern.

NOTES

1 The poem is number seven of the twenty-one that form the collection *La Bonne Chanson*, written during the winter of 1869–70 and published in 1870. I follow Jacques Robichez's 'Classiques Garnier' edition (Paris, 1969), as does Jean Chaussivert in *L'Art verlainien dans 'La Bonne Chanson'* (Paris, 1973), in dividing between ll. 10 and 11. The reasons why I support this division, which was obscured in early editions because it fell at the foot of a page, will become obvious.

2 'Discourse' here means language in use, and hence defined in, and by, the situation in which it is used, as well as defining that situation.

3 For a recent introduction to psychoanalytic criticism, see Elizabeth Wright, *Psychoanalytic Criticism* (London/New York, 1984). On the 'political unconscious', see Frederic Jameson, *The Political Unconscious* (Ithaca, NY, 1981).

4 See Michael Riffaterre, *The Semiotics of Poetry* (Bloomington, Indiana, 1978).

5 See 'Linguistics and Poetics', in *Style in Language*, ed. T. A. Sebeok (Cambridge, MA, 1960), pp. 350–77.

6 The so-called 'hermeneutic circle' is associated with the work of Hans Georg Gadamer; see his *Truth and Method* (New York, 1975), originally in German as *Wahrheit und Methode* (Tübingen, 1960).

7 On the 'fictive' discourse situation in poetry, see especially Barbara Herrnstein Smith, *On the Margins of Discourse: the Relation of Literature to Language* (Chicago, 1978), esp. chapter 2 ('Poetry as fiction'), pp. 14–40. (I have reservations, however, about her category of 'natural discourse'.)

8 See Jonathan Culler, 'Apostrophe', in *The Pursuit of Signs: Semiotics, Literature, Deconstruction* (Ithaca, NY, 1981), pp. 135–54.

9 See Pierre Fontanier, *Les Figures du discours* (Paris, 1968), p. 371.

10 'Illocutionary' because the term implies a speech-act, and hence the relevance of the agents 'I' and 'you'; 'context' because 'I' and 'you' are best thought of, however, as linguistic slots by which discourse defines itself as a vehicle of social exchange (of information), and so produces its own context.

11 See Franc Schuerewegen, 'Réflexions sur le narrataire', *Poétique*, 70

(1986–7), pp. 247–54; and 'Le Texte du narrataire', *Texte*, 5/6 (1986–7), pp. 211–23.

12 Biographically speaking, we know that the poems of *La Bonne Chanson* were written for Mathilde Mauté, who was Verlaine's fiancée at that time. Her medieval-sounding name (in poem VIII, it is a 'nom Carlovingien') certainly overdetermines the contrast readable in the poem between tradition ('Le Nom si beau, si noble et si sonore') and modernity.

13 Students of French should note that the word is now spelled without the first 'h': 'rythme'.

14 The information in this paragraph derives from Wolfgang Schievelbusch, *The Railway Journey: The Industrialization of Time and Space in the Nineteenth Century* (Berkeley, California, 1986), originally in German as *Geschichte der Eisenbahnreise* (Munich, 1977).

15 'Verse' is from Latin *versus*, designating the turn or swing of the plough at the end of a furrow.

16 For detailed metrical analysis of these lines, see Chaussivert, *L'Art verlainien*, p. 35; and *cf.* his remark, 'Ce n'est pas un affaiblissement mais une anarchie du rythme ...'

17 A reader of my draft called this point critical 'sleight-of-hand'. What do you think?

18 For a complementary account of the blurring of social identities in this period and its impact on 'impressionist' art, see T. J. Clark, *The Painting of Modern Life: Paris in the Art of Manet and his Followers* (London, 1985); and *cf.* Christopher Prendergast's review, 'Blurred Identities: The Painting of Modern Life', *French Studies*, 40, 4 (1986), pp. 401–12.

19 For a series of careful studies of comparable ambivalences in mid-nineteenth-century writing, see Nathaniel Wing, *The Limits of Narrative: Essays on Baudelaire, Flaubert, Rimbaud and Mallarmé* (Cambridge, 1986).

10

SYLLEPTIC SYMBOLS: RIMBAUD'S 'MEMOIRE'

Michael Riffaterre

I

L'eau claire; comme le sel des larmes d'enfance,
L'assaut au soleil des blancheurs des corps de femmes;
la soie, en foule et de lys pur, des oriflammes
sous les murs dont quelque pucelle eut la défense;

5 l'ébat des anges; – Non ... le courant d'or en marche,
meut ses bras, noirs, et lourds, et frais surtout, d'herbe. Elle
sombre, ayant le Ciel bleu pour ciel-de-lit, appelle
pour rideaux l'ombre de la colline et de l'arche.

II

Eh! l'humide carreau tend ses bouillons limpides!
10 L'eau meuble d'or pâle et sans fond les couches prêtes.
Les robes vertes et déteintes des fillettes
font les saules, d'où sautent les oiseaux sans brides.

Plus pure qu'un louis, jaune et chaude paupière
le souci d'eau – ta foi conjugale, ô l'Epouse! –
15 au midi prompt, de son terne miroir, jalouse
au ciel gris de chaleur la Sphère rose et chère.

III

Madame se tient trop debout dans la prairie
prochaine où neigent les fils du travail; l'ombrelle
aux doigts; foulant l'ombelle; trop fière pour elle;

20   des enfants lisant dans la verdure fleurie

leur livre de maroquin rouge! Hélas, Lui, comme
mille anges blancs qui se séparent sur la route,
s'éloigne par delà la montagne! Elle, toute
froide, et noire, court! après le départ de l'homme!

IV

25   Regret des bras épais et jeunes d'herbe pure!
Or des lunes d'avril au cœur du saint lit! Joie
des chantiers riverains à l'abandon, en proie
aux soirs d'août qui faisaient germer ces pourritures!

Qu'elle pleure à présent sous les remparts! l'haleine
30   des peupliers d'en haut est pour la seule brise.
Puis, c'est la nappe, sans reflets, sans source, grise:
un vieux, dragueur, dans sa barque immobile, peine.

V

Jouet de cet œil d'eau morne, je n'y puis prendre,
ô canot immobile! oh! bras trop courts! ni l'une
35   ni l'autre fleur: ni la jaune qui m'importune,
là; ni la bleue, amie à l'eau couleur de cendre.

Ah! la poudre des saules qu'une aile secoue!
Les roses des roseaux dès longtemps dévorées!
Mon canot, toujours fixe; et sa chaîne tirée
40   Au fond de cet œil d'eau sans bords, – à quelle boue?

✳✳✳

Symbolist poetry resists interpretation, because symbols remain
independent from any recognizable trope or figure, and thus elude
those critical approaches that have evolved from rhetorical analysis.
Even the distinction between figurative and literal discourse does
little to help, since words can symbolize while keeping their literal
acceptation. In extreme cases, words can symbolize without any
identifiable or specific symbolism of their own, representing instead
the symbolic stance itself, the mere assumption that signs stand for
something other than they appear to, and yet still convey their
expected meanings. This elusiveness alone would make the readers'
task daunting. In the case of Rimbaud, deciphering symbols has

been more problematic because the image of the poet has hidden the poetry and warped its interpretation. The substitution of writers for their writing is a widespread fallacy, but it has raised more obstacles between the readers and Rimbaud's work because of his visibility as a man and as a myth. The scandal surrounding his life, at least in the eyes of his contemporaries, and the aura of his precocious genius, have made the temptation irresistible to explain away textual difficulties as autobiographical allusions, when they actually stem from the semiotic make-up of verbal symbols. A related problem of interpretation arises from the use and abuse of his programmatic pronouncements and of those of his poems that are also manifestoes. The attention lavished on the 'Voyelles' sonnet has long caused critics to try to focus on Rimbaud's practice of synesthesia, when it is but one instance, and in fact a minor one, of his doctrine of *dérèglement de tous les sens*. Conversely, this last formula and others culled from the so-called 'Lettre du Voyant' have served to justify blanket acceptance of any departure from usage, or of non sequitur as a principle of composition, or the rash surmise that open-ended terms like *image* are adequate tools for analysis. Typically one is faced with statements like the following: 'a mere sequence of images, rather than the depiction of a specific scene' (this purports to explain the poem I am about to discuss), only to find that the one specific and therefore usable feature this assertion contains has been taken away in the next paragraph (here, the very concept of sequence from which one might have derived some rule of the poem's particular grammar).[1] Again Rimbaud's most quoted sentence, 'Je est un autre', is taken to authorize any interpretation of the lyric that defines it as the subject's taking over the Other, or conversely as the otherness of the subject. The main point of the phrase is dismissed as a stylistic emphasis, while this point (the discrepancy between a first-person subject and a verb in the third person) could be used independently of its content, thus safely free of any intentional fallacy, as a formal model for one of Rimbaud's syntactic idiosyncrasies.

My aim here is to focus on the text's formal features. No interpretation of a poem, it seems to me, can ever be specific and reliable unless based on such features. No generalization towards a definition of Rimbaud's manner can be made without such analyses as its preconditions. To that end, I have chosen a poem from *Derniers Vers*, 'Mémoire', whose obscurity is unanimously judged typical of Rimbaud, an obscurity however that all critics attempt wrongly to solve through autobiographical 'evidence'. In contradistinction to this (the easy option which is also irresponsible since it authorizes just about any hypothesis), obscurity should be seen as an index pointing to its own keys, the reason being that it controls the readers' attention and restricts their freedom of fancy. Indeed, hermeneutic hurdles, far from permitting random guesses, clearly define the areas where usage is challenged and our linguistic competence defeated. It thus forces readers to participate creatively rather than react passively. It harnesses the thrust of their efforts through a limited number of options, itself further and further limited by other hurdles to come.

'Mémoire' is especially representative for two reasons: reactions to it exemplify critics' behaviour in Rimbaud's case, and the poem itself exemplifies his writing strategies. As regards critics' behaviour: for those who know Rimbaud's life, the beginning of the poem seems to refer to the landscape around his birthplace, Charleville; the allusions to an authoritarian mother, and to her desertion by the father, coincide with the poet's family life; and the let-down at the end, when the rowboat has run aground in the mud or is anchored in still water, is consistent with Rimbaud's claustrophobic childhood. Critics are fond of pointing to similar passages in poems like 'Les Poètes de sept ans', 'Les Assis', and above all 'Bateau ivre', from which recurrence they infer that the theme's frequency is explained by the author's bitter experience. But of course the likelihood that the above is true still does not mean that it plays a role in our reading and appreciation of the poem. If we needed outside information to evaluate the poem's truth, the poem would therefore be somehow deficient. If the poem is in fact effective, convincing, and consistent with a title such as, say, 'Childhood's Memories', it is because the poem's system of verisimilitude is self-sufficient, not because it happens to be verifiable through means of information exterior to it. The only reliable criterion for judgement of the mimesis of a life is to decide whether that representation is explicitly autobiographical. In this case, it is not: most landscapes offer rivers and towns; what we do know of Madame Rimbaud (née Cuif) makes it unlikely that she pursued her errant husband, an event some critics insist is recounted in part III of the poem. Finally, the recurrence of the theme may or may not be explained by its reflecting the author's experience, but its effect on the reader is sufficiently accounted for by that recurrence itself and by its being a recognizable stereotype. On the other hand, if autobiographical representation is not explicit, the only acceptable critical position is that autobiography is precisely what the poem avoids, and that it must remain irrelevant to the poem's impact.

As for the writing strategies I have alluded to, they are:

(1) A systematic challenge to literary conventions, such as lexical restrictions excluding certain words from poetic use, and the privileging of tropes. These conventions inherited from French classicism were hardly disturbed by the romanticists despite their claims to the contrary. The rules differentiating between prose and verse in particular are abolished. In this respect 'Mémoire' is half-way between the discursive features of traditional verse and the prose poem to which Rimbaud would eventually turn as the only form suitable for his writing.

(2) The prevalence of verbal humour, both as the principal device for challenging convention, and as a substitute for the formal features of verse.

(3) An overdetermination of the verbal sequence, to compensate for the previous two categories. It is mostly achieved through verbal equivalences and tautological paradigms that visibly structure the text and make up for the loss of metre and rhetorical forms. Readers become aware of paradigms by dint of repetition or of variation on a topic within the text or through intertextuality.

(4) A referential circularity, whereby the sign–object reference may be reversed; in particular, a circularity peculiar to symbolism that prevents readers from deciding which is figurative and which is literal. The text becomes a double-entry system in which the compared and the comparing trade functions in a merry-go-round of undecidability.

'Mémoire' in fact unfolds two parallel series of images, the components of one alternating with those of the other, one describing a river, one a family or rather a woman now seen as a wife and now as a mother. Both series are commented upon by a first-person narrative voice. The reader is hard put to decide whether the river is a part of the setting or stage for that family's life, or whether it represents that family metaphorically, or whether on the contrary the family is not in fact a metaphorical code, an artful conceit to represent the river.

For the sake of clarity, or rather to identify the shifts from one image to the next, and figure out what may motivate these shifts and lead to some common factor that may open on to an interpretation, I shall sketch the to-and-fro swinging from one sequence to the next:
Description of the river in black and white (ll. 1–6).
Description of the river as a bedroom (ll. 7–8).
The river as a family scene (ll. 9–12).
The river and the sun it reflects depicted as man and wife (ll. 13–16),
    or: man and wife depicted as the sun mirroring itself in the river.
An actual family scene: an outing on the river-bank (ll. 17–21).
Sunset: the river as abandoned wife (ll. 21–4).
The past, or: bittersweet memories in a river landscape (ll. 25–30),
    alternating between regret (ll. 25, 29–30) and happy recollections
    (ll. 26–8).
Today, or: despondency and powerlessness depicted as stagnant
    water (ll. 31–40).

In the first three stanzas, the river is real but represented through an accumulation of figurative language (ll. 1–12). In stanza 4, either the river is metaphorized once more, or a couple, or a sexual relationship, is metaphorized as a river (ll. 13–16). In stanza 5, the family seems literal enough (ll. 17–21). In stanza 6, a scene of parting is metaphorized as sunset on the river (ll. 21–4). The last four stanzas clearly tell the story of a life, opposing the past and the present, which are symbolized by a real river.

The first six lines are either metaphorical or symbolic. From then on to line 24, figurative discourse seems metaphorical because equations are explicitly posited between one set of representations and another (e.g. ll. 7–8). No such equations can be drawn afterwards, and life and river are equally literal. Their parallel descriptions make the latter symbolize the former.

And now for a quick overview of the poem's repeated challenges to convention. These may not be easily related to the symbolism of the whole, or even to separate symbols. But it will soon be apparent

that the humour attendant on these gestures debunking the literariness of tradition also functions as the sign pointing to a new
literariness, as an index showing the way to interpretation.

Undermining poetic convention

The departures from conventional forms may not be drastic
enough to fall into the class of *dérèglement de tous les sens*. They
seem rather to extend to the whole (syntax *and* lexicon) of poetic
discourse a principle contrary to Boileau's doctrine of 'le mot juste
mis en sa place' which was to remain until World War I the
cornerstone of 'good' writing.

Colloquial or even vulgar forms are used where verse would have
permitted only normal, guarded usage, or literary discourse. 'En
foule' (l. 3) for instance, instead of 'beaucoup' is either vulgar or
schoolchild's talk. Verlaine uses it in the kind of poems half-way
between written formalism and spoken colloquialism that were to
culminate in the verse version of realism made popular by François
Coppée.[2] Similarly, 'ô l'Epouse' (l. 14) mixes the vulgar form of
address (with the article, instead of the normal or poetic form which
lacks it) and 'ô' of lofty style invocations; again 'Eh! l'humide ...'
(l. 9) replaces with an ejaculation of conversational parlance the *vois*
or *contemple* in the imperative mood that are the conventional
enticements to admire in the lyric.

Clichés are disturbed, a move of unfailing efficacy since the fact of
violating forms engraved complete (as lexicon and grammar
together) in our memory has more of an impact than the tampering
with a rule not yet embodied in a known stereotype. Since *ébats*,
designating a ludic hyperactivity, is used only in the plural, *l'ébat* in
the singular – in 'l'ébat des anges' (l. 5) – underscores its meaning,
emphasizing the usual connection with children at play, and thus
reinforcing the whiteness implicit in angels with the candour that
childhood metonymically suggests.

Lines 11 and 12, 'Les robes vertes et déteintes des fillettes/font les
saules', replace the normal adverbial structure of a comparison such
as 'les robes semblables aux saules'. This traditional way of comparing, the normal trope, would have kept two orders of reality apart
while illustrating one with the other. *Faire*, instead, seems to

comment on an actual transformation, as if language were magic, as if the willows were metamorphosed into little girls or vice versa. 'Déteintes', an adjective from the laundry lexicon that traditional poetic discourse would preclude (as it would 'fillettes', by the way, a word used by mothers or salesmen in children's clothing stores) confirms this actuality with the tawdriness of hand-me-downs. 'Déteintes' also fits the pale green of willows. Add to this the reversal of the expected order of comparison, 'les saules semblables à des robes': the sentence plays at verifying the not quite believable metamorphosis, suggesting a double face of things, an impossibility or illogism defused by comparison but favoured by symbol.

The mimesis of water transparency has been a favourite locus of descriptive poetry ever since the Latin pastoral. 'L'humide carreau tend ses bouillons limpides' (l. 9) at once continues this tradition and parodies it, recalling a classical phraseology that was still common-place as late as the 1830s. Nodier speaks of 'onde limpide qui roule son cristal liquide', Sainte-Beuve of a fountain's 'humides vitraux', of 'l'onde aux mobiles vitraux'.[3] Rimbaud creates a humorous stylistic clash by substituting the humble everyday windowpane for words high in a scale of prestigious associations, like *cristal* and *vitrail*. He underscores the contrast by keeping the classical epithets 'humide'[4] and 'limpides' which remind readers that *cristal* and *vitrail* are metaphors for water. He exacerbates the effect of his device with a further contrast between 'bouillons', a precise and matter-of-fact notation, and the verb 'tendre', which is more appropriate for a flat surface (one stretches a canvas over a frame, a screen across a window) than for bubbling water. It is as if his obvious intention – to achieve accuracy and relevance in the mimesis – could not be fulfilled, whether through classical stereotypes or through realism, without the verbal twist of seemingly gratuitous humour. This twist reminds readers, as verse would, that the text's primary purpose here is to create a verbal artifact rather than merely to depict things, places, and people.

It must be remembered that humour is not destructive, as satire would be. Nor is it a way of saying things *a contrario* as in the case of irony. Humour is a trope, a bizarre and usually comical turn of phrase unmotivated by content, whose very gratuitousness empha-sizes the form given to that content, whether it be tragic or comical, without erasing its seriousness or taking away from its import. Humour compels readers only to a consciousness of form, and of the fact that this form is a constant and is, therefore, capable of indicating that the text belongs to a specific genre. The relationship between humour and content is thus akin to the relationship between metre and content. In both cases, content is emphasized and marked as literary. There is a line in 'Mémoire' that corroborates the fact that this genre-denoting consistency is indeed the function of humour that will eventually enable it to replace verse in the later prose poems. The evidence that humour affects everything evenly in the verbal sequence is an instance in which it modifies forms that are already humorous in language and which, therefore, should be immune to change. 'Les saules, d'où sautent les oiseaux sans brides' (l. 12), obviously a caricature of a phrase like 'the willows from which the free birds take flight', is derived from a humorous colloquial metaphor for pointless and idle endeavours, 'brider les oies', 'to bridle geese' (the helpless court-room clerk in Beaumarchais's *Mariage de Figaro* is named Brid'oison). Rimbaud's transform extracts from the farcical gosling of the colloquial phrase a poetic hyperbole of the soaring bird.

Now the whole mechanism of humour depends upon the readers' ability to contrast the text's twisted wording with its corresponding, normal counterpart in usage. Every unconventional transform presupposes a pre-transformation state of the sentence or phrase indicating a reference to a model displayed in order to be destroyed. This trains the reader to recognize that words have two sides, that they do not just refer semantically to a content, but semiotically to an identical analogon. This awareness then prepares the reader to spot syllepses, the keys to the significance.

Generating symbols

By significance I mean the deeper meaning arrived at by a reading of the whole poem, a meaning that transcends not only the successive senses conveyed by the metaphors, but also the undecidability of what in these is the compared and what is the comparing component. Since undecidability and obscurity prevail in literal and metaphorical meanings alike, significance must be located where these meanings do not hold sway, that is, on the other side of the relevant words, the semantic aspect that is excluded by context and can be retrieved only if we assume some kind of pun. A pun is precisely what syllepsis is, with the difference that perceiving a word-play here is not left to the reader's whim or imposed by our initial perception of the word. Rather it becomes necessary when we look back at it in the light of verbal derivations from it. Syllepsis is the trope that consists in the simultaneous presence of two mutually exclusive meanings for one word. The meaning required by the context preceding the word represses the meaning incompatible with that context. But unless there is a wilful check to that dynamics, repression is compensated for by the generation of a syntagm in which the repressed sense surfaces in various guises. The sylleptic word is thus made to symbolize whatever thought, feeling or act is represented by that resurgence.

Such a resurgence can be phonetic or lexical. If phonetic, the sounds of the matrix, that is, the generating word, are repeated or echoed within derivative words so as to channel the other meaning. If lexical, different words will form a periphrasis of the matrix, but one will be referring to it only from the vantage point of the repressed meaning. In both cases, the derivation is disconcerting since it issues from the 'wrong' content. In both cases, it is overdetermined and therefore compelling because it is tautological or repetitive.

Instances of the phonetic derivation may be approximate and have been mistaken for mere alliterations.[5] Such seems to be the fact for 'les roses des roseaux dès longtemps dévorées' (l. 38). And yet the symbol, which will be the third of a series, is born here on the model of the previous line, in which the departing bird shaking down the dust of foliage provides a second symbol for the melancholy that is already represented a first time by the still water.[6] To top the first two with a more emotionally charged version, the river is made to produce beauty only for it to be symbolically destroyed. That is why *roses* are extracted from water reeds only to be devoured.

A major crux in the poem results from phonetic derivation. It remains an obstacle to comprehension, because it depends on an audible enactment of the pun rather than on the customary silent reading of the text. It is only when we say the word aloud that we have to decide between two competing oral renditions of its spelling. In 'la prairie/prochaine où neigent les fils du travail' (ll. 17–18), the cliché 'sons of toil' or 'sons of labour' to speak of the proletariat demands that we voice the final 's' of 'fils', but then we are stuck with the incompatible verb. If, on the other hand, the 's' is not voiced, 'fils', 'threads', fits the snow image, for in this sense it alludes to newly-woven linen or sheets that used to be spread on meadows to be bleached snow-white by the sun. That was before chemical bleaching was invented, and that picturesque scene was a literary cliché. Rimbaud doubles the word's evocative power by conflating the weavers and the woven fabric under one spelling for two sounds.[7]

Lexical derivation, however, is much more productive since it is not restricted to phonetic iteration. 'Le souci d'eau' (l. 14) is the marsh marigold, but its allegorical metamorphosis into an eye looking with bitter envy at the sun, its celestial rival, develops from its homonym that the watery context eliminates, 'souci' as 'worry'. This homonym also causes the speaker in the poem to reject the marigold as 'la (fleur) jaune qui m'importune' (l. 35). The clause 'the yellow flower that worries (or bothers) me' is the literal periphrasis of the psychological 'souci'. It is no wonder then that such devious overdeterminations create the temptation of autobiographical reference. As long as we do not perceive that a latent homonymy, uncovered only by derivation, is the sole root of the symbol, the apparently unmotivated 'qui m'importune' can only be rationalized away as a private whim. Any unexplained preference would seem to belong in the semiotic system of a character's mental set-up.

Because the device's generative potential is limited only by the number of available synonymous phrasings, its repercussions can spread through the whole work, producing the two major symbols on which the poem rests.

The image of the river as a bedroom, and its corollary, the river's being indifferently depicted as a stream and as the wife that an exemplary or hyperbolic or just conventional literary bedroom (a connubial one) of necessity entails, both issue from the *lit* syllepsis. The same word in French, and in English as well, may be a river bed or a bed for two. From Virgil choosing *thalamus*, the poetic term for a newlywed's couch, when he speaks of a river, to a French folkloric song putting lovers to sleep in the river bed, the *double entendre* opportunity has been exploited again and again, no doubt because the lexical repression here coincides with a psychological one. Any word whose other side lends itself to sexual fantasies multiplies tenfold its imagistic potential. Another factor, of course, facilitates the derivation: the presence of a theme from erotic poetry in which the verdant recesses of the forest are described as a natural bedroom. Rimbaud's 'Jeune ménage' provides an example of this.

Finally, but with the widest impact yet, the very title of the poem sylleptically generates its central image, and makes it possible, indeed imperative, for the river to symbolize memory. From the start, readers may have sensed a vague but lingering inappropriateness in the title, because *mémoire* designates a mental faculty rather than the images of one's past garnered by that faculty. So much so that the expected title for a poem about reminiscing should be *souvenir*, or even, *remembrance*, which latter Rimbaud selected for another text.[8]

Everything falls into place, however, when it occurs to us that the riverscape is the periphrastic equivalent of a phonetic analogon of *mémoire*: *mes moires*. In its technical sense, *moire* means watered silk or moiré, the top of the line of elegant fabric in interior decorating and in feminine apparel. In its metaphorical sense, though, *moire* designates the shifting play of light on water, silk-like reflections. Rimbaud himself re-translates watery *moires* into the silk of that word's literal definition when he speaks elsewhere of a 'source de soie'.[9]

The syllepsis here is facilitated by a theme identifying life with a river. The course of life is metaphorized by the flow of the current. The river loses itself in the sea, which may be seen as death or infinity. Rowing upstream, back to the source, represents reminiscing. The objects or places reflected in the river are the memories. Unavoidably, such a context brings together *mémoire* and *moire*. There is in fact a poem by Banville which does just that. The only difference from Rimbaud is that the equivalence between the two words, their mutual substitutability, is made explicit by the rhyme instead of being sylleptically repressed:

> Et moi, j'étais plus triste encor
> Lorsque, comme en un fleuve d'or,
> Je remontais dans ma mémoire,

Et que d'un regard triomphant
Je revoyais mes jours d'enfant
Couler d'émeraude et de moire.[10]

As comparisons and rhymes keep apart the very objects they
declare to be similar, the twain may have different functions, as
when a noun and an adjective are paired. 'Moire', 'émeraude' and
'or' are positive signs: they therefore suggest that the memories are
pleasant ones, which makes the present sad by contrast. But if
mémoire as a recollecting self, and *mes moires* as that self's own
'reflections' are one and the same, *moires* cannot assume the
function of an adjectival modifier. Consequently there can be only
one way left to contrast a depressing present to sweet memories, and
that is to replace memories by the present. In terms of the other facet
of the syllepsis, this solution should entail the vanishing of *moires*.
This is indeed what line 31 effects: 'Puis, c'est la nappe, *sans reflets*,
sans source, *grise*'. Water has lost its shimmer, a notation repeated
by 'eau morne' (l. 33), or better still by 'œil d'eau morne', an eye that
does not reflect anything, an unseeing eye. Half a century later, it
will be Paul Valéry's turn to navigate the river of memory. As *his*
oars disturb the *moire*, the wake of the rowboat is said to 'abolir la
mémoire'.[11]

The *mémoire* syllepsis thus differs from the others. Whereas *souci*,
lit and *fils* are single terms repressing similarly single homonyms,
mémoire represses a predication, comprised of a subject (*mes*) and of
a predicate (that subject is reflecting). The equation or mutual
substitution of the two facets is therefore capable of symbolizing,
and it is proven true not because two words are perfect or approximate homonyms, but because one word guarantees, as it were, or
lends the authority of its morphological model to a portmanteau
word, attesting to the grammaticality of the predication it represents
(*mes moires*).

The mechanics of authority here is the same as for Nerval's 'rose
trémière' in 'Artemis'. Nerval's stylistic problem is to solve formally
the oxymoron staked in that poem's first two lines: 'La Treizième
revient ... C'est encor la première; / Et c'est toujours la seule.' The
'mystic' proof that this paradox is true and that his first love, lost
and found again in her thirteenth incarnation, consists in a syllepsis:
'La rose qu'elle tient, c'est la Rose trémière.' At first glance, if the

lover must tell his beloved by the flower she is holding, it is too bad that her rose should be a lowly hollyhock. But the other side of the botanical adjective must be read as a portmanteau merging 'treizième' and 'première'. As a modifier, 'trémière' may indicate that this rose is not a rose. As a compound word invested with the authority of usage, it verifies the identity between the thirteenth and the first, a symbol of love impervious to the passage of time.

Dictating interpretation

When the semiotic system of a poem is so disconcerting, so much at variance with the ways of language, and made outrageously so by the resulting humorous overtones, readers need special guidance to make sense of apparent absurdity.

Two sign systems are at work which over-ride the mimesis, with its web of anomalies and of aberrant representations, and replace the mutilated referentiality of words to things with two structures, one cumulative or paradigmatic, the other narrative. This is not to say that the story so bizarrely told is clarified by amended versions. It is clarified instead by freeing the words of the poem from their anomalous grammar and making them once again meaningful by giving precedence to their significance as variants of a structural invariant over the meanings assigned to them by that grammar.

Both systems are selected by and derived from the syllepsis in the title, now functioning as a matrix. If *mémoire* represents a happy past made to look even better in retrospect by a wretched present, and if *mes moires* analyses *past happiness* versus *present despondency* in terms of a river substituted for the self and of shimmer as a synecdoche substituted for the river as a whole, then every positive representation of the river as shimmering or reflecting light will bespeak memories, and every negative or negated (that is, represented as absent) representation of the same will bespeak the bitterness of their loss.

The first system of hermeneutic guidance, the paradigm system, manifests itself from the first, with the white and black, light and dark versions of the riverscape. The initial impression of the series that goes from 'eau claire' to 'l'ébat des anges' is that of a tumultuous jumble of scenes, not unlike the painting on a medieval retable, with knights fighting under crenellated walls, Joan of Arc, convoluted standards, and in the sky angelic witnesses flying here and there in the Giotto manner. Many attempts have been made at assigning a distinct symbolism to every scene or detail. Indeed the paratactic, unorganized sequence encourages such attempts[12] in a first reading. But when no coherent picture prevails, an unbroken iteration of whiteness and light still unravels Ariadne's thread: 'eau claire', 'le sel des larmes', naked females (and therefore exemplary whitenesses), the lily-white silk of French royalty, another insistent exemplarity, and finally 'pucelle', humorous and thus the climax of the paradigm, since 'quelque pucelle' cancels out Joan of Arc herself, leaving only a virginal essence, that is, a candour that tops the whiteness. The impact of this symphony in white is doubled by the contrasting paradigm of darkness, especially after 'Non!' signals the presence of a writerly or painterly persona hesitating between two versions of his rendition of the river (themselves neatly boxed in between 'l'eau', l. 1, and the bridge, l. 8). 'Courant d'or', however, still subordinates the darkness of the depth to the overwhelming sun playing on water, either a scintillating surface or the shadowy river bottom plumbed by rays of light (curtains are needed, ll. 7–8; 'l'eau meuble d'or pâle', l. 10).

A third paradigm, ll. 25–28, harps upon emotional recollection, either by stating it explicitly ('Regret', l. 25), or by two signs both positive ('Or', l. 26; 'joie', l. 26) but both specifically dated and thus references to the past ('lunes d'avril', l. 26; 'soirs d'août', l. 28).

The depressing present balances all three paradigms with a fourth one that extends from line 31 to the last, a variation on negativity: from 'sans reflets' on, a sequence of extinguished reflections I have already discussed; from 'nappe' and 'sans source', through 'immobile' twice repeated and the multiple caesuras of l. 32, to 'fixe' and 'chaîne' and 'boue', a sequence of allusions to a dying current and to stagnation; from the old man of the river to the speaker unable to reach flowers or the bank from his boat, a declension of images of impotence and *taedium vitae*.

A closer look at the mechanism of the paradigm will show how it can confer symbolic value to all its components without involving tropes in general and metaphors in particular. All members of a paradigm are variants of some invariant. All share a certain function or semantic feature. The aforementioned paradigms, however, are not composed of synonyms or antonyms as most paradigms are. What their components all have in common is a marker, less a semantic feature than a plus or minus sign, an index of negative or positive value. This marker, derived from the matrix title, modifies similarly every word it applies to, irrespective of what this word may represent in isolation or in different contexts. Thus every word so modified becomes a symbol of what the title's latent portmanteau stands for. The shape the marker takes may change but not its function which is defined by the matrix: e.g. in the fourth paradigm, the repetition of 'sans', the implicit opposition that makes 'nappe' and 'immobile' the contraries of 'courant' in 'water' code, etc., all refer to the lack of light and motion signalling the displacement of memories by a tawdry present.

This system is thus free of the limitations of conventional or 'natural' symbols, and free as well of any need to resort to a tropological framework. There is no need for a representation to be figuratively or literally ready to assume a symbolic function. To be symbols, the 'oriflammes' do not have to resemble the play of light on the water. 'Canot immobile' does not have to suggest the absence of *moire*. Nor is there any necessity for the reader to evaluate the symbols before accepting them, as he must when faced with a metaphor. Instead of figurative equivalences that may be questionable as tropes often are, the mere physical fact of the paradigm's iteration is all that has to be perceived, and enacted by reading, for symbolism to operate. Symbolism created thus is performative, and therefore always effective, always safe from readers' misgivings.

All this of course only applies to descriptive discourse, to the mimesis. It cannot apply to the narrative aspects of the poem, namely the story of the wife's misfortune and of her runaway mate, because that episode cannot be derived from the matrix title as one more of its variants. The story is a rationalization, purporting to explain the disappearance of light. We suppose it to be a sunset. But nowhere is it said that the departed husband is the sun, nor can we hypothesize or extract from the text a structural authority for that interpretation.

The matrix which generates the narrative is, as we saw, the *lit* syllepsis. In the same fashion that the weavers and the fruit of their loom were together inscribed in 'fils', the river is at once bedroom and that bedroom's occupant, a woman since the French words for river and water are in the feminine. The logic or continuity of the derivation demands that the reflections on the water be feminine as well. Hence an exchange of gazes between the male sun and the female personification who locks eyes with him. It makes sense that the eye of water, the same eye we will soon find dulled by despair, its sparkle gone after the lover's departure (ll. 33, 40), should be a flower similar in shape and colour to the sun so often pictured as a sunflower. Furthermore, it is an established motif of mythical discourse that flowers have faces and eyes, a whimsy attested to in the naive animism of fairy tales, in the not-so-naive fantasies of Lewis Carroll, in the drawings of Granville, and in Rimbaud's own 'Après le Déluge': 'Oh! ... les fleurs qui regardaient déjà'.

A combination of sexist stereotypes, of a narcissistic mirroring structure, and of the negative connotations of 'souci', translate the gaze of love into one of jealousy. Jealousy in turn generates the portrayal of an overbearing wife and its narrative consequence, her spouse's desertion, and now the abandoned wife in hot pursuit.

Here, however, the superimposition of the fugitive husband on to the retiring sun and of the woman racing after him on to racing water is threatened by the arbitrariness of figurative discourse. For the text's parallel images invite an explicit comparison and soon a metaphor whose arbitrariness is compounded by the tendency of sustained metaphors to veer away from verisimilitude, as their own logic gradually distances them from an initially acceptable given.

This is where a model becomes necessary, an authority – like that of the portmanteau syllepsis – the authority of a reference to an already established wording, to a tableau complete with its ready-made interpretation and its ready-made valorization, to an intertext so familiar that it would be pointless for Rimbaud to name sun and water before metaphorizing them.

The intertext does exist, the explicit counterpart of our text, a sonnet where metaphors are spelled out as a commentary before the fact. It is a poem by Baudelaire which contains all the ingredients of the Rimbaud narrative (see my italics), including the link between memory and light as beauty and a tragic change from luminous recollection to sombre actuality. The sun is an eye already, causing his admirers to swoon. These, a flower and a spring of water, are the very components that 'souci d'eau' will combine into one compound word. Spurned lovers pursue the setting sun (the authority for Rimbaud, ll. 21–4), and a victorious night demotes the landscape to the degraded level of a swamp (the authority for the last three stanzas of 'Mémoire'):

Le Coucher du soleil romantique

> Que le soleil est beau quand tout frais il se lève,
> Comme une explosion nous lançant son bonjour!
> – *Bienheureux celui là qui peut avec amour*
> *Saluer son coucher plus glorieux qu'un rêve!*
> 5 *Je me souviens! J'ai vu tout, fleur, source, sillon,*
> *Se pâmer sous son œil comme un cœur qui palpite ...*
> *– Courons vers l'horizon, il est tard, courons vite,*
> *Pour attraper au moins un oblique rayon!*
>
> *Mais je poursuis en vain le Dieu qui se retire;*
> 10 *L'irrésistible Nuit établit son empire,*
> *Noire, humide, funeste et pleine de frissons;*
>
> Une odeur de tombeau dans les ténèbres nage,
> Et mon pied peureux froisse, au bord du marécage,
> Des crapauds imprévus et de froids limaçons.

Moreover another intertext deep in the unconscious of language lends its authority to the amorous pursuit, guaranteeing that this Baudelaire symbol of anxiety is genuinely rooted in the rituals of the libido. Racing to a hill to catch a last glimpse of the sunset was a practice of nineteenth-century literary lovers, a token of shared emotions. So do Sainte-Beuve's lovers in chapter 16 of *Volupté*, so do lovers chapter after chapter, hill after hill, in Jules Verne's *Le Rayon vert*.

The return from intertext to text is just as overdetermined as are all other transitions in the poem. Indeed, once the intertext's work is done, authority reverts to the sylleptic system. The lover's race in Rimbaud conflates the breathless chase (l. 24) and the river's current ('le courant d'or en marche', l. 5, now hurries up). By being sylleptically identified, anguish and running water 'prove' the aptness of the river symbol, despite the split at the mimetic level which makes 'l'Epouse' run on the road as a woman and in the riverbed as a stream. The linkage of two incompatible scenes is seamless at the very point where visualizing is most difficult.

Making words into things

The wrenching change from happy recollections of the past to the slough of despond of the present is a stereotype of elegy, and that is indeed the genre to which 'Mémoire' belongs. But the interest of the piece rests not on what it is about, but on what it is as a verbal artifact, on the circuitous path that destroys meanings to achieve significance, and cancels out metaphors to create symbols.

Rimbaud's characteristic humour prevents his readers from ever becoming inured to verbal scandal. The rigorous overdetermination of the sylleptic linkages enables each successive image to blossom forth into a full representation, irrespective of those details of the tableau that do not fit into the overall significance of the poem. A descriptive entropy results, an apparently wasteful consumption of mimetic riches which traditional aesthetics would have eliminated as foreign to the topic.

These irrelevancies make it hard for readers to find their way, but that very difficulty increases their dependency on the letter of the text. More importantly, irrelevant derivations increase the feeling of reality, thanks to the verbal scissiparity that makes each syllepsis beget two representations for one word, and a triple persona for one character: the river as water, the river as wife, and that wife's double, 'Madame ... trop debout dans la prairie/prochaine'. Her function is to embody the narrative motivation of the story, thus providing the symbolic lexicon with the syntactic means to shift from meanings to significance. Thus Rimbaud's symbols acquire an opaqueness that is justly recognized as essential to the definition of that category of signs, except that this opaqueness is not the result of their materiality as things, but of their semantic two-ply thickness.

Rimbaud's symbols remain, therefore, equally verbal in their function as signs and in their presence as things, whether we perceive their semiotic or their mimetic side. Indeed, their apparent materiality is a purely linguistic *effet de réel*. It is as if Rimbaud actualized two definitions, at least, for each dictionary entry, or even the encyclopaedic part of that entry. Only the Surrealists will go further than Rimbaud, saturating their texts with automatic writing instead of focussing, as he does, on discrete symbols.

The immediacy of the vision, the grasping together of images that tradition, commonsense and verisimilitude would keep separate, the momentary absurdity we therefore experience when reality seems to crowd our perceptions – all this Rimbaud achieves by using his dictum: 'Je est un autre' as a model for text production. 'Je' is found in the linearity of the verbal sequence, whereas the Other is steeped in the alternate reference systems of textual paradigms and of the intertext.

NOTES

1 'Ces vers assemblent des images' says Antoine Adam after speaking of the 'pure succession d'images', adding self-destructively 'mais il est difficile d'en découvrir le lien', in Rimbaud, *Œuvres complètes*, ed. Antoine Adam (Paris, 1972), p. 944, note 7. *Cf.* R. Etiemble and Y. Gauclère, *Rimbaud* (Paris, 1950), pp. 165–6: 'Rimbaud ne prend pas la peine d'établir un lien entre ces images diverses qui se succèdent en lui à la vue du souci' (l. 13). The assumption is clear that poetry is born through spontaneous generation or as a result of a passive acceptance of verbal associations motivated by nothing more than phonetic or lexical similarities.

2 *Cf.* Verlaine, *Romances sans Paroles*, 'Bruxelles': 'Du mal en masse et du bien en foule'.

3 Charles Nodier, *Poésies* (1829), Sainte-Beuve, *Poésies de Joseph Delorme (1830)*, 'Le Creux de la Vallée', quoted in Gérald Antoine's critical edition of the latter (Paris, 1956), p. 207, note 385.

4 'Humide' does not refer as it would in plain French to an objective physical fact (moisture). It is one of the conventional poetic words used to transform any appropriately large, but not marine, object into an image of water: e.g. Virgil's *umida regna*, 'the sea'. There is no way the text can be understood even as a mimesis without this opposition; ignoring it causes commentators to resort to grotesque hypotheses, e.g. Robert G. Cohn, *The Poetry of Rimbaud* (Princeton, 1973), p. 232.

5 Some are, for instance the opposition between 'joie' (l. 26) and 'jouet' (l. 33) underscoring the shifting mood from euphoria to dysphoria. Some are only in the imagination of eager interpreters, but in going too far they still testify to the overwhelming thrust of the text's generation, e.g.

Jean-Luc Steinmetz extracting the blue flower (l. 36) from the wrong stress in 'meuble' (l. 10) (meubleu!), in André Guyaux, ed., *Lectures de Rimbaud* (*Revue de l'université de Bruxelles*) (Brussels, 1982), p. 59. On *roses/roseaux*, see Etiemble and Gauclère, p. 197.

6 Half-way between the colloquial 'secouer la poussière de ses souliers' and Robert Frost: 'The way a crow shook down on me/The dust of snow/From a hemlock tree/Has given my heart/A change of mood.'

7 For a more developed demonstration of this, see Riffaterre, 'Hermeneutic Models', *Poetics Today*, 4 (1983), pp. 7–15.

8 In an ironical piece of *Album zutique*, 'Remembrances du vieillard idiot'.

9 *Illuminations*, 'Nocturne vulgaire'.

10 Théodore de Banville, *Les Cariatides, Songe d'Hiver* (1842), I, ll. 7–12. Banville returns time and again to the moiré image for water, e.g. in *Roses de Noël* (1857), 'Silence'.

11 Paul Valéry, *Charmes* (1922), 'Le Rameur'.

12 E.g. Ross Chambers, 'Mémoire de Rimbaud: essai de lecture', *Essays in French Literature*, 5 (1968), pp. 22–37, especially p. 29; A. L. Amprimoz, '"Mémoire": la fête de l'oubli d'Arthur Rimbaud', *Orbis Litterarum*, 40 (1985), pp. 111–24, especially pp. 119–20.

POETRY AND CLICHÉ: LAFORGUE'S 'L'HIVER QUI VIENT'

Peter Collier

I have not art to reckon my groans ...
Thine evermore, most dear lady, whilst this machine is to
him.

J. L.

OPHELIA: He took me by the wrist, and held me hard;
    Then goes he to the length of all his arm,
    And, with his other hand thus o'er his brow,
    He falls to such perusal of my face,
    As he would draw it. Long stay'd he so:
    At last, – a little shaking of mine arm,
    And thrice his head thus waving up and down, –
    He rais'd a sigh so piteous and profound,
    That it did seem to shatter all his bulk,
    And end his being. That done he lets me go,
    And with his head over his shoulder turn'd:
    He seem'd to find his way without his eyes;
    For out o' doors he went without their help,
    And to the last bended their light on me.
POLONIUS: This is the very ecstasy of love.

L'HIVER QUI VIENT

1   Blocus sentimental! Messageries du Levant! ...
    Oh, tombée de la pluie! Oh! tombée de la nuit,
    Oh! le vent! ...
    La Toussaint, la Noël et la Nouvelle Année,
5   Oh, dans les bruines, toutes mes cheminées! ...
    D'usines ...

On ne peut plus s'asseoir, tous les bancs sont mouillés;
Crois-moi, c'est bien fini jusqu'à l'année prochaine,
Tant les bancs sont mouillés, tant les bois sont rouillés,
10 Et tant les cors ont fait ton ton, ton taine! . . .

Ah, nuées accourues des côtes de la Manche,
Vous nous avez gâté notre dernier dimanche.

Il bruine;
Dans la forêt mouillée, les toiles d'araignées
15 Ploient sous les gouttes d'eau, et c'est leur ruine.

Soleils plénipotentiaires des travaux en blonds Pactoles
Des spectacles agricoles,
Ou êtes-vous ensevelis?
Ce soir un soleil fichu gît au haut du coteau
20 Gît sur le flanc, dans les genêts, sur son manteau,
Un soleil blanc comme un crachat d'estaminet
Sur une litière de jaunes genêts
De jaunes genêts d'automne.
Et les cors lui sonnent!
25 Qu'il revienne . . .
Qu'il revienne à lui!
Taïaut! Taïaut! et hallali!
O triste antienne, as-tu fini! . . .
Et font les fous! . . .
30 Et il gît là, comme une glande arrachée dans un cou,
Et il frissonne, sans personne! . . .

Allons, allons, et hallali!
C'est l'hiver bien connu qui s'amène;
Oh! les tournants des grandes routes,
35 Et sans petit Chaperon Rouge qui chemine! . . .
Oh! leurs ornières des chars de l'autre mois,
Montant en don quichottesques rails
Vers les patrouilles des nuées en déroute
Que le vent malmène vers les transatlantiques bercails!
40 Accélérons, accélérons, c'est la saison bien connue,
        cette fois.

Et le vent, cette nuit, il en a fait de belles!
O dégâts, ô nids, ô modestes jardinets!
Mon cœur et mon sommeil: ô échos des cognées! . . .
Tous ces rameaux avaient encor leurs feuilles vertes,

45   Les sous-bois ne sont plus qu'un fumier de feuilles
      mortes;
   Feuilles, folioles, qu'un bon vent vous emporte
   Vers les étangs par ribambelles,
   Ou pour le feu du garde-chasse,
   Ou les sommiers des ambulances
50   Pour les soldats loin de la France.

   C'est la saison, c'est la saison, la rouille envahit les
      masses,
   La rouille ronge en leurs spleens kilométriques
   Les fils télégraphiques des grandes routes où nul ne
      passe.

   Les cors, les cors, les cors – mélancoliques! ...
55   Mélancoliques! ...
   S'en vont, changeant de ton,
   Changeant de ton et de musique,
   Ton ton, ton taine, ton ton! ...
   Les cors, les cors, les cors! ...
60   S'en sont allées au vent du Nord.

   Je ne puis quitter ce ton: que d'échos! ...
   C'est la saison, c'est la saison, adieu vendanges! ...
   Voici venir les pluies d'une patience d'ange,
   Adieu vendanges, et adieu tous les paniers,
65   Tous les paniers Watteau des bourrées sous les
      marronniers,
   C'est la toux dans les dortoirs du lycée qui rentre,
   C'est la tisane sans le foyer,
   La phtisie pulmonaire attristant le quartier,
   Et toute la misère des grands centres.

70   Mais, lainages, caoutchoucs, pharmacie, rêve,
   Rideaux écartés du haut des balcons des grèves
   Devant l'océan de toitures des faubourgs,
   Lampes, estampes, thé, petits-fours,
   Serez-vous pas mes seules amours! ...
75   (Oh! et puis, est-ce que tu connais, outre les pianos,
   Le sobre et vespéral mystère hebdomadaire
   Des statistiques sanitaires
   Dans les journaux?)

   Non, non! C'est la saison et la planète falote!

80 Que l'autan, que l'autan
    Effiloche les savates que le temps se tricote!
    C'est la saison, oh déchirements! c'est la saison!
    Tous les ans, tous les ans,
    J'essaierai en chœur d'en donner la note.

✳✳✳

Before 1886 Jules Laforgue was a clever, not unsuccessful young poet. His *Complaintes* and his *Imitation de Notre Dame la Lune* (1885) were a firework display of cynical wit and linguistic tricks. His celebration of the moon symbolized an attack on conventional acceptance of nature and desire, his posturing as clown guaranteed detachment from his own emotions. In 1886 his friend Gustave Kahn founded the review *La Vogue*, publishing well-known poets like Mallarmé and Verlaine, but also some translations of Walt Whitman's *Leaves of grass* by Laforgue,[1] and some of Rimbaud's *Illuminations*. Perhaps Whitman's revolutionary *souffle*, rather than Verlaine's smoother harmonies, was to help him develop his aim of 'une poésie qui serait de la psychologie dans une forme de rêve, avec des fleurs, du vent, des senteurs, d'inextricables symphonies avec une phrase (un sujet) mélodique dont le dessin reparaît de temps en temps'.[2] And if that programme sounds close to an amalgam of Baudelaire's synaesthesia, as announced in 'Correspondances', with the musical principle of the Wagnerian 'leitmotif', it is certainly no accident.

The keynote which Laforgue takes from Baudelaire and Wagner, however, is not only the interweaving of the senses and the symphonically structured aesthetic totality, but also the subjectivist, expressionist aesthetic (as we would see it now), where emotional impulse ('mouvements lyriques de l'âme'), imaginative expansion ('ondulations de la rêverie') and intellectual disturbance ('soubresauts de la conscience')[3] provide the very structure of the poetry, rather than remaining mere themes or premises, and where musicality transcends the organization of agreeable sonorities and rhythms, exploits phonetic assonance and dissonance as self-generating, creative forces, and moves beyond regular rhyme and metre to explore the possibilities of a wider phrasal rhythm, a modulation of argument, a harmonics of thought.

Gustave Kahn, writing after Laforgue's death, noted perceptively the link between Laforgue's deconstruction of the stanza and his ideological freedom: 'Mes efforts porteront surtout sur la construction de la strophe, et Laforgue s'en écartait délibérement, volontairement, vers une liberté idéologique plus grande qui le devait conduire à cette phrase mobile et transparante, poétique certes, des poignantes *Fleurs de bonne volonté*'.[4]

In the pages that follow I shall be examining the first poem of Laforgue's final collection of verse, presented after his untimely death as his *Derniers vers*. In my commentary on 'L'Hiver qui vient', first published in *La Vogue* on 16 August 1886, I shall try to look carefully at what structural principles might still be operating within apparently 'free' verse, I shall suggest that Laforgue's writing uses painting and music as anti-discursive aesthetic models, and I shall try to offer ways of describing self-conscious and parodical writing in terms of a generalized rhetoric of the intertextual and the anti-rhetorical, that is, loosely speaking, a rhetoric of cliché.

Each poem seems to express a different mood, an alternative universe. 'L'Hiver qui vient', with typical Laforguian irony, seems to announce the end of the series at its beginning, and since it starts with a longish quotation from Shakespeare, appears to defer even that inverted overture. The opening quotation immediately places Laforgue's poem under the sign of Hamlet, the Hamlet of hesitation and despair, of hopeless desire shot through with yearnings for lost purity: the Hamlet whose manic-depressive feelings can only be assimilated to normal desire by the unperceptive Polonius, and yet a Hamlet whose discourse is refracted through that of Ophelia and Polonius, before being framed by Laforgue's appropriation of Hamlet's declaration of passionate but agonizing love.[5] Thus the voice that opens 'L'Hiver qui vient' is already the twice-mediated voice of a tragic, self-doubting and misinterpreted lover. And as if in deliberate contrast to Ophelia's dramatic, dignified blank verse, Laforgue's poem immediately expostulates, stutters, repeats itself and fades: its 'oh's and suspension marks and its staccato, verbless clauses seem to perform in linguistic terms a hypnotic vision, a paralysed signalling of emotion together with an inability to act. This does not mean that Laforgue's poem will not be a serious comedy. On the contrary, just as Hamlet's acting out of madness represents a tragedy of self greater than that of simple madness, so Laforgue's exploration of varieties of discursive disguise will show the tragic ontological doubt underlying his emotional troubles.

'L'Hiver qui vient' opens with a punning reference to the 'continental blockade' of Napoleon ('le blocus continental'). But this historical reference, giving a geopolitical status to the problem of emotional frustration, seems at once too extreme and too playfully self-conscious and controlled not to deflate its overt pessimism through its own textual inflation. Meanwhile, however jocularly, it announces a sub-current of almost military violence. This violence will keep surfacing throughout the poem, but often obliquely: the sun is buried (l. 18), borne on a stretcher (l.22), the clouds are the remains of a defeated army (l. 38), dead leaves will serve to stuff mattresses for wounded soldiers (l. 49). We recognize the leitmotif as the expression of an inner violence; we also recognize the discursive, descriptive play itself as another kind of evasion, as a projection of the inner emotional blockage out into contingent natural description. Metaphor is no longer innocent. It transports tension out from the self into decor. Thus the whole poem, with its constant interruptions to its own incipient lyricism, acts out the sort of nervous blockade of emotion it announces at the outset. The imagination of the poet is not a transcendental faculty which transforms feeling through its privileged references and images. The poem itself becomes a drama where each reference and each image is the result of a struggle in the poet's 'imaginary' order to find and express himself.[6]

The mode of which these devious motifs partake is that of irony – the paradoxical expression of experience through its negation. One of the first aspects of a Laforgue poem to strike the reader is this playful but destructive self-irony. Playful, in that the voice of the poem often seems to be less an authentic vehicle of emotion than a series of theatrical roles, playing games with discourse. Destructive, because these games in their turn become the anxious source of new discursive questioning, where the speaking subject finds that he nowhere centrally inhabits his own discourse. The themes of that discourse – Love and Nature – are themselves largely public discourses: the sensitive, original soul feels wounded the moment he moulds his feelings into their straitjacket. As he names them, he protests at the need for that naming (ll. 27–8, 58–61). The poet addresses himself, but his personal 'tone' ('ton ton') starts blaring tritely like a hunting horn ('ton ton, ton taine'); the romantic echoes of autumn hunts are recognized as being produced by the self-writing listener rather than being given as meaningful natural signs ('as-tu fini').

Among other important features of modernism – even in Laforgue, one of the first figures of modernism – is that it calls into question the romantic criterion of originality. The theme of the poet's creative originality is savagely mocked in Laforgue. And indeed one of the features of Laforgue's poetry is constantly to question the language that articulates the poem, through that same language. The productive poetic voice inhabits – or is inhabited by – a range of public voices (Shakespearean, historical, popular); it moves constantly along the frontiers of cliché, but it manages to avoid total immersion in public banality by courting self-conscious excess: as for instance through exaggerated repetition (the apparent drama of 'Oh, tombée de la pluie!' becomes immediately suspect when the literal fall of rain is embarrassingly repeated in a suddenly reactivated dead metaphor: 'Oh! tombée de la nuit'), or through bathetic deflation, as when this potentially lyrical appeal to nature is itself swiftly infiltrated by factory chimneys: 'Oh, dans les bruines, toutes mes cheminées! ... D'usines'. (We expect the romantic fireside, but are confronted with a modernist mixture of nature and technology, as in one of Laforgue's favourite paintings, 'De Sisley, la Seine avec poteaux télégraphiques et ciel de printemps').[7] In a strange way the intrusion of banal urban imagery into the hackneyed romantic vision (which latter is based on the 'pathetic fallacy', where private emotion is projected on to, and read back from, landscape) does not redouble the deadness of the language, but invests cliché with an implicit quality of knowingness. Another emotional cliché, 'Crois-moi, c'est bien fini', is undercut with a social cliché, 'jusqu'à l'année prochaine', turning the failure of love into a kind of comic annual festival, recurring regularly in the accelerated cycle of Whitsun, Christmas and the New Year announced in the first stanza. Neither the language of emotional despair nor the language of social knowningness is allowed full control. Each undercuts the other.

In another way too Laforgue's understanding of Impressionist painting may be relevant here. He championed its rejection of any artificial intellectual restructuring of the vibrant complexity of experience.[8] In this light, Laforgue's attempt to give voice to as many different strands of verbalization as possible is his way of trying to express the subjective, contradictory physicality of experience in the least distorted way possible. Thus, although Laforgue demands instantaneous expression of the fleeting mood in painting,[9] he shows in *Derniers Vers* that he does not believe in some shallow model of the mind passively reflecting a series of ever-changing visions; rather, he believes in a dynamic, conflictual model of the production of sense.

Unlike the traditional poem, where, if not always recollected in tranquillity, the emotion is at least usually reorganized from a fixed retrospective stance, the whole tone of this poem is that of a contingent voice, an uncertain, moody, subjective voice. The speaker expostulates with 'oh's and 'ah's, rather than producing measured, elegant judgements; he turns his attention capriciously from apparently trivial details of his surroundings ('les bancs sont mouillés') to more general observations. But whether describing nature, love or society, there is the same cynical refusal to take his own debate seriously: the tone and phrasing are those of an ongoing argument with the self, where lyrical or sentimental flights are constantly arrested (ll. 33, 73–8).

And yet we feel that the ironic self-dramatization is also a sign of being wounded, and also a defence, as with Hamlet. The kind of self-mocking intertextual interplay of voices operated by Laforgue is given a further twist in the reference to Little Red Riding Hood in line 35: she is invoked only to point out the fact that she is absent from Laforgue's winter landscape, which refuses to decant mythical atmospheres or figures. This negation of myth is an important strategy for the modernist writer, since myth and allegory tend to instil recuperative, reintegrationary structures into our reading of a text, reconciling us with painful experience: Laforgue's kind of negative naming depends for its effect on a critically alert and participatory reader – it anticipates our process of 'readerly' association, that constant provisional mental writing, unwriting and re-writing.[10] It exploits, but also alerts us to, our tendency to integrate any discourse, however novel, into pre-established models. Here,

Laforgue mocks his own (and perhaps our) expectation that the gloomy winter might develop features of the fairy tale, as in other lines he mocks his and our amorous temptations. Such self-mockery of the romantic impulse is not straightforwardly anti-romantic: it is part of the inherent romantic ironic defence against the failure of the necessarily impossible romantic ideal. But Laforgue pushes the procedure to the point where self-doubt, as in Hamlet, becomes the founding principle of the self; the series of hypothetical propositions and the consequent verbal echoes are the only evidence heard by the self of its thoughts and feelings. There is not even an ultimate, unproblematic sincerity in his ruthlessly questioning the sincerity of his emotions, but rather an exposition of the way in which all postulations of the true self are in fact rhetorical constructs, and thus the best hope of locating, experiencing and expressing the authentic self is not to seek some chimerical ultimate level of sincere discourse, but rather to scrutinize closely the process of polyphonic construction itself. The problem exposed by Laforgue is therefore not so much how to control feeling with irony,[11] but how to discover the limits of desire within the self by subjecting it to the test of contradictory formulae, how to explore the ways in which the self is created as a desiring self by its attempts to transcribe desire. The self appears to be riven with textual effects, but it none the less proceeds from them, rather than precedes them.[12]

Proceeding through a twin subversion of the colloquial and the mythical, homely words like 'tricote' and 'falote' fail to evoke the domestic or psychological topoi we would expect; not only is there no Penelope weaving or Hélène spinning, but there is not even the wan Pierrot figure, often used by Laforgue in earlier verse, which we might expect, given the reference to a Watteau painting. Pierrot, like Hamlet, is inextricably comic and sad, solemn and extravagant, but the comfort afforded by the mask of the Commedia dell'arte or the circus is now eschewed: Laforgue lets his own identity crisis take the stage and obliterate the Watteau character. And Laforgue's 'Notre Dame la Lune' of Les Complaintes and L'Imitation had already been a baroque and decadent figure, an amalgam of tumescent reverie and vague Graeco-Roman figures of elegantly feminized sterility. In the Derniers Vers the literal figures of the melancholy, amorous, ridiculous clown and the beautifully, viciously, erotically

PETER COLLIER

indifferent moon have been dissolved into a more subterranean and allusive presence within the rhetorical figuration of the text. It is Time itself which knits, and it is the whole planet which has become affected with the poet's apathy, not merely some convenient character or archetype. The Watteau landscape is used more surreptitiously to evoke subliminally the typical 'Embarquement pour Cythère' (the decorously amorous neo-classical picnic nostalgically recalled in Nerval's *Sylvie* and savagely ironized in Baudelaire's 'Voyage à Cythère').

The mapping of intertextual echoes in the poem might include the reference to Don Quixote, who attacked a flock of sheep thinking them to be enemies. Laforgue's anti-original originality, as with his deflation of the dangerously erotic fairytale forest, is to track down the literary origins of his own fabricated feeling of excitement as the wagon trails appear to chase after the racing clouds (ll. 36–9). He produces a potentially expressive image of mental panic, but shows that the image itself, however natural an objective correlative for emotion the landscape may seem, is the product of a determined discursive posture.

In these circumstances there can be no unique or even any privileged poetic discourse. And indeed, like Victor Hugo and like Rimbaud, Laforgue rejects any idea of a specifically noble or poetic diction. He is ready to use a whole range of archaisms, scientific terms, colloquial speech and cliché. But whereas Hugo had wanted to expand the linguistic resources of poetry in order to expand the range of the poet's representation of experience, Laforgue exhibits a playful energy which refuses to obey this mimetic principle. In earlier poems Laforgue had delighted in showing off his anti-bourgeois impropriety and iconoclastic energy in neologisms such as 'sexciproques', 'violuptés', 'sangsuelles', 'éternullité', as if linguistic creativity, delightfully and powerfully, could negate the ordered lie of the bourgeois–Christian cosmos. But in *Derniers Vers* a more subtle creative energy demands a more reflective reading. In his essays on Impressionist painting Laforgue justifies, in terms of his cherished ideals of anarchy and nihilism,[13] the new aesthetic with its destruction of a falsely rationalized artistic restructuring of nature and experience. His poetic writing, too, demands interpretation in terms of a deconstructionist ideology, with his disjointed phonemes performing the same task for poetry that self-conscious brush-strokes and abrupt splashes of raw colour performed for painting.[14]

Use of neologism, for instance, may paradoxically convey the difficulty of categorizing modern feeling. In this apparently elegiac poem, we find neologistic adjectives such as 'don quichottesques' and 'kilométriques' taking their literary and technical references from two extreme poles of the romantic problematic (where industrial society elicits a contradictory, fantasy ideal), and transforming them into epithets which neatly ironize their context by a process of semantic exchange – it is the technology ('don quichottesques rails') which is fantasized (and mocked for that fantasy), and it is the melancholy feelings ('spleens kilométriques') which are metallically extruded into the unfeeling form of the rusty telegraph-wires, and perhaps even echoed in the syncopated lines and rhythms of Laforgue's poem.

When other kinds of specialized vocabulary – whether diplomatic ('plénipotentiaires'), mythical ('Pactoles', from Pactolus, the legendary golden river where Midas bathed), medical ('phtisie pulmonaire'), botanical ('folioles') or slang ('savates') – intrude, it is still often antithetically. Diplomacy has already been introduced as blockade and rout. We guess flowers to be wind-beaten in suburban gardens; we know trees are leafless. The grandiose sun and its cornucopian splendour are no sooner evoked than deflated, when we realize that they referred merely, despite their deliberately grandiloquent rhetoric, to the rustic routines of ploughing, sowing and harvesting. They are then doubly deflated, when we realize that even that season of ideal wealth, light and power is now buried and unobtainable. Everything in Laforgue's linguistic fantasia tends to suggest the inability of a prepackaged system of discourse to articulate or contain feeling.

Likewise, the colloquial in Laforgue is not a simple matter of representing popular speech, or affecting intimacy with the reader, although the refusal of an intellectual rhetoric and of privileged, prophetic insight distinguishes Laforgue from even the most violent romantic poets. Only Rimbaud – and then not always – dared destroy the privileged position accorded by possession of the Verb. Indeed, I wish to draw attention to what I see as Laforgue's deliberate alternative, the rhetoric of cliché. A conversational gambit ('On ne peut plus s'asseoir, tous les bancs sont mouillés') is given a kind of melancholy dignity by its sheer, echoing persistence ('Tant les bancs sont mouillés, tant les bois sont rouillés'). Where semantic precision (the 'mot juste') was for the classical age the hallmark of fine writing and of universal relevance, the romantics were the first deliberately to seek the *different*, or the *original* word, as a mark of individual self-expression. But now in Laforgue both semantic precision *and* rhetorical difference yield to the slow, hypnotic, repetitive unreeling of vaguely similar sonorities, of faintly fading meaning, as if language were somehow weakly resisting the attempt to express – this is a kind of Impressionism, the verbal equivalent of the slow, overlapping gradations of colour in a Renoir or a Monet painting, where an interplay of light, colour and texture over-runs the known contours of objects; so here the groundswell of emotion washes its irrationally motivated tonal modulations over the outlines of would-be distinctive statements.

Similar in function to the phenomenon of repetition is the phenomenon of juxtaposition. A single cry, 'Oh, tombée de la pluie!', could be a moving metonymy for melancholy. But, as I have suggested, when the same grammatical structure is re-echoed in a different idiom – 'Oh! tombée de la nuit' – it seems excessive, and when repeated in triplicate – 'Oh! le vent!...' – it seems self-deflating, especially when that triple structure of lament is itself twice repeated:

> La Toussaint, la Noël et la Nouvelle Année,
> Oh, dans les bruines, toutes mes cheminées! ...
> D'usines ...

Such juxtaposition of similar syntactic structures is reinforced by the juxtaposition of objects perceived: 'lainages, caoutchoucs, pharmacie, rêve ... Lampes, estampes, thé, petits-fours', where the relentless equivalence of the objects destroys the potentially evocative force of each separate object, leaving us face to face with the resistant, or at least the indifferent, otherness of matter. The paraphernalia of domestic sickness, instead of being lovingly invested with emotional recognition and fantasy as they were to be in Proust, are cruelly dedramatized as they had been in Flaubert's *Madame Bovary*. Moreover, what might have been a spiritual alibi for realistic listing, a transcendental motive for the foregrounding of the objective and bodily – that is, the dream – is reified and detached as merely another object. This principle of collage had already been the structuring force behind one of Laforgue's most original *Complaintes*, the 'Complainte de la ville de Paris', where the heteroclite listing, complicated by a semantic and syntactic breakdown, seems clearly shown as the effect of a generalized capitalist commodification of experience.[15] Laforgue's effect of demystification through montage is increased by the effect of phonetic generation, whereby we feel that items named are evoked less for their intrinsic significance than for their phonetic patterning ('Lampes, estampes'). Laforgue's lamps and prints thus lose both the reality *and* the symbolic force that they had in, for instance, Baudelaire's 'Le Voyage', and his dream loses the redemptive force of Baudelaire's.

Laforgue's colloquialisms, reinforced by their effect of unwriting the conventionally poetic, tend to denote moments of an emotion unable, as it were, to sustain rhetorical differentiation: the list of trivialized interests – lainages, caoutchoucs, pharmacie, rêve – is also highlighted as an unpoetic collage by its sing-song rhythm and careless grammar (eliding the 'ne' of 'serez-vous pas mes seules amours!'). *Mutatis mutandis*, the emotional intimacy of the aside ('Oh! et puis, est-ce que tu connais') is immediately shown to be merely another rhetorical device for gaining the sympathy of the reader, as it engenders an elegant afterthought ('outre les pianos') and some highly wrought syntactical inversion ('Le sobre et vespéral mystère'). Where all is riven with cliché, all is potentially rhetorical, and traditional rhetorical devices become especially suspect.

Laforgue's inversion recalls the kind of anglicized placing of the adjective before the noun which in Laforgue's older contemporary Mallarmé had signalled the presence of high culture, of mandarin poetry. But the rhetorical ploy is doubly deflated by Laforgue, with his mischievous equation of the promisingly symbolic and metaphysical ('sobre et vespéral mystère') with the most down-to-earth aspect of death and disease ('Des statistiques sanitaires / Dans les journaux'), and the implied destruction of Mallarmé's sanitized syntactic antics.

As the poem develops, the poet offers colloquial protests to the mocking elegiac echoes of hunting-horns or of vestigial romantic verse, which, as they sound through his voice, seem to mute the lost summer sun he would like to revive (ll. 24–9). The very simplicity of the 'as-tu fini' and the 'Et font les fous' shows the inability of the poet to produce the kind of convincing rhetoric which would sustain images of warmth. At times the diction appears to use the colloquial in attempting an avoidance of melancholy by developing random observation ('Et le vent, cette nuit, il en a fait de belles!'; 'Feuilles, folioles, qu'un bon vent vous emporte'), but a conflicting, perhaps unconscious, discursive force wrenches the topic back to the central question of emotional suffering: thus a comment on storm damage cruelly reverts to an expression of emotional chaos, and the disturbance of self-questioning:

> O dégâts, ô nids, ô modestes jardinets!
> Mon cœur et mon sommeil: ô échos des cognées!;

and thus the conventional image of autumn leaves is converted through an apparently random series of associations into images of drowning, burning, killing (ll. 47–50).

It is certainly true that Laforgue develops a 'stream-of-consciousness' style in *Derniers Vers*,[16] but the label might give a false idea of smoothness. In fact, like Joyce and Woolf after him, Laforgue writes in a mode of extreme tension. Every phrase seems the result of a compromise between several competing layers of sense and feeling, every phrase enunciated seems to imply several more; forgotten, suggested, repressed. In fact, rather than a simple proto-Freudian dialogue between two layers of consciousness, or even a conflict between different interpretative strategies (realist versus romantic, for example), we have more the impression that there is a protean struggle to produce the self *through* meaning, to discover the mind through provisional fragments of enunciation. So much is unsaid: 'Oh! le vent!'; so much is oddly invested with inappropriate emotion: 'toutes mes cheminées'; so much seems out of control: 'as-tu fini! ... Et font les fous'; or part of a self-induced hypnotic investigation: 'Accélérons, accélérons, c'est la saison bien connue, cette fois ... Mon cœur et mon sommeil: ô échos des cognées!' And the potential symbolic power, the plenitude of meaning of the topoi evoked are deviously undermined: the harvest is turned into loss by concentration on the presence of its empty traces alone ('leurs ornières des chars de l'autre mois'); the potential grace and warmth of woman is vestigially indicated, but indicated as lacking, in the crinoline-type skirts of a Watteau painting ('les paniers Watteau'). If they *had* been there, the women would have been creatively harvesting and also providing a real human harmony and charm with their traditional dancing ('bourrées'), as they do, say, for the hero of Nerval's *Sylvie*, as well as providing a focus for the poem's desultory erotic velleities, perhaps hinted at in the lost 'vendanges' and the absent Red Riding Hood, perhaps quoted at a distance in the discreetly contextualized 'mon cœur et mon sommeil', allegedly disturbed by the storm, and in the disruption of the 'modestes jardinets', a traditional image in medieval writing for female modesty.

Since I have raised the question of the Freudian unconscious I should distinguish it from the Schopenhauerian-cum-Darwinian collective unconscious which Laforgue interpreted, the *Philosophy of the Unconscious* of the German philosopher Hartmann, much in vogue since its translation into French in 1877. For the fastidious and sensitive Laforgue, the grossness of natural desire and the inevitable disappointments and disparities of love between individuals come to be tritely symbolized in the fertility cycle of the changing seasons or the rites of courtship of polite society (the teasing piano-playing of the nubile cohorts is out of reach beyond the boarder's dormitory; the lovers' benches are too wet to sit on; illness and formal teas isolate the individual from the ocean of other, desired, individuals). But there is a point at which Laforgue's persona, however overwhelmed by its fatalistic appreciation of the collective unconscious, struggles to regain control, and it appears to operate through the exercise of capricious free association, the free association that was soon to become Freud's panacea ('the talking cure') for neurosis.

In Laforgue the freeedom of speech is noticeable above all as a freedom from traditional poetic forms. As well as its larger discursive strategies, the poem uses its microscopic texture to reinforce its self-consciously libertarian performance. Just as Laforgue's Impressionists liberate seeing from given, intellectualized forms, and restore the physical vibrancy and chaos of sentient experience through their painting, so one might argue that Laforgue liberates words from conventionally learned contours. Rather than the brash liberation of sense in striking neologisms, or the arrogant assertion of power through acrobatic rhyming, which he had used in previous poetry, Laforgue now uses more the liberation of association and dissociation. Dissociation of sound from sense, of word from connotation, of image from emotion; liberation of poetry from fixed rhyme and rhythm, from fixed symbolic systems.

The revolution in prosody of the late nineteenth century in France, with the prose poetry of Baudelaire, Rimbaud and Mallarmé, introduced into French poetry a suppleness of rhythm which seemed to at last allow the poet to develop the rhythms of breathing, of feeling, of consciousness, which English poets had taken for granted. Laforgue, in the wake of Whitman, is able to develop a phrasal rhythm, a rhythm of argument, which sets up its own internal forms: the bathetic collapse of lines 3 and 6 after the alexandrines of 1 and 2, 4 and 5; the abrupt observation of line 13, followed by two lyrical alexandrines developing the idea in lines 14 and 15; the sudden *huitains* of lines 47 to 50 as Laforgue allows his own sentimental depression to be guyed in the form of a popular song. Laforgue, then, develops a highly subjective, psychologically motivated rhythm, articulating the intermittences of breathing or the heartbeat or the oscillations of the emotions and the intellect directly, rather than using regular patterning to suggest them.

But the most powerful forms of liberation are often those which, rather than being entirely unstructured, use parody or other forms of transgression to draw attention to the rules being flouted. Thus Laforgue plays with rather than obeys or ignores regular verse forms. The whole enterprise is clearly pointed by his long quotation from Hamlet at the start of his *Derniers Vers*, with Ophelia's supple argument weaving three complex sentences through the space of fourteen iambic pentameters. Laforgue then launches into alexandrines which (despite some apparent conversational padding – which would be precisely what poor poets might use to sustain a regular metrical system) keep collapsing into irregular verse, thus made more expressive.[17]

Laforgue is a virtuoso of rhyme, with a facility perhaps equalled only by Gautier before him and Apollinaire after him. But rhyme in

Laforgue is neither a regular decorative pattern nor even the stiffening structure set up only to be overcome that it is for many sophisticated poets. There are rhyming couplets (ll. 4 and 5, 11 and 12), and even a rhyming triplet ('faubourgs'/'petits-fours'/'amours'). Elsewhere Laforgue will happily use *rimes croisées* (ll. 7, 8, 9, 10). Just as often, however, the rhymes are spaced out irregularly so that they appear to echo faintly rather than to match (l. 6: 'usines' > l. 13: 'bruine' > l. 15: 'ruine'). There are also half-rhymes like 's'amène' and 'chemine', and much-separated rhymes: 'routes' (l. 34) ... 'déroute' (l. 38). In the end, however, as it would be tedious merely to list the combinations, so it would be inadequate even to talk only of transgressional rhyming. There is also a process of phonetic generation, whereby, for instance, certain diphthongs (ui, ue, oui, oi) associated with palatals (l, r) appear to direct the production of language and to overdetermine its sense. The word 'nuit' is modulated into a whole series: 'bruines', 'usines', 'ruine', 'lui'; branching out from this series there develops a related series: 'rouillés', 'mouillés', 'nuées'; 'toiles', 'crois', 'bois'. Laforgue's exploitation of the half-rhyme and assonance gives his discourse a powerfully forward-moving impulse: 'personne' ... 's'amène' ... 'chemine' / 'cou' ... 'routes' ... 'rails' / 'mois' ... 'fois' ... 'feuilles vertes' ... 'sous-bois' ... 'feuilles mortes'.

This intricate network of internally re-echoing sonorities establishes a climate of fluidity and musicality which helps to suggest the rustling of autumn leaves and the dripping of rain, and leads carefully into an atmosphere of rich auditory evocation, with the plaintive call of the horns and hunters wafted intermittently on the autumn wind: 'Taïaut', 'hallali'. The whole poem is dominated by the 'l' and 'r' sounds:

> Il bruine;
> Dans la forêt mouillée, les toiles d'araignées
> Ploient sous les gouttes d'eau, et c'est leur ruine;

in the above lines one can both hear the droplets in the carefully interwoven sequence of plosives, palatals and mute 'e''s of 'toile', 'ploient' and 'gouttes', and see enacted in the intercalation of a series of foreshortened lines full of palatals and nasals the running of the rain off the linear web. Similarly, fricative sibilants intrude when the missing Red Riding Hood, imagined tripping through the leaves, introduces a modulated series of 'ʃ' and 'dj' sounds:

> Et sans petit Chaperon Rouge qui chemine! ...
> Oh! leurs ornières des chars de l'autre mois,
> Montant en don quichottesque rails.

Self-generating sonorities significantly invade even the poet's own attempts to break out of his repetitive melancholy and his attempt to utter a more logical narrative statement; so that we feel there is no self independent of discourse, able to control the discourse which produces the self:

> Allons, allons, et hallali!
> ... Accélérons, accélérons.

In traditional poetry the division into stanzas and lines of similar length and shape gave a visual image of order and control which reassured the reader, by overdetermining the ability of the poet to restructure experience into sense. Correlatively, the free verse of Laforgue displays its freedom visually. There are actually quite a few alexandrines, but the overall impression is of a rather random line-length, shifting according to mood. Perhaps he is not quite the 'impressionist recorder of passing moods ... the rapidity of whose change leads him into that strange elliptical style, that violent alternation of opposites' noted by Pound,[18] for, as I have argued, Laforgue does not just observe his inner flux – he interferes with, and is created by, its productive process, and it is a richly dialectical verbal progress, rather than a straight transcription of an experiential oscillation.

The process of visualization of form (made graphically explicit a little later in Mallarmé's 'Un Coup de dés' of 1897) is cleverly pointed by various semantic signals – Laforgue sets up an expectation in his reader of reading his horizontal lines against the grain in terms of vertical fall (with the abrupt collapse of the metrical system after the evocation of rainfall, then of chimneys); he then evokes a series of linear contradictions with the horizontal benches, the racing line of clouds, the round sun stretched on to a flat bed, and the arachnid tracery crossed with droplets, remobilized again by the crossroads, the ruts, the rails, the troops, the branches, the stretchers and the telegraph-wires. We are obviously tempted to read the lines here as 'ribambelles', there as 'statistiques', now as 'pharmacie', now as 'rêve', so much do his 'feuilles' seem by turns diagnostic and therapeutic. Laforgue suggests that his poetry echoes and ebbs like open-air music, like erratic gusts of wind. Thus, for instance, in lines 75–8 we are invited to feel a performative force in the progressive slimming down of the syllabic count from twelve (and a repetitiously structured, quadruply inchoate alexandrine, at that) to four, from the contingent music of the 'pianos' to the abruptly lethal prose of the 'journaux' a psychological force struggling with its own potentially lyrical expression, still vestigially present in the rhyme scheme.

By wrenching sound and sense apart, by liberating expression from simple feeling and imagery from sense, Laforgue might tempt a reading in terms of pure form, pure musicality. This was an explicit aim for poets like Gautier and Verlaine, and certainly the poem as a whole can be seen to be organized according to musical principles with its structuring assonance, and the musical anology is invited by the repeated references to 'cors', 'ton', 'antienne', 'note', 'échos', 'bourrées', 'pianos', 'musique', 'chœur'; but we must not ignore the symphonic structuring of argument and reference, as well as the more obvious phonetic harmonies. The potentially Wagnerian leit-motifs are dispersed and reorganized, they are self-consciously questioned, as if *not* producing the 'Gesamtkunstwerk' they suggest. Musical motifs in particular are questioned for their superficial lyricism (the horns and pianos with their facile associations of autumn mellowness and well-bred, even artistic romance), and the whole poem is sent up in the last line as a one-man choir.

Laforgue's distinction between superficial musicality and deeper symphonic structure is, I believe, persuasive.[19] It may be that the organization of the poem is deliberately that of the tone poem of his contemporary Debussy (who set Mallarmé's 'L'Après-midi d'un faune' to music) – but this implies more than the appearance and disappearance of motif, or the notation of impressionistic sensory and emotional experience, although they count; rather it is the repetitions and interruptions, the elliptical or garbled syntax which we have to take as showing the force of mood behind their explicit

message. Thus Laforgue seems to move beyond the colour harmonics of Whistler's painting or the graduated clusters of imagery of
Gautier's 'Symphonie en blanc majeur', and create a new kind of
writing, where semantic associations provide strange harmonies
threatening to negate the rational line of argument, where the
chordal texture of the prosody, imagery and syntax works in
counterpoint to the verbal melody.

But impressionist (or expressionist) phrasing and argument
suppose the presence of unconscious obsessions, the obsessions, in
fact, which are the repressed, unspoken 'themes' of a poem which
appears to have abandoned thematic focus, or to use it only
contrapuntally – images of illness and death break through com-
ments on weather, desire erupts anarchically, deviously, at the turn
of a phrase. In Laforgue's earlier verse the unconscious was named
as a force over-riding individual choice, and desire was expressed
more explicitly and more acutely. In some of the *Complaintes*
Laforgue was more openly hostile to God ('Infini, gare de trains
ratés ... Infini, montre un peu tes papiers'), and his sexual fears and
longings were more violent.

In 'L'Hiver qui vient' there is a more covert clash between desire
and disgust for desire, between ridicule and pathos. And the
emptiness of any metaphysical transcendence is hinted at rather than
stated. Obviously the reference to Hamlet invites us to read between
the lines. We suspect that Hamlet's hysterical, half-feigned horror at
Ophelia's love is an unacknowledged projection of an unrecognized
self-disgust, his own desire being somehow contaminated, just as
much as Ophelia's pure love is, by his mother's unacceptable
sexuality. If in Laforgue's poem desire seems both disappointing and
trivial, it is no doubt by way of hinting at the greater tragedy, that
desire is both inescapable and unacceptable, (self-)destructive even.
Laforgue's modernist expression of desire refuses to accept either
desire or the failure of desire as capital, and symptomatically his
bland disclaimers are belied by occasional outbursts of melancholy
(ll. 73–4), by sudden linguistic slips (baskets abruptly evoking skirts
by the association of 'paniers' with the 'paniers Watteau' of the girls
carrying them), by the eruption of apparently unpremeditated
visions (the rain momentarily figured as angels, because of the
tensely elliptical syntax – the foreground meaning 'les pluies [qu'il

faut supporter] d'une patience d'ange' becoming lost in the surge of impressionistic meaning 'les pluies que l'on regarde en rêvant patiemment d'un ange'), by the aggressive repression of fantasy ('caoutchoucs, pharmacie, rêve'), by a kind of phonetic subtext (the strange emphasis on 'Les cors, les cors, les cors' invites simultaneous interpretation of an unconscious sub-text 'les corps, les corps, les corps'), and a submerged world of erotic fantasy where Little Red Riding Hood and angels signal their absence as they skip or dissolve away, where windrocked heartbeats and ruffled gardens sound their *double entendre*, and pianos and dreams are muffled by rival systems, the noise of sanitary statistics and the static of sensible autumn clothing.

Readers of poetry from any age before the modern period will expect images or symbols to focus the meaning of the poem, however subversive. There are epic or narrative poems whose message is in various ways contained in their stories, but more usually some image will encapsulate the formula, such as the lake in Lamartine's 'Le Lac', or the carcass in Baudelaire's 'Une Charogne', which are both introduced metonymically but developed metaphorically. And here, sure enough, we find a melancholy autumn scene, with a windswept landscape merging into the decor of an invalid's bedroom. But Laforgue infiltrates the conventional rustic landscape with urban imagery: the autumn wind, rain, leaves and spiders' webs suggesting sadness are overlaid with the city-dweller's contingent, unevocative park bench, rust and telegraph-wires. Hunting-horns and harvest baskets yield to tubercular coughing, winter clothing and medicine.

More disturbingly, the symbolic systems interfere. Leaves should not rust. The sun should not be a small, wet, cold, pale and dirty bodily product. But even this conflictual symbolic imagery yields to a more dense and intractable descriptive clutter, which starts filling up the poem towards the end. This erodes and displaces but does not quite negate the impact of the central image of the poem – where the urban convalescent and the sickly autumn landscape merge in the figure of the dying sun, partly a symbol, partly a projection of the state and feelings of the poet, dying ('fichu'), stretched out as if dead ('gît'), looking like a discoloured mess of spittle coughed up on the floor of a tavern ('blanc comme un crachat d'estaminet'), a vision no doubt expressing the state of the sick speaker, with the yellow broom forming a bed for this stretcher case, an unheroic version of Vigny's Roland.[20] The slow punning link ('qu'il revienne ... / qu'il revienne à lui') between the loss of the sun, hoping it will return next year, and the loss of consciousness of the poet foregrounds the performative aspect of the symbolism, as if the metaphorical structure were largely a linguistic accident.

The horns interrupt the vision again (ll. 27–9) – and this intermittence of the image is a very bold, modernist feature, disrupting the coherence of the allegory which a sustained network of metaphors previously tended to produce in poetry, as the subject's very consciousness of his suffering wanes – and then the image of illness and suffering bursts in again; the dying sun with its opaque white smudge running into a rough yellow haze is likened horribly to a gland torn out of a neck (l. 30). The image is difficult to visualize, for all its apparently graphic and explicit unpleasantness, for by now the sun stands for both the person and the purulent neck, both the body and the phlegm expectorated. This illogical over-running of image, which veers uncontrollably between an analogical and a contextual function, anticipates Freud's theory of the overdetermined, displaced, condensed imagery of dreams, and indeed, the progression of Laforgue's poem is full of illogical shifts, repetitions and co-agulations of this sort. In the end we have the feeling of a poetry of vision, like that of Rimbaud, where it is not possible to distinguish between reality and fantasy – everything is bathed in a subjective perceptual fantasy, rather as an Impressionist painting revises reality in terms of its own colours and textures.

It has been argued that Laforgue is not a Symbolist in the sense of Baudelaire and Mallarmé, that he does not believe in a hidden world of correspondences giving meaning to the superficial images employed, that he does not believe in the possibility of meaningful, essential knowledge.[21] There is a fine distinction here, but it is worth drawing. The reasons for Laforgue's dying sun or echoing horns seeming non-symbolic are perhaps not qualitative but functional: Laforgue has tied up his images into such an extended and contingent network that, as Lawrence Watson argues,[22] their sheer extension (and, I would add, their mutual motivation, denying any element of the image originary status) destroys any feeling of a

pantheistic investment of significance in Nature behind the individual images; even the modern Nature of the city is denied
privileged symbolic meaning by this kind of textual proliferation:
park benches, rainwear and petits-fours drown the lamps and prints
and immerse them in urban meaninglessness, rather than the
morally significant squalor and excitement evoked by Baudelaire's
moral hell. The link between the weak, smoky sun and the gobbet of
spittle is both a visual accident and a material cause (via the damp
dormitory); the roofs happen to look like a sea of water. Other kinds
of drive than the truly metaphorical and metonymic seem to be at
work in the relation between sun and sickness, rain and rust (for
example the repressed urges for travel, or perhaps for drowning,
surfacing momentarily in the figuring of the wet roofs as the ocean).
Laforgue's landscapes are no doubt a kind of objective correlative,
as Eliot invented the term in his essay on 'Hamlet',[23] and certainly
this oblique figuring of a state of mind is very like Mallarmé's
ambition to evoke states of mind rather than reality itself, but
through the procedure of montage we have an impression of the
whole process of mental symbol-forming and relation-founding
being scandalously exposed and simultaneously upset: we are
moving towards an aesthetic based on fragmentation and disjunc-
tion, rather than one based on analogy and organic harmony.

The use of shock imagery, of surprising associations, was first
developed systematically by Baudelaire, in poems like 'Métamor-
phoses du vampire' or 'Un Voyage à Cythère'. Already in Baudelaire
such techniques implied the self-conscious presence of the poet,
aware of his production of imagery and his sense of a performance.
But Laforgue adds to this shock the new casualness of modernism,
as, unlike Baudelaire, he allows himself to be distracted by the
apparent background description ('De jaunes genêts d'automne'),
and allows his attention to fluctuate ('Oh! les tournants des grandes
routes'). Even his melancholic appeal to drowning and burning
seems to wallow in an almost sensory pleasure of enumeration, of
assonance (ll. 44–6).

Now intermittence of theme has become the theme; the person is
spoken by his despair. In this fluctuation of viewpoint, this intermittence of thematic concentration, the poet is no longer a voice judging
retrospectively, but a presence exploring experience and language as

they develop. With this major shift from 'emotion recollected in tranquillity', a non-retrospective, hesitantly developing narrative stance explores its own implications as it creates them, and listens to them. Its lyrical phrasing is interrupted by short phrases; then its staccato statements are overtaken by a rhetorical afflatus providing its own emotional impetus.

Thus it is the casual, flippant treatment of a serious theme, the variable attitude of the persona to his own themes and emotions, which is new here. The subject is not central to his discourse; he is sometimes an alienated observer, sometimes the creature of his language, sometimes a fragmented, polyphonic participant. Laforgue's planet earth is 'falote' – merely dull and silly, not even graced with the grandeur of metaphysical ennui; his sun expectorates in a pub, his angels are merely a figure of patience in the depressing tendency of the heavens to open. Yet such humour is not even a consistent register, as it was with the coruscating irony of Rimbaud's 'Les Assis' or 'Les Pauvres à l'église'. It is one of a number of available registers, and again it is the mixture which is modernist. Similarly with the intertextual echoes of other poets: taken together, Laforgue's virtual parodies of Mallarmé, Vigny and Baudelaire enact a subversion of poetry and the poetic genre altogether, making them appear to be a suspicious congealing of discourse. Yet it is impossible to say to what degree the poetic voices are borrowed or attacked, displaced or privileged, and here again Laforgue announces modernism. For perhaps Laforgue, Hamlet in his own play, mocks his own self-mocking posturing as the Pierrot of symbolist poetry, in pastiching his peers too earnestly in earlier poems. He is conscious that every vision he is tempted to evoke as a significant reflexion of natural meaning, every discursive falsification he wishes to expose, is in fact already a discursive performance by himself, thus the '*spectacles* agricoles'.

Yet finally, if we enjoy reading Laforgue lingeringly, meditatively, digressively even, rather than puzzle to reconstruct some overall or original meaning, if we hear dissonant music rather than discordant noise, if we feel invigorated by his exploration of melancholy and the difficulty of expressing it, it is because, for all his discursive deconstruction, perhaps even because of it, Laforgue has captured some essential mental rhythm. He has created that fluid lyricism of the modern soul which was beautifully defined by Baudelaire in his preface to the 'Petits Poèmes en prose', and which, very soon after Laforgue's writing, was to be most quintessentially captured in the improvised variations of jazz, and the great explosion of visual fantasy and rhythm provided by the mobile collages of the silent cinema screen. 'L'Hiver qui vient' is a kind of early blues, ragtime, or Chaplin. In another mode, it is even more akin to the Cubist painters' attempts to express simultaneously conflicting planes of time and space, intellectual, emotional and sensory perception, or the unrealistically expressive plastic forces of the Fauves and the Expressionists, than to the Impressionists' homogenizing techniques. Laforgue's poetry demands a demanding reader – but it may well create that reader.

NOTES

1 See Walt Whitman, *Œuvres choisies* (Paris, 1918) ('Dédicaces', p. 57; 'Enfants d'Adam', p. 68; 'Ruisseaux d'automne', p. 250).
2 Laforgue, (in a letter to Charles Henri in 1881), *Œuvres de Jules Laforgue*, Vol. IV, *Mélanges posthumes* (Paris, 1923), p. 66.
3 See Baudelaire's preface to his *Petits poèmes en prose*, in his *Œuvres complètes* (Pléiade edition, Paris, 1975) Vol. I, pp. 275–6.
4 G. Kahn, *Premiers Poèmes* (Paris, 1897), p. 17.
5 Laforgue has telescoped Hamlet's original words: 'I have not art to reckon my groans; but that I love thee best, O most best! believe it. Adieu. Thine evermore, most dear lady, whilst this machine is to him, HAMLET' (*Hamlet*, Act II, scene ii).
6 According to the French psychoanalyst Jacques Lacan, our personalities are informed by the public symbolism of language to such an extent from early infancy, that we can only attain conscious selfhood by projecting our thoughts and feelings into given discursive models (into the 'symbolic' order), and we are obliged to read back the result in order to perceive ourselves as whole selves (in the 'imaginary' order), as if externally, reflected in a mirror. See J. Lacan, 'Le Stade du miroir comme formateur de la fonction du Je', in *Ecrits*, I (Paris, 1970), pp. 89–97.
7 Laforgue (in a letter to Charles Ephrussi in 1881), *Mélanges posthumes*, p. 225.
8 Laforgue, 'L'Impressionnisme', in *Mélanges posthumes*, pp. 136–7.
9 Laforgue, 'L'Impressionnisme', pp. 140–1.

10 See Jean-Paul Sartre, *Qu' est-ce que la littérature*, (Paris, 1964); Roland Barthes, *Le Plaisir du texte*, (Paris, 1973).

11 Laforgue, *Derniers Vers*, ed. M. Collie and J. M. L'Heureux (Toronto, 1965).

12 The idea that a text is not a transparent expression of reality, but a constant re-echoing of always pre-existing texts, was made fashionable by a brief book by Julia Kristeva called *Le Texte du roman* (The Hague, 1970). She was inspired by the earlier twentieth-century Russian theorist Bakhtin, who argued that Dostoievski's characters and the narrator were not separate speaking entities, but dialogic partners in one polyphonic whole. She later developed her idea in relation to symbolist poetry in *La Révolution du langage poétique* (Paris, 1974).

13 'L'Impressionnisme', p. 142.

14 'L'Impressionnisme', pp. 134–5.

15 For a translation and analysis of this poem, see my chapter, 'Nineteenth-Century Paris: Vision and Nightmare', in E. Timms and D. Kelley, eds., *Unreal City: Urban Experience in Modern European Art and Literature* (Manchester, 1985), esp. pp. 40–2. For an exposition of the subversive effect of montage, particularly in the theatre, see W. Benjamin, 'What is Epic Theatre?', in *Understanding Brecht* (London, 1983).

16 P. Broome and G. Chesters, *The Appreciation of Modern French Poetry 1850–1950* (Cambridge, 1976), p. 113.

17 As T. S. Eliot says in his 'Reflections on *Vers libre*' (1917): 'the ghost of some simple metre should lurk behind the arras in even the 'freest' verse ... freedom is only truly freedom when it appears against the background of an artificial limitation'. (*Selected Prose* (London, 1963), p. 85).

18 Ezra Pound, 'Irony, Laforgue and Some Satire', *Poetry*, xi, 2 (1917), pp. 93–8.

19 'Corbière ne s'occupe ni de la strophe ni des rimes ... J'ai voulu faire de la symphonie et de la mélodie'. Laforgue, *Œuvres*, Vol. V (Paris, 1925), p. 137.

20 *Cf.* Laforgue's echoing of Vigny's 'Dieu! que le son du Cor est triste au fond des bois'.

21 M. Collie, *Jules Laforgue* (London, 1977), pp. 98–9, 119.

22 L. Watson, *L'Hiver qui vient*: poème manifeste', in J. Hiddleston, ed., *Laforgue aujourd'hui* (Paris, 1988), pp. 135–53.

23 T. S. Eliot, '*Hamlet*' (1919), in *Selected Prose*, p. 102.

GENIUS AT NIGHTFALL: MALLARMÉ'S 'QUAND L'OMBRE MENAÇA DE LA FATALE LOI ...'

Malcolm Bowie

Quand l'ombre menaça de la fatale loi
Tel vieux Rêve, désir et mal de mes vertèbres,
Affligé de périr sous les plafonds funèbres
Il a ployé son aile indubitable en moi.

5   Luxe, ô salle d'ébène où, pour séduire un roi
Se tordent dans leur mort des guirlandes célèbres,
Vous n'êtes qu'un orgueil menti par les ténèbres
Aux yeux du solitaire ébloui de sa foi.

Oui, je sais qu'au lointain de cette nuit, la Terre
10   Jette d'un grand éclat l'insolite mystère,
Sous les siècles hideux qui l'obscurcissent moins.

L'espace à soi pareil qu'il s'accroisse ou se nie
Roule dans cet ennui des feux vils pour témoins
Que s'est d'un astre en fête allumé le génie.

✳✳✳

This sonnet (published in its final form in the 1887 edition of the *Poésies*) is unusual among Mallarmé's many ceremonial tributes to the dying or the dead in that its entire funerary drama is internal to the mind. Elsewhere, in his *hommages* and *tombeaux*, death is something that happens to other people, out there in the world, and that sets the poet-narrator's mind echoing with its own frailty. Here, it is an inward monition, many-voiced and not to be stilled. Elsewhere, a painful path leads from the moment of loss, through the work of mourning, towards an eventual reassertion of the survivor's potency: Mallarmé in 'Toast funèbre' is less Attic and less copious than Milton in 'Lycidas' or Shelley in 'Adonais' or Arnold in 'Thyrsis', but he shares their sense that bereavement provides the poet with an artistic education not easily to be had elsewhere. But here, in 'Quand l'ombre . . .', the play between loss and creativity is conducted with fine savagery by the introspective intelligence acting upon itself, educating itself in the face of its own approaching destruction. Could anyone – least of all a much loved friend or an admired fellow-artist – ever incontrovertibly *die* in a world where death is so perfectly immanent to the poet's thinking? Could news of such a death ever impinge, other than as the faintest *fait divers*, upon a mind so elaborately apparelled in its own mortality?

Mallarmé's death-haunted monodrama makes a grand cosmological claim. The poem adheres in its imagery to the funeral conventions of Christian Europe and reads at first as an only slightly laicized *leçon de ténèbres*. Yet the claim that Mallarmé makes is not Christian, and not really psychological, despite his fondness for mind-space over physical space: it concerns the generative and regenerative power of human desire within the cosmos. The poem's rhetoric too is grand, and, from a philosophical viewpoint, risky. For while it postulates and declares on the one hand, and counter-postulates and concedes on the other, 'Quand l'ombre . . .' does not do anything that could be called, however charitably, arguing. The sonnet comprises four complex propositions, each of which is co-extensive with one of the quatrains or tercets. This convergence of syntactic and metrical structure at the end of each stanza produces an air of fullness and finality four times over, and if we confine ourselves to the surface unfolding of each stanza-sentence this quality seems quite unmitigated by doubt or indecision. Indeed if the poem is looked at as a sequence of rhetorical gestures devoid of precise content, it begins to resemble a machine for producing assertions and for proclaiming the virtues of the assertive mode.

But beneath the surface things are different: each sentence gathers into a formulaic final shape a sequence of volatile image-fragments and the reader's passage through these can scarcely be other than cautious and doubtful. In the first quatrain, for example, which narrates a failure of creativity, the idea of death is ingeniously overdetermined: it casts its shadow upon human endeavour, has the force of austere legality, is the unshakable destiny beneath which all action takes place; our hopes, fated to perish, are pursued in a décor that is already funereal; death is not one option among others but the choice already made for us that underlies all our choosing. And 'Rêve', the idea which alone has the power to oppose death in this first formulation of the poem's central conflict, is presented as fragile and intermittent. It is an instinctual appetite and a bodily affliction ('désir et mal de mes vertèbres') but may at any moment be driven into eclipse. The capital 'r' of 'Rêve' suggests that this is some essential, emblematic gift – the power of surmise, say, or the mind's ability to propose ideal models of the world – yet the initial 'Tel' of line 2 has already introduced a doubt: this 'dream', even capitalized, is no more, perhaps, than one model randomly chosen, the product of one unremarkable mental fidget. 'Vieux' gives the dream at once the dignity of age and the tiresomeness of unrelieved repetition ('here it is again, the same old dream'); and resistance to extinction, figured as the concerted action of muscle and bone, has its own creaturely impermanence and smallness of scale: even if the wing were re-extended for flight, it would still be just a wing. Mallarmé's first assertion has accumulated so much doubt by the time its point of completeness is in sight that 'indubitable' itself may begin to hesitate: is this an expression of knowledge secure and beyond doubt, or a grander version of the conversational 'doubtless' by which a speaker may politely or guilefully disguise a doubt that is still real?

Mallarmé has a particular fondness for syntactic suspension, and uses parentheses, ablative absolutes, appositional strings and inter-polated proleptic or analeptic clauses as if they were the obvious and 'natural' vehicles for playfully self-aware thought. This first qua-train could be regarded as a text-book case. An extended central portion, from 'désir' to 'funèbres', comprises material of this suspen-ded kind and contains both elements of the acoustically and semantically rich rhyme 'vertèbres'/'funèbres'. 'Rêve' is doubly qualified, first in a pair of appositions (l. 2) and then in an adjectival phrase introduced by a past participle (l. 3). But, in both cases, this is subordinate material that will not stay subordinate. These phrases do not simply supply sense to the main proposition, but act powerfully upon each other: death is an affliction, but that which alone rises up against it ('Rêve') is an affliction ('mal') too. Similarly, it is from the 'subordinate' material that we learn, in advance of the dream-wing's withdrawal from flight in line 4, that any attempt at flight, any proud emancipatory gesture of the human mind, is already doomed ('Affligé de périr sous les plafonds funèbres'). By way of these simultaneously backward- and forward-looking central phrases, Mallarmé is able to suggest what his sentence nowhere plainly declares: that a complicity exists between death and its already ghostly human antagonist, and that death may act upon the individual not simply as a threat to passion but as a passion in its own right.

The aberrant energies that Mallarmé's suspended material releases within the controlling framework of his assertions are even more prominent in the second quatrain. Line 5 introduces the kaleidoscopic interplay of light and darkness that is to be sustained in all but one of the remaining lines (l. 12), and it does so in a way that invites the reader from the start to be uncertain in his or her syntactic and moral scansions of the text. 'Luxe' and 'salle d'ébène' pose the problem: which is figure and which ground? Both are vocatives, the two of them are in apposition, and either or both of them together can act as addressee for the expostulation of line 7: 'Vous n'êtes qu'un orgueil . . .' But this seeming symmetry does not mean that we get the same sort of answer if we place each in turn in the dominant position. If we read 'Luxe . . . Vous n'êtes qu'un orgueil' and place the 'salle d'ébène' in an inferior role, sepulchral darkness and the luminous tracery which crosses it are one representative instance of sumptuous sensory appeal – the most impressive instance, perhaps, but luxury rather than the stars and the interstellar spaces is the main polemical target. If, on the other hand, we read 'ô salle d'ébène . . . Vous n'êtes qu'un orgueil' and give 'Luxe' the force of a simple preliminary flourish, the narrator may be seen raising an indignant fist at the whole light-dark pageant of the heavens: they have become an overarching *vanitas* symbol. The two readings produce two different moral intensities, and the first reading, unlike the second, has a decided air of sinfulness upbraided. Those who overvalue 'luxe' are guilty of encouraging not only pride ('orgueil') but lust ('luxure'). Line 5 has already told us that an attempt at seduction is under way.

What is there in the spectacle of the night sky that a royal personage might find dangerously alluring (l.5)? The main proposition, contained in lines 7 and 8, gives the official story: the heavens are grand but the faith of the solitary is grander; the radiant stars do not survive the test of darkness, but this faith – for reasons that are still obscure – does. Yet once again the adjacent mass of 'subordinate' material contains a very different account of the narrator's desires and motives. The 'guirlandes célèbres' are destined to be extinguished and to have their apparent authority countermanded, by the surrounding darkness, but long before this happens they are already in their death-throes: the price they pay for their radiance is the eventual exhaustion of their combustible matter; the light they emit is lethal to them. These stars, which die at once from external and internal causes, are seductive not just because, inlaid into ebony, they offer a striking decorative display but because they provide an *ars moriendi* for the creative intelligence. The already dying Dream of the first quatrain is strongly echoed in the already self-consuming energy-source of the second, and the unofficial and unasserted story that they together tell is one of death no longer resisted but become an object of rapt pursuit.

Remembering the central trance of Keats's Nightingale Ode, we could say that Mallarmé's narrator too is half in love with death, but with a death that is neither easeful nor rich nor free of pain. Mallarmé has contrived in the first eight lines of his poem a violently disrupted verse-texture in which the terrors and allurements of death are variously aligned and interconnected. A deeply disturbing complexity of perception is brought to bear upon matters that are in one sense too brutal to deserve such delicacy and nuance. And the mortuary lyricism of it all is made more shocking by a further internal disproportion. Whereas the cancelling hand of death, whether castigated or secretly colluded with, is shown in the grim diversity of its powers, the redeeming impulses of the human individual are vastly underspecified – a dream, a desire, a faith – and no sooner named than queried. Even the inner certainty that faith offers has its own dissonance (l. 8): dazzle, we remember, is an impairment not an enhancement of vision.

Of the poem's four propositions, the second pair, contained in the tercets, are much more plainly affirmative than the first in their structure and in their general import. Affirmation is extracted from mere dazzle at the start of the first tercet: 'Oui' retrospectively clarifies the 'ébloui' that it echoes. The radiance of faith was the

beginning of knowledge: 'Ebloui, je sais...' In addition, both tercets
have the courtesy to begin directly with their subjects and to adhere
strictly to the subject–predicate pattern: Mallarmé's two culminating professions of faith coincide with a regaining of faith in everyday
grammar.

Alternative readings are to some extent still encouraged, but at the
level of word order rather than sentence order. The genitive in
particular has its share of ambiguity to impart. Do we construe line
10 as

> Jette, d'un grand éclat, l'insolite mystère

or as

> Jette l'insolite mystère d'un grand éclat?

Do we construe line 14 as:

> Que le génie d'un astre en fête s'est allumé

or as

> Que le génie s'est allumé d'un astre en fête?

Without seeming too lazy-minded about matters of detail, one could
say that the differences involved here are small. Each of the tercets
makes a proud boast about the luminiferous power of the 'solitary'.
From having been a mere receptor of light, a retina, at the end of
quatrain 2, he is now to become its sole worthy transmitter: the
Earth, privileged among planets, borrows its effulgence from him
and, by virtue of his presence, is suddenly less darkened by the
hideous procession of human epochs (ll. 9–11). When Mallarmé
switches back from historical time to the incalculable vastness of
space, the opprobrium that had been attached to the secular human
world is transferred to the procession of the stars: they are as vile as
the centuries had been hideous, and bear witness in their turn to the
cleansing moral efficacy that genius alone possesses (ll. 12–14). The
grandeur of these claims is such that the multiple constructions
invited by lines 10 and 14 can all be seen as conducing to a single
end. Whether the Earth casts a mystery brightly or a brightness
mysteriously in line 10, and whether mystery is cause or effect of the
definitive 'éclat' to which the narrator now lays claim, the hyperb-

olic force of his self-description is unaltered. Being the sole source of value in the world, he is also – in his essential gift if not in his fallible person – the first cause from which all beneficial moral effects spring. Similarly, in line 14, it does not much matter whether the fire of genius is figured as a festive star or as having been kindled by a festive star external to itself, for in this scenario external forces can expect, at best, to act as no more than a trigger or a catalyst upon the now transcendentalized human mind. In each case, these unruly genitives may be thought of as sending minor seismic waves through a verse texture in which the single source and single destination of meaning are already firmly in place.

We could say, then, that this sonnet, while being affirmative throughout, discovers its full capacity for affirmation as it goes on. The movement from the quatrains to the tercets is a movement from indulgence to strictness in the handling of fantasy: subordinate material is eventually resubordinated, and its counter-suggestive recalcitrance brought back under the control of a single idea, boldly proclaimed. But if the poem as a whole leaves us with a sense that knowledge and the syntactic forms most appropriate to its expression have been threatened and, with a considerable show of triumph, regained within the fourteen-line span, we should nevertheless remind ourselves of the mobile semantic and acoustic field in which this overall progression takes place. The rhyme-axis itself is extraordinarily rich, even by Mallarmé's standards. The five inter-laced sequences 'loi'–'moi'–'roi'–'foi', 'vertèbres'–'funèbres'–'célèbres'–'ténèbres', 'terre'–'mystère', 'moins'–'témoins' and 'nie'–'génie' bear so much of the poem's drama and bring into focus so many of its ironies that they can at moments become a narrow, column-shaped poème-objet in their own right, contiguous to a Mallarmé sonnet but offering the reader an independent kind of satisfaction. The rhymes in -oi, for example, offer a microcosmic reduction of the human self and its dominant states and dispositions. The 'moi' is at once a subject and a would-be sovereign; the implacable legalities by which its subjecthood is defined are at once external and internal to its sphere of action; its claims to kingship are sustained by faith (but not by reason, primogeniture, public assent or divine authority) and falter as faith itself falters. The second four-term rhyme-drama, launched at the end of line 2, continues this play of contrasts between the private and public faces of selfhood: death and darkness attack not just the body but the very backbone of us, and, not content with this violation, they act upon our social personalities too. All memory of us, and the afterlife of celebrity which once spurred us on, are to be removed from the record.

Yet beyond this grimly playful final column of text, the rhyme words have another quite different disruptive effect upon the propositional flow of the poem. In their combined acoustic and semantic richness they supercharge each line-ending, and in so doing freeze and singularize each alexandrine in turn. To a certain extent, this process accords smoothly with the overall movement of the syntax. The main syntactic units or sub-units may be self-contained in any one of four obvious ways: (a) as complete propositions, (b) as grammatical subjects, (c) as predicates or (d) as qualifying clauses or phrases. All but five of the alexandrines coincide exactly with one or other of these syntactic measures:

> (a) Il a ployé son aile indubitable en moi
>
>   Se tordent dans leur mort des guirlandes célèbres
>
>   Vous n'êtes qu'un orgueil menti par les ténèbres
>
> (b) L'espace à soi pareil qu'il s'accroisse ou se nie
>
> (c) Jette d'un grand éclat l'insolite mystère
>
>   Roule dans cet ennui des feux vils pour témoins
>
> (d) Affligé de périr sous les plafonds funèbres
>
>   Aux yeux du solitaire ébloui de sa foi
>
>   Sous les siècles hideux qui l'obscurcissent moins

Of the five exceptions, one (l. 14) is barred from (a) by a single syllable only:

> (Que) s'est d'un astre en fête allumé le génie

and another (l. 2) can claim honorary membership of (b) by virtue of its being both the object of 'l'ombre menaça' and the subject-in-anticipation of 'Il a ployé ...':

> Tel vieux Rêve, désir et mal de mes vertèbres

This leaves only three lines that are from the syntactic viewpoint incomplete or heterogeneous:

Quand l'ombre menaça de la fatale loi

Luxe, ô salle d'ébène où, pour séduire un roi

Oui, je sais qu'au lointain de cette nuit, la Terre

And it can be said of these that they occupy the position of least danger within their respective stanza-sentences: each is an opening line, far removed from the moment of closural fit between metre and syntax towards which each stanza is directed; and the incompleteness of each dramatically restarts the quest for the affirmative mode that each stanza enacts.

Yet in the eleven seemingly well-adjusted cases I listed a moment ago this same sense-rhythm may be driven off course in a number of ways. For the alexandrine cannot tell the difference between those syntactic units that do and those that do not serve the general movement of sense. Two of the four main propositions, for example, are contained in single lines (4 and 7), but in line 6 a lesser proposition is promoted to near-main or main-sounding status by the double pressure of metre: the line is both a metrical entity in itself and the first half of a larger metrical entity, a couplet. The syntactic parallelism between the two successive propositions, though partially disguised by the inversion of subject and verb in line 6, receives a compensatory highlight from the ultra-rich end-rhyme and the pre-rhymes that announce it:

Se tordent dans leur mort des guirlandes célèbres
Vous n'êtes qu'un orgueil menti par les ténèbres

Similarly, subjects and predicates may become detached from each other, and individually monumentalized, by the segmenting and framing action of metre, and those lines in which mere qualities are specified may by the same means be endowed with substance of their own. The closing lines of the second quatrain and the first tercet – 'Aux yeux du solitaire ébloui de sa foi' and 'Sous les siècles hideux qui l'obscurcissent moins' – are the most notable cases of the latter kind. Grammatically speaking, these lines are simply adverbial indications of mental viewpoint or physical locality, but metre turns them into unofficial propositions. In each of them a claim is finalized that is both crucial to Mallarmé's account of creative potency and not to be found elsewhere in the work: that an inward 'faith' may outshine the splendour of the heavens (l. 8) and that the possessor of such faith redeems the otherwise miserable record of humanity (l. 11).

Among the eleven single-line monuments, however, none is more remarkable than the following, which is a subject not simply severed from its predicate but given its own terse predicative authority:

L'espace à soi pareil qu'il s'accroisse ou se nie

Whereas the claim that is soon (in l. 13) to be made about this space – that it contains merely celestial and therefore rather shabby stars – has already appeared in quatrain 2, this 'subject-only' line says something that is new and astonishing. Space, shrink or expand as it may, whether in the eye of the beholder or in obedience to its own physical laws, is always self-identical. Here, many years in advance of *Un Coup de dés*, is the 'neutralité identique du gouffre' that overarches and undercuts the petty differentiations to which the human mind is so devoted. A bold idea has found compact expression, and an intricate phonetic pattern further increases its formulaic intensity. Each hemistich has a sumptuous display of sibilance:

L'e*s*pace à *s*oi pareil qu'il *s*'accroi*ss*e ou *s*e nie

and, less equitably distributed, of assonance upon [a]:

L'es*pa*ce *à* *s*oi *pa*reil qu'il s'*a*ccroisse ou se nie

This sound-mirroring between the two halves of the line culminates in the near-palindrome connecting 'l'espace à soi' with 'qu'il s'accroisse'. Indeed the inversion of *soi* into *-oiss-* may be thought to contain another sobering lesson for self-aggrandizing selfhood: grow and you will stay the same size, seek variety and you will discover uniformity wherever you look. In its multiple play of variation within constancy, this line is autotelic and complete – a self-bounded galaxy within the cosmos of the text.

An additional factor contributes to the disruptive individualism of Mallarmé's alexandrines. Phonetically, the rhyme-words are of course the markers of impending metrical closure, but their performance of this time-honoured role coincides with a quite separate kind of event: the rediscovery, line-ending after line-ending, of semantic equilibrium. Mallarmé crowds nouns and adjectives into the rhyme-position and sets against this repeated grammatical cadence a volatile array of opening gestures. Wherever the line begins from – whether from an active verb, a vocative, a pronoun, a connective or a preposition – an insistent magnetism draws it towards a final stabilizing notation of objects and their attributes. There are only three exceptions to the pattern (ll. 4, 11, 12), and, of these, one almost espouses it: 'moi' in line 4 is to a large extent nominalized under pressure from its nominal rhyme-partners 'loi', 'roi' and 'foi'. Line 12 is doubly exceptional in that it provides the only instance of an active verb in the rhyme position and the only instance of a noun-as-subject at the opening of a line:

> L'espace à soi pareil qu'il s'accroisse ou se nie

This line thus acquires a further poignancy by breaking two of the text's byelaws while proclaiming that a higher edict remains ubiquitously in force. But the general tendency of Mallarmé's lines is unmistakable: irrespective of each individual alexandrine's rank within the syntax of its sentence, the line-ending is overdetermined as a place of suspended animation and rediscovered amplitude of meaning.

It could, I suppose, be claimed that all this is a story of syntax amicably threatened by the counter-syntax of rhyme and metre, and that each of Mallarmé's stanzas eventually stages a complete reconciliation between parties who were never particularly belligerent in the first place. But does this describe what is going on? It certainly does not catch the tumult that each stanza is called upon to subdue. I shall summarize my own version of the story so far. The grammar of the poem is itself subject to distortion and delay and has to be worked for as we read. This already disrupted grammar is contested not by one alternative mode of organization but by several, and these do not harmonize smoothly with each other. The line is at once: a trajectory along which the object-directed arrow of sense flies; a device for creating pseudo-propositions from the dissociated subjects and predicates of 'real' propositions; and, in its ending, a section of the rhyme-based vertical axis of meaning. These competing dispositions are all still palpable at the end of each stanza, and the lines effecting closure are themselves still mobile in their allegiances. Each ending is a truce passed off as a victory. If we are to understand why Mallarmé's proudest pronouncements about the creative power of the mind should be made with this air of ironic reservation – why his claims should sound so much like retractions– we must begin by looking again at what is being advanced.

In this poem, Mallarmé makes a solitary return journey from a heliocentric to a geocentric model of the solar system and the spaces beyond it. But 'la Terre', now restored to the centre of the known universe, is entitled to its privileged position, its radiance and its capital letter not by virtue of any intrinsic merit or luminiferous capacity that it may be thought to possess, and still less because it has found favour with the deity, but because a chance representative of humanity has chosen to declare his desire. The narrator's desire is, however, without externally visible features or impact. Being the possessor of it, or its momentary vehicle, produces a number of internal effects, and these can be named: a capacity to dream, a resilient certainty, a faith, and a moral vision according to which everything that lies outside the individual's desiring orbit is benighted, hideous and vile. The sum of these effects is finally to be glorified as 'genius', and the narrator needs neither to do anything further, nor to possess any further aptitude, in order to win this designation. This is *ingenium* perfectly drained of ingenuity. Indeed we are faced with a poem which, while having 'the poet' or 'the creative artist' as its main invisible and unnamed referent, has nothing to say about poesis or about the resistant medium upon which the artist's craft is exercised. If we discount the ostensive definition that is no doubt hidden here somewhere – 'being a genius means being able to write like *this*' – we are left with an elaborate account of desire as desirous, of human creativity, in its quintessential form, as a radiance that radiates. No spark, no goad, no demon, no imp, no genie is required to get it going: creativity triggers itself, fuels itself, and its luminosity ceases when its self-consumption is complete.

Mallarmé's refurbished geocentrism is set forth in splendidly insolent terms. Desire is the strongest force in the new cosmology he proposes. The periodicities, intensities and modes of discharge characteristic of human sexuality are projected upon the cosmos as boldly as in any primitive creation myth. Arousal, inflammation, pleasure-spasm and deathly self-surrender, Mallarmé's conceit tells us, are things that happen to heavenly bodies too, and even the empty envelope of space ('qu'il s'accroisse ou se nie') may find itself subject to an all-too-human rhythm of tumescence and detume-scence. But it is the peculiarity of desire in this scenario that it should be objectless and intransitive. Even 'ébloui de sa foi', which seems for a moment to suggest that a sensorium is being (over-)stimulated by an external agent, is internal to the workings of the desiring mind: this *foi* is not the inner echo of a force 'out there', not a belief in the efficacy of a shared and publicly accredited principle, but the mind's self-security in its own passion, now fully recognized and reappropriated. The only remnants of the communicative and transactional content of human affairs to be found in the poem are the threat of line 1 and the threatened seduction of line 5. In the first case the 'fatal law' of nature (that all creatures die), and in the second the charm of the 'celebrated' starry sky, are portrayed as holding sway outside as well as inside the mind. Yet in these reminders of human exchange, no exchange occurs, for the mind, having received threats from without, answers with a blank reasser-tion of its own power. One kind of light – the photon-stream that stars emit – can be 'menti par les ténèbres', but another kind – the desire-light that only minds emit – knows no *démenti* and is the sole source of truth.

Much as one may admire simplicity and elegance in scientific explanation, one may still feel that Mallarmé's cosmology has left too much out to be entirely convincing. If the human order is to have a demiurgic role within the world-picture, it could be expected to act multifariously upon material things, to be endowed with calculation as well as prowess in the exercise of its redemptive power. But the human order has two incarnations only and a very limited repertory of behavioural styles: it is to be found either in the drudgery and mean-spiritedness of 'les siècles hideux' or in the magical self-transformation of passion into genius. And genius has as its sole function the bringing to realization, by an unspecified route, of an equally unspecified dream. Performing this function may be the finest, fullest and most demanding form of agency that the human mind can aspire to, yet in the intricate world of human exchange the performer has nowhere to reside and nothing to do. Self-declaration is the only task of genius, and the interiority of the mind its only breeding-ground.

It may seem at first as if the voice of the lyric poet has reached a preposterous level of self-alienation from the social order in 'Quand l'ombre . . .', and that to speak from this imagined point of classlessness and craftlessness about the potency of the artist is to be a ranter and a humbug. But class and craft, although they are not directly ascribed to Mallarmé's narrator, are actively present in the poem and give a topical frame of reference to its talk of timeless mental effulgence.

The sonnet took shape during the heyday of the International Exhibitions, and Mallarmé reported on two of them – those held in London in 1871 and 1872 – for Le National and L'Illustration.[1] Walter Benjamin speaks of the Exposition universelle held in Paris in 1867 as the place where the 'phantasmagoria of capitalist culture attained its most radiant unfurling', but eye-witness accounts suggest that these later London events were easily its equal in phantasmagoric splendour. Mallarmé's reportage contains many lexical pre-echoes of the sonnet: luxe, salle, ébène, séduire, guirlande, célèbre, éblouir, hideux, éclat, mystère are all used in describing the opulent display of artefacts, and certain pieces of virtuoso gold-work prompt Mallarmé to resurrect 'l'épithète démodée de "royales"'. Indeed it does seem as if Mallarmé's mighty attack in quatrain 2 on the heavenly vault and its stars, by which a royal personage might be seduced, had been verbally prepared for in the vicinity of the newly-erected vault of the Royal Albert Hall. But a much more striking connection between these prose writings and the sonnet is to be found in the qualified enthusiasm with which he describes the goods on display. In Mallarmé's account the commodity hovers between use-value and exchange-value, and the tension between the two is now dissolved and now re-exposed by the category of 'the aesthetic' which presides indecisively over the entire pageant:

Nos exposants ne s'étonneront pas de notre sollicitude pour leur tentative – vraiment celle de l'âge moderne tout entier – d'une fusion de l'art et de l'industrie. N'est-ce pas un réciproque devoir, que l'art décore les produits requis par nos besoins immédiats, en même temps que l'industrie multiplie par ses procédés hâtifs et économiques ces objets embellis autrefois par leur seule rareté? Je me propose de rechercher, sous l'heureuse inspiration de votre programme . . . toutes choses participant de ce double aspect.[2]

The 'double aspect' of the objects on display, and the 'reciprocal duty' which binds together art and industry, do not make things easy for the spectator, however. On the one hand, it is good to find that figurines which until recently had been mere 'fétiches esthétiques' in the domestic interior have been given something useful to do – to support a brass candelabrum, say.[3] But, on the other hand, these objects often seem determined to outgrow their uses: once a chest, a casket or a pedestal table has reached a certain level of 'somptuosité extérieure', contemplation by the fetishizing eye begins again to seem the only activity worthy of it.[4] 'Maintenant: un mystère', Mallarmé announces in the last of his 1871 reports. He had discovered a piano in the main French exhibition room, but in what capacity was it there? As an item of furniture to be admired, or as a mere instrument from which admirable music might flow? There are, for Mallarmé, two clear exit-routes from what seems at first an impasse in the relationship between usefulness, beauty and monetary value. One leads towards the creation of luxuries – goods that do not serve the needs of the artisan-producer and that are too expensive for him to own. Such objects are at once repellent and exciting. The other leads towards the creation of beautiful things which in themselves recapitulate and pay tribute to the producer's shaping labour. But here again, faced with these alternative routes, Mallarmé hesitates.

Mallarmé's career as an observer of capitalism in spate, far from stopping at the threshold of his lyric poems, reaches in 'Quand l'ombre ...' a new grandeur and a new mordancy. The satirical brush-stroke of 'Luxe, ô salle d'ébène ...' is of course broad: over and against the awesome constellations that Mallarmé elsewhere in his works invokes with such force, here is that vanity of vanities, a Great Exhibition laid out not in Kensington but in the universe at large. The firmament itself has been annexed by the bourgeoisie; it has become, in the opening words of *Das Kapital*, 'an immense collection of commodities'. Yet together with Mallarmé's disdainful rejection of these commodified stars runs an equally powerful sympathy with them, for, like the narrator himself, they too have the chill of mortality upon them; they too are a process seeking its term, a mechanism running down.

The lyric poet of 'Quand l'ombre ...' relives the perplexity and indecision that the journalist had experienced in London, but something very much more intimate and urgent is now at stake. For he himself is the artisan whose wares are on display; his own poem is the unstable commodity pulled in two directions at once – towards luxury and towards the active recapitulation of productive work. How can it any longer be possible to write a poem in good faith and with a responsive recipient in mind? How can the poem's refinements of structure and minute gradations of tone avoid being swallowed up by a society whose appetite for trinkets, and mechanized production processes, now seems insatiable? One answer to this problem as we have already seen, is to remove the poet from the verbal workshop once and for all, to promote him to such sublime potency that his pen need never again travel across the page. But against this answer – which may be thought of as the poem's central, sustaining fantasy – Mallarmé provides another, and on this occasion a thoroughly 'writerly' one. As the narrator projects himself beyond the exactions of poetic craft and satirizes those who are still slave to merely *artisanal* modes of awareness and action, Mallarmé the poet steps forward as an artisan fiercely loyal to the laborious complexities and contrivances of his calling. His manipulations of verbal matter – the staggering, suspension, superimposition, intrication and recursion to which he insistently subjects his verbal messages – undermine the surface affirmativeness of the text, reaffirm the virtues of caution and doubt and set a tragic limit to the narrator's culminating conceit. Such a display of artifice in a work that disowns artifice is at one level perfectly straightforwardly motivated: it reminds the reader of work, sets him to work, and protects the poem from shallowness and euphoria. But at another level the motivation is much more hazardous. For the artificer is propelled by a dangerous as well as by a defiantly optimistic passion. In his quest for elaborated structure and richly interfused meaning, he builds bridges and breaks them, proclaims desire and thwarts it, offers himself to the reader not just as a light-bearer but as an exemplary victim, an emblem of wounded hope. Human passion, in this sonnet, is pursued under intolerable conditions of duress – *beneath* the sky's funereal ceilings, *beneath* the hideous centuries. But it has its own 'fatal law' too, a love of darkness that also seeks outlet in the creative task and threatens to turn the intricate mechanism of the text into an instrument of destruction.

In previous pages, I have been separating the strands of Mallarmé's contrapuntal texture and mapping at a very slow speed its unusually rapid dynamics of thought and feeling. There is, of course, a level of meaning to which analysis of this kind has only limited access, and it is all the more unfortunate that this should be the level inhabited by the 'ordinary' reader as he or she reads – between the lines of counterpoint, between the alternative semantic axes, between the poet's conflicting drives, and always in movement and under pressure. We need an analytic method that, having frozen the poem's individual moments and tendencies, can unfreeze them again in order to rediscover its dialectic. Hegel, in his *Phenomenology*, brings inexhaustible literary ingenuity to his models of consciousness-in-process, tugged at once forwards and backwards by the desire that actuates it:

The individual who is going to act seems ... to find himself in a circle in which each moment already presupposes the other, and thus he seems unable to find a beginning, because he only gets to know his original nature, which must be his End, *from the deed*, while, in order to act, he must have that End beforehand. But for that very reason he has to start immediately, and, whatever the circumstances, without further scruples about beginning, means, or End, proceed to action; for his essence and *intrinsic* nature is beginning, means and End, all in one.[5]

What Mallarmé criticism needs is a way of articulating the all-in-oneness of 'beginning, means and End' that is to be found, in textualized form, in each of his great poems. In the case of 'Quand l'ombre ...', such analysis would attend to the collapse and reconstruction of hierarchical systems within the text; to its premature and belated discoveries of meaning; to its constant play between simultaneity and sequence; to its hesitation between sense effect and sound effect; to its ingenious interweaving of philosophical motifs; and, beyond ingenuity, beyond the indirections of poetic language, to the grand prospects – of pleasure and of disaster – that the text affords.

NOTES

1 *Œuvres complètes* (Paris, 1945), pp. 666–79 and 680–6.
2 *Ibid.*, pp. 666–7.
3 *Ibid.*, p. 671.
4 *Ibid.*, p. 672.
5 G. W. F. Hegel, *The Phenomenology of Spirit*, trans. A. V. Miller (Oxford, 1977), p. 241.

FRENCH VERSIFICATION:
A SUMMARY

Clive Scott

(All examples in this appendix are drawn from nineteenth-century verse and, whenever possible, from the poems analysed in the body of the book).

The regular alexandrine

Ainsi,/toujours poussés//vers de nouveaux/rivages,	2+4+4+2
Dans la nuit/éternelle//emportés/sans retour,	3+3+3+3
Ne pourrons-nous/jamais//sur l'océan/des âges	4+2+4+2
Jeter l'ancre/un seul jour?	3+3

The stanzas of Lamartine's 'Le Lac' are each composed of three alexandrines followed by a hexasyllable, i.e. 12, 12, 12, 6. The scansion of the first stanza immediately makes several things clear about the regular alexandrine:

1 It has a fixed medial caesura (marked //) after the sixth syllable, which enforces an accent (stress) on the sixth syllable. The only other *obligatory* accent in the line falls on the final (twelfth) syllable.

2 The caesura is a *metrical* juncture which usually coincides with a significant syntactical juncture (and thus a pause), for reasons which will become apparent. But it is first and foremost the line's principal point of rhythmic articulation, not its most obtrusive syntactic break. It divides the alexandrine into two half-lines (*hémistiches*). Each half-line *usually* contains one other accent apart from the one on its final syllable. This 'secondary' accent is mobile and may fall on any of the hemistich's other syllables. A schematization of the metre of the regular alexandrine would thus be:

$$\_\,\overset{(\prime)}{\_}\,\_\,\_\,\_\,\overset{\prime}{\_}\,// \,\_\,\_\,\overset{(\prime)}{\_}\,\_\,\_\,\overset{\prime}{\_}$$

The brackets round the secondary accents indicate that these accents are both mobile and optional. In other words, the alexandrine may have only two accents (on 6 and 12), or three (say on 2, 6 and 12, or 6, 9 and 12), but it normally has four which is why the regular alexandrine is called the *alexandrin tétramètre* (i.e. with four measures). There are thirty-six different possible rhythmic configurations of the regular alexandrine, ranging from the basic two-accent 6+6, through tri-accentual patterns (6+4+2, 3+3+6, etc.) to the tetra-accentual combinations (1+5+4+2, 3+3+2+4, 4+2+1+5, etc.).

3 The fact that the obligatory accents fall at the end of the half-lines indicates that French accent is by nature terminal (oxytonic): it falls on the last accentuable syllable of the word or word-group. During the course of its phonetic development, French accent has gradually weakened, so that it is not so much individual words which have accents as word-groups (syntactic segments) (i.e. accent is reinforced by intonation, by the rising or falling pitch of the voice). Thus a word which in one collocation might receive accent because it is the final unit will be without accent in other collocations in which it is not the final unit – 'un stýle' but 'un style orné'. Because verse intensifies our sense of rhythmicity and tends to increase the segmentation of utterance, it will usually accentuate more elements than 'normal' speech would; for example, it is unlikely that Lamartine's 'nouveaux' or 'nuit' would receive accents in non-verse contexts.

4 The weakness of French accent partly explains why, up to the latter years of the nineteenth century, rhyme was considered indispensable to French verse: rhyme gives more audibility to the final, line-demarcative accent of the line. The rhyme-scheme of 'Le Lac' is *rimes croisées* (alternating rhyme: abab); the other principal rhyme-schemes are *rimes plates* (couplets: aa, bb, etc.) and *rimes embrassées* (enclosed rhyme: abba).

5 When looking for the accentual pattern of a regular alexandrine, therefore, we can confidently place accents on syllables 6 and 12 and then identify the principal syntactic divisions (word-groups) within each hemistich, assigning an accent to the last accentuable syllable of any group which obtains. Thus we might describe our scansion of the first line of 'Le Lac' as

Adv. (governing whole stanza)/Adj. phrase describing 'nous'
Adv. of time+past part.//Adv. phrase of place
Prep.+adj./Noun

We then notate the rhythm of the line by indicating the number of syllables within each syntactic segment, thus 2+4+4+2.

6 Syllables. Two major problems beset the counting of syllables: do two contiguous vowels, as in 'nuit', count as one syllable (synaeresis) or two

(diaeresis), and does one count mute 'e's' or not? The standard way of resolving the first problem, in classical verse at least, is etymological: since *nuit* derives from the Latin *nox, noctem*, which has only one root vowel, so *nuit* is counted as only one syllable (/nɥi/) rather than two (/nyi/). This principle is of course complicated as verse becomes freer and admits changes in current pronunciation.

As far as the mute 'e' (*e atone*) is concerned, a distinction must be made between line-terminal 'e's' and line-internal ones.

(i) Line-terminal 'e's'. These are not counted as syllables (though they may attract some degree of enunciation); they indicate that the rhyme is feminine. Thus *rivages* has two syllables and *âges* has one, and together they constitute a feminine rhyme. From the middle of the sixteenth century up to the latter half of the nineteenth century, poets rigorously observed the alternation of masculine and feminine rhymes (*la loi de l'alternance des rimes*): i.e. a masculine rhyme-pair must be followed by a feminine one, and vice versa.

(ii) Line-internal 'e's'. A line-internal 'e' is counted as a syllable, and pronounced, when it is immediately followed by either a consonant (even if mute) or an aspirate 'h'. A line-internal 'e' is elided (not counted) when it is immediately followed by a vowel or a mute 'h'. Thus in the first stanza of 'Le Lac', the final 'e's' of both 'éternelle' and 'ancre' are elided before a following vowel.

Summary to date and differentiation with English verse

The regular alexandrine has two obligatory accents on syllables 6 and 12, and usually two other accents, mobile and optional. Because it is fixed, the medial caesura is a *metrical* element, governing the rhythmic and syntactic distribution of the line. Often the caesura coincides with the major syntactic juncture within the line, but it need not do so. Above all, it acts as a fulcrum for the line, a rhythmic pivot encouraging relationships of symmetry, chiasmus, antithesis, complementarity, parallelism, between the two half-lines (*hémistiches*). In the English iambic pentameter, on the other hand, the caesura is mobile because it occurs at the major syntactic juncture within the line wherever that may be. It thus has no *metrical* significance, but does contribute to the rhythmic variety of a sequence of lines. Grammatically significant French words (nouns, verbs, adjectives, adverbs) do not consistently enjoy a right to accent, do not have accent built into them, whereas their English equivalents do. French accent is directly related to syntactic structure, to word-group; English stress is word-related before it is phrase-related. Thus, very crudely put, in French verse rhythm derives from syntax, whereas in English verse a syntax or word-sequence is fitted to a metre.

Because of this distinction, variability of syntactic structure does not, in English verse, lead to metrical variety. In English syllable-stress metre, an iambic, or trochaic, or anapaestic foot is a repeated unit, repeated through thick and thin, albeit with conventional variations; and because English metre is constructed on repetition and recurrence, so the metrical structure of one line predicts that of the next. In French verse, on the other hand, although we may predict that one sequence of twelve syllables will be followed by another, we cannot predict the particular rhythmic configuration of a particular alexandrine on the basis of the alexandrine which precedes it; just as we cannot predict the rhythmic configuration of a second hemistich on the basis of the first. After the 2+4 of 'Le Lac's' first hemistich could we foresee the 4+2 of the second? After the 2+4+4+2 of the first line, could we predict the 3+3+3+3 of the second line? Because French accent is word(-group)-terminal, so in French verse there is a natural tendency for the end of the line to coincide with a syntactic break. This inevitably makes enjambement an unlikely phenomenon and together with the rhythmic unpredictability just described endows each alexandrine with a peculiar autonomy. But in English verse, thanks to the repetition of the foot and the continuity of the metre from one line to the next, enjambement is rhythmically non-disruptive, an unexceptional resource of verse. French verse is syllabic, and one syllable more or less is the difference between one kind of line, one set of possible rhythmic segmentations, and another; French verse thus necessitates very precise rules about pronunciation and the values of syllables. Whether contiguous vowels count as one or two syllables is a crucial question, as is the status of the *e atone* (mute e). English verse is less sensitive to the syllable, and whether certain syllables are pronounced or not ('heav'n' or 'heaven', 'stagg'ring' or 'staggering', 'tow'r' or 'tower') matters little as long as the underlying metrical pulse is maintained; an iambic pentameter may vary between eight and twelve syllables without the English ear being unduly troubled.

Armed with these findings, let us turn to the second and third stanzas of 'Le Lac':

O lac!/l'année à peine//a fini/sa carrière	2+4+3+3 f.
Et, près des flots/chéris//qu'elle devait/revoir,	4+2+4+2 m.
Regarde!/je viens seul//m'asseoir/sur cette pierre	3'+3+2+4 f.
Où tu la vis/s'asseoir.	4+2 m.
Tu mugissais/ainsi/sous ces ro:/ches profondes;	4+2+3+3 f.
Ainsi/tu te brisais//sur leurs flancs/déchirés;	2+4+3+3 m.
Ainsi/le vent jetait//l'écu:/me de tes ondes	2+4+2+4 f.
Sur ses pieds/adorés.	3+3 m.

Five further points should be added to the foregoing list of verse-features:

7 The bar-line which we use in scansion to divide one measure from the next is called a *coupe*, and since the accentuated vowel of the word-group closes the rhythmic measure, the *coupe* falls immediately after the accentuated vowel. The *coupe* is a fiction, a convenience of scansion, and does not bear on the enunciation of the line, other than where an articulated (unelided) e is involved.

8 The *e atone*, as its name suggests, cannot bear an accent. This is why, in speaking of the terminality of French accent, we needed to specify the 'last *accentuable* syllable of the word or word-group', since the accentuated word may end with an *e atone*. When the accentuated word does indeed end with an articulated, post-tonic 'e', the *coupe* usually continues to fall immediately after the accentuated vowel, thus pushing the final *e atone* into the following measure. This is called a *coupe enjambante*, because the accentuated word straddles or enjambs the *coupe* (see the first and third lines of the third stanza). The *coupe enjambante* helps to create a seamless continuity in the line, an intonational suppleness, an undulating ease.

9 On rare occasions, however, an *e atone* after an accentuated vowel cannot be assimilated into the following measure, for expressive or syntactic reasons. In these instances the *coupe* falls *after* the *e atone* and coincides with a pause, with a rupture in the rhythmic and syntactic chain. This kind of *coupe* is called a *coupe lyrique* (or *coupe féminine*). 'Regarde!' in the third line of the second stanza is an unsuppressible interjection, an interruptive imperative, bitterly requiring the lake to witness the poet's dispossession. How compromised and conciliatory it would sound were it to be enunciated with a *coupe enjambante*:

Regar:/de! je viens seul//m'asseoir/sur cette pierre   2+4+2+4

Instead we choose a 3'+3+2+4 reading, where the *coupe lyrique* is indicated by the apostrophe which accompanies the first 3.

10 It would be easy to assume that all rhythmic decisions relating to the classical alexandrine are cut and dried, that there is no room for interpretative choice. This is not true. For example, the third stanza takes up the 'Ainsi' of the first stanza and makes it an insistent, self-torturing refrain. I have treated it throughout the stanza as a separate measure. But may it not be that this word develops not so much a mechanical intensity as an exasperated weariness, becomes something taken for granted? Thus perhaps not:

Ainsi/le vent jetait//l'écu:/me de tes ondes   2+4+2+4

but

Ainsi le vent/jetait//l'écu:/me de tes ondes   4+2+2+4

as the poet's attention shifts from his lingering sense of injustice to the natural theatre, highlighting the violence of the wind's activity. Equally we might wish to read the third line of the first stanza not as 4+2+4+2 but as 6+4+2, so that the whole construction of the modal verb – 'ne pourrons-nous jamais' – is rhythmically undifferentiated, flat, will-less.

11 Of the even-syllabled (parasyllabic) lines, only the alexandrine and the decasyllable have caesuras. The octosyllable and, as here, the hexa-syllable do not.

This completes our rapid exploration of the regular alexandrine. Before moving on to deal with other lines, we should mention some of the liberties taken with this metrical institution by nineteenth-century poets.

The 'alexandrin trimètre'

The principal 'transgression' practised is the substitution of a three-measure alexandrine (*alexandrin trimètre*), for the four-measure one (*alexandrin tétramètre*), or the substitution of a ternary structure for the standard binary one. This involves the erasure of the medial caesura and the consequent dislodging of the hemistich as the basic rhythmic building block. The alexandrine is invaded by syncopation, and the conceptualizing tendency of binarity yields to the contingent and intractable amalgam of three:

> Je vis trembler/leurs traits | confus/et par degrés   4+4+4
> Blanchir l'écume,/ou creuse | une on:/de dans les blés   4+4+4
> (Hugo: 'La Pente de la rêverie', ll. 43, 124)

In both of these examples, even though the sixth syllable remains potentially accentuable and a spectral caesura still survives, the demands of the syntactic grouping over-ride the binary structure and argue for a three-measure segmentation. The *alexandrin trimètre* is to be found in seven-teenth-century dramatic verse, particularly comedy, in La Fontaine, in the work of the late eighteenth-century poet André Chénier. But it achieves a polemical value and a concerted use only with the romantics, especially Hugo, and for this reason is often referred to as an *alexandrin romantique*.

It is generally assumed, and with much justification, that the *trimètre* of the romantics is itself conservative, that the ghost of a caesura is maintained by the continuing accentuability of the sixth syllable, as above, and that it most frequently falls into a 'regular' 4+4+4 pattern. This is why it is often difficult to decide, in one's reading of such lines, whether to treat them as *alexandrins trimètres*, or as *alexandrins tétramètres* with enjambement at the caesura, the central phrase straddling the two hemistichs. Thus, should one read:

Les deux pôles!/le monde | entier!/la mer, la terre
('La Pente de la rêverie', l. 57)

that is 4'+4+4, with a *coupe lyrique* at 'pôles', further separating the three elements and allowing the exclamation to die away in its own expansiveness? Or should one opt for:

Les deux pô:/les! le monde//entier!/la mer, la terre   3+3+2+4

where the *coupe enjambante* emphasizes the dynamism of the vision, its onrush as it encompasses vast spaces, a vision which suddenly comes to a suspended halt at 'monde', so that, triumphantly, the crescendo can release itself in 'entier'? Each reader will make up his own mind.

But we occasionally find a more asymmetrical distribution of the *trimètre*'s measures in romantic poetry:

Se réfléchit/avec ses riviè:/res de moire   4+5+3
('La Pente de la rêverie', l. 66)

'Avec', it should be noted, has a capacity for accentuation which one might not expect and which derives from its acoustic fullness (compare the archaic form 'avecque'). This line of Hugo's should be compared with Vigny's:

Que l'homme a fait/avec les animaux/serviles   4+6+2
('La Mort du Loup', l. 70)

and with Baudelaire's:

Qui l'observent/avec | des regards/familiers   4'+5+3
('Correspondances', l. 4)

Here, too, I favour a *coupe lyrique* at 'observent', to imbue this look with something sinister, penetrating, a look whose strangeness creates a piquant oxymoron with 'familiers'.

But it is only in the *vers libéré* (see below) of the post-romantic, proto-symbolist poets, poets such as Verlaine and Rimbaud, that the *trimètre* accomplishes a complete eradication of the caesura and fully exploits its capacity to assemble irregular combinations. Although the opening line of Verlaine's 'Le Paysage dans le cadre des portières':

Le paysa:/ge dans le ca:/dre des portières

falls into a 4+4+4 pattern, 'dans' does not allow even the ghost of a caesura on the sixth syllable. And although the lines

Vont s'engouffrant/parmi le tourbillon/cruel
Où tom:/bent les poteaux min:/ces du télégraphe
Dont les fils/ont l'allure étran:/ge d'un paraphe

APPENDIX

from the same poem, offer accentuability at the sixth syllable, the configurations which emerge from the trimetric readings they encourage are as
varied as 4+6+2, 2+5+5, 3+5+4.

Hitherto we have dealt only with the alexandrine. We should now attend
briefly to those even-syllabled lines which come next in order of descent, the
decasyllable and the octosyllable.

The decasyllable

If we cast our eye over the first stanza of Baudelaire's 'La Mort des amants':

Nous aurons des lits//pleins d'odeurs légères,	5+3+2
Des divans profonds/comme des tombeaux,	3+2+5
Et d'étranges fleurs//sur des étagères,	3+2+5
Ecloses pour nous//sous des cieux plus beaux	2+3+3+2

we might suppose that the decasyllable, like the alexandrine, has a fixed
medial caesura, after the fifth syllable, and that it usually has three accents
per line (obligatory accents on 5 and 10, plus a mobile and optional third
one), but may have as few as two and as many as four. Such a supposition
would be largely mistaken. The 5//5 division is just one version of the decasyllable, a version particularly cultivated by nineteenth-century poets, and if
we read on in 'La Mort des amants' we can see why Baudelaire has chosen it:

Nos deux cœurs seront//deux vastes flambeaux,
Qui réfléchiront//leurs doubles lumières
Dans nos deux esprits,//ces miroirs jumeaux.

Baudelaire's images of reflection, of perfect reciprocity and complementarity, call for the symmetry of 5//5. But the classical divisions of the
decasyllable are in fact 4//6 or 6//4, with the hexasyllabic element usually
containing two accents, and the tetrasyllabic element one.

The octosyllable

Much of the rhythmic ambiguity and fluidity of the octosyllabic line derives
from its lying between the three-accent-per-line norm of the decasyllable
and the two-accent norm of the hexasyllable; it thus frequently invites both
a two-accent and a three-accent reading:

A l'horizon monte une nue,	4+4/4+1+3
Sculptant sa forme dans l'azur:	4+4/2+2+4
On dirait une vierge nue	3+5/3+3+2
Emergeant d'un lac au flot pur	5+3/3+2+3

(Gautier, 'La Nue')

250

Whereas the alexandrine is the line of sustained discourse, usually enjoying a certain syntactic completeness, the movement of the octosyllable outstrips the development of syntax and parcels it into a sequence of momentary tableaux, near-autonomous images or cryptic utterances, which are able to stand in a variety of potential relationships with each other. These are the qualities which made the octosyllable attractive to Gautier (*Emaux et camées*, 1852) and to the symbolist poets after him. The rhythmic volatility of the octosyllable – it has only one fixed accent, on its eighth syllable – and the swift return of its rhymes have also given it a reputation for alertness, zestfulness, impertinence even, suitable for lighter varieties of verse. Henri Morier describes the octosyllable as 'un vers que nous avons déclaré capricieux et insubordonné par définition'.

The alexandrine, the decasyllable and the octosyllable are the three principal (parisyllabic) lines of classical French prosody. Before moving on to the imparisyllabic lines (*vers impairs*) which are associated with the liberated verse (*vers libéré*) of the latter half of the nineteenth century, we should give some further consideration to rhyme.

Rhyme

As already mentioned, rhyme was, until the end of the nineteenth century, considered indispensable to French verse. It was a device which clearly marked verse's status as verse, by strengthening the line-terminal accent and itself performing a line-demarcative function with its homophonic mechanism. French rhyme distinguishes itself from English rhyme in three important respects: rhyme gender, terminality of accent and rhyme degree.

Not only does French verse differentiate between masculine and feminine rhymes, it systematizes the differentiation by insisting on the alternation of rhyme-pairs of different gender (see 6(i) above). Many commentators feel that masculine and feminine rhymes have different expressive tonalities too: masculine rhymes are abrupt, peremptory, hard, uncompromising, while feminine rhymes are gentle, melting, yielding, evanescent. This prosodic sexism cannot be applied very convincingly to the stanza from Gautier's 'La Nue' quoted above, but then the rhymes here are unusual in that the feminine rhymes 'nue'/'nue' end in vowels (when it is more usual for masculine rhymes to do so) and the masculine rhymes 'azur'/'pur' in consonants (when it is more usual for feminine rhymes to do so).

The terminality of French accent and the relatively high inflectedness of the language mean that rhyme falls more often than not on suffixes and endings. This automatically increases the rhyme vocabulary available in French (as opposed to English). It also means that rhyme tends to semanticize endings, to underline the modality of tenses and to invest suffixes with more than a purely suffixal meaning.

French verse analysis differentiates between different degrees of rhyme: *rime pauvre* (or *faible*), *rime suffisante*, *rime riche* and *rime léonine*. In the nineteenth and early twentieth centuries, rhyme classification distinguished between phonemic material following the tonic (rhyming) vowel and phonemic material preceding it, producing the scale:

(a)   rhyme of tonic vowel alone: *rime pauvre (faible)*
(b)   rhyme of tonic vowel + following consonant(s): *rime suffisante*
(c)   rhyme of tonic vowel + preceding consonant(s) (*consonne(s) d'appui*) + any following consonants: *rime riche*
(d)   rhyme of tonic vowel + preceding syllable(s): *rime léonine*

The incidence of *rime riche* increased with the romantic poets and became an important plank in the aesthetic platform of the Parnassians (e.g. Banville: 'Sans consonne d'appui, pas de Rime et, par conséquent, pas de poésie'). In the hands of these poets, rich rhyme was looked to to provide more resonance, colour, dramatic presence, to guarantee the depth and authenticity of thought and feeling, and to safeguard the rigour of the poetic vocation. But to twentieth-century analysts, the nineteenth-century system of classification has seemed too crude, particularly as it classes rhymes like 'bonté'/'cité' as rich, while denser accumulations of phonemes (e.g. 'tordre'/ 'mordre', 'arche'/'marche') are merely *suffisantes*. Accordingly a purely numerical approach to rhyme-classification has been adopted, whereby the more identical phonemes there are, whether preceding or succeeding the tonic vowel, the richer the rhyme. Thus in Leconte de Lisle's 'Midi', 'bleu'/'feu' (/ø/), 'fin'/'divin' (/ɛ̃/) are *rimes pauvres* (identity of one element, the tonic vowel), 'dorée'/'sacrée' (/Re/), 'rire'/'maudire' (/iR/) are *rimes suffisantes* (identity of two elements, the tonic vowel + consonant, but note that 'dorée'/'sacrée' would be *riche* under earlier classification), and 'plaine'/ 'haleine' (/lɛn/), 'd'ombre'/'sombre' (/ɔ̃bʀ/) are *rimes riches* (identity of three or more elements in tonic syllable; but note that 'd'ombre'/'sombre' would be *suffisante* under earlier classification). For examples of *rime léonine* (identity of two or more vowels/syllables, the tonic syllable and one or more vowels/syllables preceding it) we might turn to Nerval's 'El Desdichado' ('abolie'/'Mélancolie', 'consolé'/'désolé'). Variation in rhyme degree may have a structural function, or may affect the focus of images (from soft to sharp) or may be expressive in other ways: weaker rhymes suggest the prosaic, the unassuming, the weary, the deprived, the impoverished, etc.; richer rhymes suggest the confidently poetic, the authoritative, the alert, the abundant, the opulent, etc.

The 'vers impair'

The imparisyllabic line, the *vers impair* (13, 11, 9, 7 or 5 syllables), is remarkable by its scarcity in the classical canon of verse. It occurs intermittently throughout French verse history – e.g. *Aucassin et Nicolette*, sixteenth-century ode, Malherbe, La Fontaine, Marceline Desbordes-Valmore, Hugo – but it is particularly associated with the *vers libéré* of poets such as Verlaine, Rimbaud and Laforgue, because in their work it is exploited more frequently and more tendentiously. Because of its lack of self-assured equilibrium – Leconte de Lisle was of the opinion that 'le vers français vit d'équilibre, il meurt si on touche à sa parité' – the *vers impair* can be seen as intrinsically anti-oratorical and peculiarly suited to the depiction of moods which are unstable, nervous, indeterminate, or ironic and mischievous. Slightly 'out of true', a kind of *vers faux*, the *vers impair* provokes a tentative, exploratory reading appropriate to vague, even anxious feelings; but at the same time, by increasing the reader's alertness to syllabic values, it can achieve modal and tonal effects of great subtlety. Verlaine's 'Art poétique', in lines of nine syllables (enneasyllables), advocates the *vers impair* in these terms: 'De la musique avant toute chose, / Et pour cela préfère l'Impair / Plus vague et plus soluble dans l'air, / Sans rien en lui qui pèse ou qui pose.'

'Vers libéré'

Vers libéré was not liberated by virtue of its cultivation of the *impair* alone. It also made more uninhibited use of the *alexandrin trimètre*, eradicating the caesura and favouring rhythmically asymmetrical configurations, as we have seen. And it flaunted its increasingly bold enjambements. All these developments contributed to the rhythmic destabilization of the line and undermined its integrity. Rhythms lost their firm contours and consequently their aptitude for eloquent and lapidary utterance. Instead they acquired a certain looseness, fluidity, indeterminacy which favoured the intimate, the prosaic, the impromptu, the *fantaisiste*. But this was not all. The poets of *vers libéré* (Baudelaire, Corbière, Verlaine, Rimbaud, Laforgue) also took liberties with the classical rules of rhyme. From time to time they disregarded the *loi de l'alternance des rimes*, pairing masculine with feminine or exploiting the expressive potentialities of single-gender rhyme sequences. They did not scruple, when necessary, to rhyme singulars with plurals. And in more extreme instances, half-rhyme was resorted to (e.g. Verlaine: 'vêpres'/'cortège', 'mauves'/'jaunes', 'liturgiques'/'mélancolie'; Rimbaud: 'facile'/'elle', 'étonne'/'infortune', 'auberge'/'perche').

But for all its erosions of traditional practice, *vers libéré* stopped short of dislodging those two factors which are the very foundation of regular verse: the principle of syllabic regularity (isosyllabism) – which also meant, of course, that the poets of *vers libéré* observed the conventions concerning the syllabic status of the *e atone* (see 6, above) and contiguous vowels (synaeresis and diaeresis, see 6 above) – and the principle of rhyming, where rhyme, whatever its degree or gender, is seen as an indispensable demarcator of the line, a guarantor of the line's integrity and the sole source of stanzaic structure.

'Vers libre'

The emergence of *vers libre* (free verse) occurred in 1886, in the pages of the review *La Vogue*, edited by Gustave Kahn, where in rapid succession were published Rimbaud's free-verse *Illuminations* 'Marine' and 'Mouvement' (1872–3), translations of Whitman by Laforgue, poems by Kahn later to be published in his *Les Palais nomades* (1887), the first *collection* of *vers libre*, ten of Laforgue's own free-verse poems (to be collected in his *Derniers Vers*, 1890) and other specimens of the new verse by Jean Moréas and Paul Adam. To this list of initiators, Jean Ajalbert, Édouard Dujardin, Albert Mockel, Francis Vielé-Griffin, Henri de Régnier, Adolphe Retté and Maurice Maeterlinck added their names in the years immediately following.

The poets of *vers libre* undermined syllabicity either by claiming that they did not count syllables any more (they only counted accents and measures) or by casting doubt on the syllabic status of the *e atone*, allowing it to be counted in the conventional way, but equally allowing its suppression both at the ends of words (*apocope*) or within words (*syncope*); additionally they impeded the urge to count by indeterminate and inconsistent practice in relation to synaeresis and diaeresis. Laforgue's line:

> Oh! et puis, est-ce que tu connais, outre les pianos
> ('L'Hiver qui vient', l. 75)

might be as long as fifteen syllables or as short as twelve syllables, a ragged 3 + 5 + 4 *trimètre*:

> Oh! et puis, est-c' que tu connais, outr' les pianos (/pjɑno/)

or anything between. So the *verslibristes* felt free to use lines of any length (where length can no longer be reliably determined) in indiscriminate combination. And the indiscriminate combination of lines was abetted by free-rhyming stanzaic structures. By 'free-rhyming' I mean not only the freedoms introduced into rhyming by *vers libéré*, but also freedom with rhyme patterning, and the freedom to use repetition and rhymelessness as the occasion demanded. In the opening lines of 'L'Hiver qui vient',

> Blocus sentimental! Messageries du Levant! . . .
> Oh, tombée de la pluie! Oh, tombée de la nuit!
> Oh, le vent! . . .
> La Toussaint, la Noël et la Nouvelle Année,
> Oh, dans les bruines, toutes mes cheminées! . . .
> D'usines . . .

'nuit' apparently has no end-rhyme partner – instead it creates an internal rhyme with 'pluie' (/ɥi/); but 'nuit' and 'usines' form a half-rhyme on /i/, a half-rhyme validated and mediated by the line-internal 'bruines' (/ɥin/) (i.e. 'nuit' (/ɥi/) → 'bruines' (/ɥin/) → 'usines' (/in/), itself, like 'usines', enjoying an acoustic kinship with 'cheminées'. Rhyme freedoms permit an intrication of acoustic association. They also enable the poet to vary the intervals between rhymes in order to situate the poem at different levels of consciousness. Thus the real end-rhyme partners of 'usines' are 'bruine' (l. 13) and 'ruine' (l. 15), but the distance between them means that the connections are made lower in the consciousness, subliminally even, compared with the highly self-conscious irony of the couplet:

> Ah! nuées accourues des côtes de la Manche,
> Vous nous avez gâté notre dernier dimanche!

where our awareness of the traditional enemy's hand in undoing the poet's sentimental adventure ('Blocus sentimental/continental' → 'des côtes de la Manche') is rendered more piquant by the fact that the 'Manche' compels the poet self-righteously to ally himself and his amatory hopes with a day – 'dimanche' – which represents all he abominates.

Vers libre can claim, with some justification, to have 'psychologized' verse-structure, to have made the act of writing apparently simultaneous with the changing movements of mind: 'Une poésie n'est pas un sentiment que l'on communique tel que conçu avant la plume. Avouons le petit bonheur de la rime et les déviations occasionnées par les trouvailles, la symphonie imprévue vient escorter le *motif*' (Laforgue, *Mélanges posthumes*). By allowing the aleatory and the improvised to inhabit verse, by exploiting the psychological layering produced by variable rhyme-interval and variable margin, by locating verse at the intersection of multiplied co-ordinates (rhyme, rhymelessness, repetition, the metrical, the non-metrical, etc.), by using linguistic structures to attract and activate paralinguistic features (tempo, pause, tone, accentual variation, emotional colouring), *vers libre* established its affinities with the stream of consciousness of contemporary fiction and proposed a stream of consciousness of reading.

REFERENCES AND SUGGESTIONS
FOR FURTHER READING

Adorno, T. W., 'Lyric Poetry and Society', *Telos*, 20 (1974) pp. 51–71.
Aprimoz, A. L., '"Mémoire": la fête de l'oubli d'Arthur Rimbaud', *Orbis Litterarum*, 40 (1985), pp. 111–24.
Austin, L. J., *L'Univers poétique de Baudelaire* (Paris, 1956).
Barrell, J., *Poetry, Language and Politics* (Manchester, 1988).
Barthes, R., *Critique et vérité* (Paris, 1966).
  La Chambre claire: Note sur la photographie (Paris, 1980).
Bénichou, P., *Nerval et la chanson folklorique* (Paris, 1970).
Benjamin, W., *Charles Baudelaire: A Lyric Poet in the Era of High Capitalism* (London, 1973).
Bersani, L. *Baudelaire and Freud* (Berkeley, 1979).
Birkett, M. E., *Lamartine and the Poetics of Landscape* (Lexington, KY, 1982).
Bloom, H., *The Anxiety of Influence: A Theory of Poetry* (New York, 1973).
Bowie, M., *Mallarmé and the Art of Being Difficult* (Cambridge, 1978).
Bowman, F. P., 'The Poetic Practices of Vigny's *Poèmes philosophiques*', *Modern Language Review*, 60 (1965), pp. 359–68.
Brereton, G., *An Introduction to the French Poets: Villon to the Present Day* (London, 1973).
Broome, P., and G. Chesters, *The Appreciation of Modern French Poetry 1850–1950* (Cambridge, 1976).
Chambers, R., '"Mémoire" de Rimbaud: essai de lecture', *Essays in French Literature*, 5 (1968), pp. 22–37.
Champigny, R., *Le Genre poétique: essai* (Monte-Carlo, 1963).
Chatman, S., *A Theory of Meter* (The Hague, 1965).
Chaussivert, J., *L'Art verlainien dans 'La Bonne Chanson'* (Paris, 1973).
Clark, T. J., *The Painting of Modern Life: Paris in the Art of Manet and his Followers* (London, 1985).

Cohen, H. L., *Lyric Forms from France: Their History and Use* (New York, 1922).

Cohen, J., *Structures du langage poétique* (Paris, 1966).

Cohn, R. G., *The Poetry of Rimbaud* (Princeton, 1973).

Collie, M., *Jules Laforgue* (London, 1977).

Culler, J., 'Commentary', *New Literary History*, 6 (1974), pp. 219–29.

The Pursuit of Signs: Semiotics, Literature, Deconstruction (Ithaca, NY, 1981).

'Reading Lyric', *Yale French Studies*, 69 (1985), pp. 98–106.

Damisch, H., *Théorie du nuage, pour une histoire de la peinture* (Paris, 1972).

de Man, P., *The Rhetoric of Romanticism* (New York, 1984)

The Resistance to Theory (Minneapolis, 1986).

Easthope, A., *Poetry as Discourse* (London, 1983).

Eliot, T. S., *Selected Prose* (London, 1963).

Elwert, T., *Traité de versification française des origines à nos jours* (Paris, 1965).

Etiemble, R., and Gauclère, Y., *Rimbaud* (Paris, 1950).

Fontanier, P., *Les Figures du discours* (Paris, 1968).

Gadamer, H. G., *Truth and Method* (New York, 1975).

Gaucheron, J., 'Vigny en poésie', *Europe*, 589 (1978), pp. 3–18.

Gaudon, J., *Le Temps de la contemplation* (Paris, 1969).

Genette, G., *Mimologiques: voyages en Cratylie* (Paris, 1976).

Germain, F., *L'Imagination d'Alfred de Vigny* (Paris, 1961).

Gevovali, S., *Baudelaire, o della dissonanza* (Florence, 1971).

Grammont, M., *Le Vers français* (Paris, 1923).

Petit Traité de versification française (Paris, 1965).

Grossvogel, A., *Le Pouvoir du nom: essai sur G. de Nerval* (Paris, 1972).

Harari, J., ed., *Textual Strategies: Perspectives in Post-Structuralist Criticism* (Ithaca, NY, 1979).

Hegel, G. W. F., *The Phenomenology of Spirit*, trans. A. V. Miller (Oxford, 1977).

Hirsch, E. D., *Validity in Interpretation* (New Haven, NJ, 1967).

Ince, W. N., 'Some Simple Reflections on the Poetry of Alfred de Vigny', *Symposium*, 23 (1969), pp. 277–83.

Jakobson, R., 'Linguistics and Poetics', in *Style in Language*, ed. T. A. Sebeok (Cambridge, MA, 1960), pp. 350–77.

Questions de poétique (Paris, 1973).

Jameson, F., *The Political Unconscious* (Ithaca, NY, 1981).

Johnson, W. R., *The Idea of Lyric: Lyric Modes in Ancient and Modern Poetry* (Berkeley, 1982).

King, R. S., '*Emaux et camées:* sculpture et objets-paysages', *Europe*, 57, no. 601 (1979), pp. 84–9.
Kristeva, J., *Semiotiké* (Paris, 1969).
  La Révolution du langage poétique (Paris, 1974).
Le Hir, Y., *Esthétique et structure du vers français* (Paris, 1956).
Leakey, F. W., *Baudelaire and Nature* (Manchester, 1969).
  Sound and Sense in French Poetry (London, 1975).
Levin, S., *Linguistic Structures in Poetry* (The Hague, 1962).
Lewis, C. D., *The Poetic Image* (London, 1947).
Lewis, R., *On Reading French Verse: A Study of Poetic Form* (Oxford, 1982).
Mazaleyrat, J., *Eléments de métrique française* (Paris, 1974).
Meschonnic, H., ed., *Poétique du vers français* (Paris, 1974).
Morier, H., *Dictionnaire de poétique et de rhétorique* (Paris, 1961).
Nowottny, W., *The Language Poets Use* (London, 1962).
Osmond, N., 'Rhetoric and Self-Expression in Romantic Poetry', *French Literature and its Background*, Vol. 4: *The Early Nineteenth Century*, ed. J. Cruickshank (Oxford, 1969), pp. 18–36.
Pater, W., *Appreciations* (London, 1889; New York, 1900).
Pommier, J., *La Mystique de Baudelaire* (Geneva, 1967).
Poulet, G., *La Distance intérieure* (Paris, 1952).
Pound, E., 'Irony, Laforgue and Some Satire', *Poetry*, 11, 2 (1917), pp. 93–8.
Richard, J.-P., *Etudes sur le romantisme* (Paris, 1970).
Richards, I. A., *Practical Criticism: A Study in Literary Judgement* (London, 1929).
Riffaterre, M., *Essais de stylistique structurale* (Paris, 1971).
  The Semiotics of Poetry (Bloomington, Indiana, 1978).
  'Hermeneutic Models', *Poetics Today*, 4 (1983), pp. 7–15.
Ruskin, J., 'On Modern Landscape', in *The Genius of John Ruskin*, ed. J. D. Rosenberg (London, 1980), pp. 83–90.
Ruwet, N., *Langage, musique, poésie* (Paris, 1972).
Sartre, J.-P., *Qu'est-ce que la littérature?* (Paris, 1964).
Schievelbusch, W., *The Railway Journey: The Industrialization of Time and Space in the Nineteenth Century* (Berkeley, California, 1986).
Schor, N., *Reading in Detail* (New York, 1987).
Scott, C., *French Verse-Art: A Study* (Cambridge, 1980).
  A Question of Syllables (Cambridge, 1986).
  The Riches of Rhyme. Studies in French Verse (Oxford, 1988)
Sontag, S., *A Barthes Reader* (New York, 1982).
Todorov, T., *Théories du symbole* (Paris, 1977).
Wing, N., *The Limits of Narrative: Essays on Baudelaire, Flaubert, Rimbaud and Mallarmé* (Cambridge, 1986).
Wright, E., *Psychoanalytic Criticism* (London/New York, 1984).

INDEX